Content and Language Integrated Learning

Language policy and pedagogical practice

Edited by
Yolanda Ruiz de Zarobe

LONDON AND NEW YORK

First published 2016
by Routledge
2 Park Square, Milton Park, Abingdon, Oxon, OX14 4RN, UK

and by Routledge
711 Third Avenue, New York, NY 10017, USA

Routledge is an imprint of the Taylor & Francis Group, an informa business

© 2016 Taylor & Francis

All rights reserved. No part of this book may be reprinted or reproduced or utilised in any form or by any electronic, mechanical, or other means, now known or hereafter invented, including photocopying and recording, or in any information storage or retrieval system, without permission in writing from the publishers.

Trademark notice: Product or corporate names may be trademarks or registered trademarks, and are used only for identification and explanation without intent to infringe.

British Library Cataloguing in Publication Data
A catalogue record for this book is available from the British Library

ISBN 13: 978-1-138-95659-9

Typeset in Times New Romon
by RefineCatch Limited, Bungay, Suffolk

Publisher's Note
The publisher accepts responsibility for any inconsistencies that may have arisen during the conversion of this book from journal articles to book chapters, namely the possible inclusion of journal terminology.

Disclaimer
Every effort has been made to contact copyright holders for their permission to reprint material in this book. The publishers would be grateful to hear from any copyright holder who is not here acknowledged and will undertake to rectify any errors or omissions in future editions of this book.

Contents

Citation Information vii
Notes on Contributors ix

Introduction – CLIL implementation: from policy-makers to individual initiatives 1
Yolanda Ruiz de Zarobe

1. Listening to learners: an investigation into 'successful learning' across CLIL contexts 14
Do Coyle

2. The power of beliefs: lay theories and their influence on the implementation of CLIL programmes 37
Julia Hüttner, Christiane Dalton-Puffer and Ute Smit

3. CLIL in junior vocational secondary education: challenges and opportunities for teaching and learning 55
Jenny Denman, Rosie Tanner and Rick de Graaff

4. CLIL in Sweden – why does it not work? A metaperspective on CLIL across contexts in Europe 71
Liss Kerstin Sylvén

5. Curricular models of CLIL education in Poland 91
Anna Czura and Katarzyna Papaja

6. Learning to become a CLIL teacher: teaching, reflection and professional development 104
Cristina Escobar Urmeneta

7. How CLIL can provide a pragmatic means to renovate science education – even in a sub-optimally bilingual context 124
Maria Grandinetti, Margherita Langellotti and Y.L. Teresa Ting

8. Genre-based curricula: multilingual academic literacy in content and language integrated learning 145
Francisco Lorenzo

9. Discussion: towards an educational perspective in CLIL language policy and pedagogical practice 159
Jasone Cenoz

CONTENTS

Supplementary Material for Chapter 7   165
Maria Grandinetti, Margherita Langellotti and Y.L. Teresa Ting

Index   175

Citation Information

The chapters in this book were originally published in the *International Journal of Bilingual Education and Bilingualism*, volume 16, issue 3 (May 2013). When citing this material, please use the original page numbering for each article, as follows:

Introduction
CLIL implementation: from policy-makers to individual initiatives
Yolanda Ruiz de Zarobe
International Journal of Bilingual Education and Bilingualism, volume 16, issue 3 (May 2013) pp. 231–243

Chapter 1
Listening to learners: an investigation into 'successful learning' across CLIL contexts
Do Coyle
International Journal of Bilingual Education and Bilingualism, volume 16, issue 3 (May 2013) pp. 244–266

Chapter 2
The power of beliefs: lay theories and their influence on the implementation of CLIL programmes
Julia Hüttner, Christiane Dalton-Puffer and Ute Smit
International Journal of Bilingual Education and Bilingualism, volume 16, issue 3 (May 2013) pp. 267–284

Chapter 3
CLIL in junior vocational secondary education: challenges and opportunities for teaching and learning
Jenny Denman, Rosie Tanner and Rick de Graaff
International Journal of Bilingual Education and Bilingualism, volume 16, issue 3 (May 2013) pp. 285–300

Chapter 4
CLIL in Sweden – why does it not work? A metaperspective on CLIL across contexts in Europe
Liss Kerstin Sylvén
International Journal of Bilingual Education and Bilingualism, volume 16, issue 3 (May 2013) pp. 301–320

CITATION INFORMATION

Chapter 5
Curricular models of CLIL education in Poland
Anna Czura and Katarzyna Papaja
International Journal of Bilingual Education and Bilingualism, volume 16, issue 3 (May 2013) pp. 321–333

Chapter 6
Learning to become a CLIL teacher: teaching, reflection and professional development
Cristina Escobar Urmeneta
International Journal of Bilingual Education and Bilingualism, volume 16, issue 3 (May 2013) pp. 334–353

Chapter 7
How CLIL can provide a pragmatic means to renovate science education – even in a sub-optimally bilingual context
Maria Grandinetti, Margherita Langellotti and Y.L. Teresa Ting
International Journal of Bilingual Education and Bilingualism, volume 16, issue 3 (May 2013) pp. 354–374

Chapter 8
Genre-based curricula: multilingual academic literacy in content and language integrated learning
Francisco Lorenzo
International Journal of Bilingual Education and Bilingualism, volume 16, issue 3 (May 2013) pp. 375–388

Chapter 9
Discussion: towards an educational perspective in CLIL language policy and pedagogical practice
Jasone Cenoz
International Journal of Bilingual Education and Bilingualism, volume 16, issue 3 (May 2013) pp. 389–394

For any permission-related enquiries please visit:
http://www.tandfonline.com/page/help/permissions

Notes on Contributors

Jasone Cenoz is Professor of Applied Linguistics in the Department of Research Methods in Education at the University of the Basque Country, UPV/EHU in Donostia/San Sebastian, Spain. Her research focuses on the acquisition of English as a third language, bilingualism, multilingualism and education. She has recently co-edited two books: Minority Languages and Multilingual Education (Springer, 2014) and *Multilingual education: between language learning and translanguaging* (Cambridge University Press, 2014).She is the President of the International Association of Multilingualism..

Do Coyle is Head of the School of Education at the University of Aberdeen, UK. Her goal is to bring together research, scholarship, teaching and learning involving technology-enhanced/enabled learning in formal contexts with a focus on social and linguistic capital. Her most recent book is *Content and Language Integrated Learning* (with Philip Hood and David Marsh, 2010).

Anna Czura is an Assistant Professor in the Institute of English Studies at the University of Wroclaw, Poland. She researches foreign-language education, learner autonomy, assessment, and content-based language teaching (CLIL).

Christiane Dalton-Puffer is a Professor in the Department of English at the University of Vienna, Austria. Her research interests lie in the fields of content-based language teaching (CLIL), classroom discourse, and bilingual education, amongst others. She has published articles in journals such as the *European Journal of Applied Linguistics*, *Language Teaching* and *International Journal of Bilingualism and Bilingual Education*.

Rick de Graaff is a Professor of Bilingual Education in the Institute of Linguistics OTS, and the Department of Languages, Literature and Communication, at Utrecht University, The Netherlands. His research focuses on effective pedagogy and learning outcomes in content and language integrated learning, and on foreign language pedagogy, professional development of language teachers and task design for communicative competence.

Jenny Denman is based in the Research Centre for Urban Talent at Rotterdam University of Applied Sciences, Rotterdam, The Netherlands.

Maria Grandinetti is based in the English Department at IPSSS L. Da Vinci, Cosenza, Italy.

Julia Hüttner is an Associate Professor in the School of Modern Languages at the University of Southampton, UK. Her main research interests lie in second and foreign language learning, and foreign language education. She is the co-editor of *Theory and Practice in EFL Teacher Education: Bridging the Gap* (with Barbara Mehlmauer-Larcher, Susanne Reichl and Barbara Schiftner, 2012).

NOTES ON CONTRIBUTORS

Margherita Langellotti is based in the Science Department at Liceo Scientifico 'Galileo Galilei', Calabria, Paola, Italy.

Francisco Lorenzo is a Lecturer in the Department of Philology and Translation at Universidad Pablo de Olavide, Seville, Spain.

Katarzyna Papaja is based in the Department of Applied Linguistics at the University of Silesia, Sosnowiec, Poland. Her research interests include content and language integrated learning (CLIL), bilingualism and multilingualism, and teaching English as a foreign language. She is the Vice Editor-in-Chief of the *International Journal of Studies in Applied Linguistics and ELT*.

Yolanda Ruiz de Zarobe is Associate Professor in Language and Applied Linguistics at the University of the Basque Country, UPV/EHU, Spain. Her research focuses on the acquisition of English as a second and a third language, multilingualism, and Content and Language Integrated Learning (CLIL). Her work has appeared in books, edited books and international journals.

Ute Smit is an Associate Professor in the Department of English at the University of Vienna, Austria. Her research interests lie in the fields of classroom discourse, English as a lingua france (ELF), English-medium education in universities and language attitudes, amongst others. She is the author of *English as a Lingua Franca in Higher Education: A Longitudinal Study of Classroom Discourse* (2010).

Liss Kerstin Sylvén is an Associate Professor in the Department of Education and Special Education at the University of Gothenburg, Sweden. Her research areas include interaction technologies, bilingualism, and educational pedagogy. She has published articles in journals such as *Journal of Immersion and Content-Based Language Education, Moderna Språk* and *ReCALL*.

Rosie Tanner is a freelance education consultant specialising in content and language integrated learning (CLIL), and English language teaching. She has previously worked in the Centre for Learning and Teaching at Utrecht University, The Netherlands, and at WideWorld, in the Harvard Graduate School of Education, USA. She is currently based in Amersfoort, The Netherlands.

Y.L. Teresa Ting is an Assistant Professor of English Applied Linguistics at the University of Calabria, Cosenza, Italy. Her research focuses on optimizing the CLIL potential within CLIL-learning materials that move the content curriculum forward and are thus useful for teacher-development: the materials presented here received the 2013 ELTons for Innovative Writing in Education while others have been published (Zanichelli) as textbooks for supporting Italian upper secondary students and their teachers who, albeit Content experts, manage "only" B1-level English.

Cristina Escobar Urmeneta is a Professor in the Department of Language Education at the Universitat Autònoma de Barcelona, Spain. She has served as a consultant to several national and regional education departments and agencies in the design of foreign language curricula and teacher-education programmes for multilingualism, and the assessment of foreign language competencies.

CLIL implementation: from policy-makers to individual initiatives

Yolanda Ruiz de Zarobe

Department of English Studies, University of the Basque Country, UPV/EHU, Vitoria-Gasteiz, Spain

Since Do Coyle and Hugo Baetens Beardsmore published their volume on 'Research on Content and Language Integrated Learning (CLIL)' in the *International Journal of Bilingual Education and Bilingualism* in 2007, there has been a great deal of interest and debate about the approach, which under the umbrella term of Content and Language Integrated Learning refers to contexts where language is used as a medium for learning content, and the content is also used as a resource for learning languages.

As has quite often been pointed out in the literature (Dalton-Puffer 2011; Hüttner, Dalton-Puffer, and Smit, this volume; Shohamy 2006), the implementation of CLIL has been supported, on the one hand, by language policy-makers, stakeholders and European institutions and, on the other, by individual initiatives undertaken by school communities, teachers and parents, all of them seeking to improve foreign-language competence in a world where globalization and the knowledge society are encouraging foreign-language learning and communication. Education policy has a central part to play in this new knowledge-based economy, and language learning is crucial to this.

As regards language policy and implementation, in 2003 the European Commission brought out an Action Plan for language learning and linguistic diversity, where CLIL was encouraged as one of the innovative methods to improve the quality of language learning and teaching. In that respect, the European Union (EU) was committed to safeguard this linguistic diversity and promote language learning for reasons of cultural identity and social cohesion. Since then, numerous European strategies have been fostered to promote CLIL, with different countries responding in different ways, although today almost all EU states have implemented some form of CLIL with varying degrees of success in compulsory education (Eurydice 2006; Eurydice Network 2012).

What becomes clear after looking at CLIL in different educational contexts is that it has become a visible trend which is spanning geographically as a truly European/international approach. Most of the EU member states have devised action plans, upon recommendation of the European Commission, to achieve the objective of learning two languages in addition to the mother tongue (mother tongue + 2 objective), an objective which had already been set out in the Barcelona

European Council meeting held in 2002 to promote linguistic diversity and increase the degree of multilingualism among European citizens. In recent years, numerous European initiatives at different educational levels have been undertaken in that joint effort to integrate subject matter and foreign languages:

> CLIL is already taking place in several European schools and has been found to be effective in all sectors of education from primary through to adult and higher education. Its success has been growing over the past 10 years and continues to do so [...] the dual focus of learning both language and content is realized optimally, as language and content are integrated in CLIL. (European Commission 2010)

To study the developments concerning language learning, language knowledge and language attitudes in the EU, which encompass these educational changes, the European Commission has carried out several surveys (2001, 2006 and 2012). One of the latest reports, undertaken in 2012 in almost 27 European countries, presents socio-demographic and behavioural variables based on the activities of the 27,000 people interviewed in terms of their language learning.

Among other issues, the report shows that Europeans have a very positive attitude towards multilingualism:

- almost all Europeans (98%) think that mastering foreign languages is useful for their children's future; 88% see it as useful for themselves.
- almost three-quarters (72%) agree with the EU objective that everybody should learn at least two foreign languages; 77% think that improvement in language skills should be a policy priority.
- 67% see English as one of the two most useful languages for themselves. Among the others most frequently cited as useful are German (17%), French (16%), Spanish (14%) and Chinese (6%). (European Commission, Eurobarometer survey 2012)

This positive attitude towards foreign-language learning and multilingualism is stimulating further educational and societal changes. However, we appreciate that there is a discrepancy between EU policies and beliefs, and the implementation of the approach nationwide. Although CLIL has been encouraged by EU agencies, educational and language policies are the responsibility of individual countries, each deciding on their own terms how they want to apply the approach, with little guidance at European level in relation to research, implementation parameters or teacher education. This would explain why, as the CLIL approach evolves from country to country, we find a wide variety of applications rooted in different contexts. Such diversity of models becomes apparent in this volume where clearly CLIL in Poland, the United Kingdom or the Netherlands will differ from CLIL in Spain, Sweden or Italy due to social and cultural differences which emerge when implementing the approach, as does the linguistic diversity in all the communities or the attitudes and strength of the foreign language (however, see Dalton-Puffer 2011, for similarities across CLIL programmes in Europe, South America and parts of Asia).

Under the acronym CLIL we recognize a wide range of models, which show divergences as regards the age of implementation of the model or the intensity of the exposure to the foreign language (see also Sylvén, this volume), to name but a few differences. Thus, several countries include at least one foreign language from the first or second year of primary education, at the age of 6–7 (Italy, Luxembourg, Austria, France, Norway, Malta, Poland, Portugal, Estonia, Finland and Sweden). In some cases, there is an even earlier start: in some autonomous communities of Spain, children learn a foreign language from the age of 3 (Ruiz de Zarobe and Lasagabaster 2010) and that rule also applies to the German-speaking community in Belgium. Other countries generally start later (8–10 years old). As regards the intensity of the approach, the time devoted remains limited, at less than 10% of the total teaching time in most cases, although that number also varies considerably between countries, from under 5% to 40% (Eurydice Network 2008).

Needless to say, in the majority of cases the foreign language is English, which is by far the most popular target language. English is learnt on average by 90% of all European students at some stage of their compulsory education. When a second foreign language is taught, it is usually French or German. In some countries, depending on the national context, other languages predominate: Spanish (France and Sweden), Italian (Malta), Danish (Iceland) or Russian (Bulgaria, Estonia, Latvia and Lithuania), among others.

However, despite implementation differences in the international scenario when responding to CLIL, a common goal will also be found to apply throughout the different contexts: most countries try to find a coherent answer to the need for language competence and communication in this globalized world, with the knowledge of languages as a key factor for job opportunities and promotion. For this reason we also find numerous bottom-up actions undertaken by educational institutions, parents, teachers and employers to promote language development, because multilingual citizens are better placed to take advantage of the educational and professional opportunities created by an integrated Europe. Therefore,

> the fire of CLIL has been fuelled from various sides: high-level policy and grass-roots actions [. . . . . .] and if one was to decide which of the two came first, we are inclined to think that it was actually the grass-roots beliefs and activities of parents and teachers which, practically simultaneously at countless locations, ignited the CLIL engine and keep it going. (Dalton-Puffer, Nikula and Smit 2010b, 4)

In recognition of this, we include some of the chapters in this volume which present grassroots actions from a myriad of educational settings, which illustrate the research and educational projects that are being conducted internationally.

All in all, and despite the hegemony of English as a global language, CLIL has been conceived to enhance language competence and communication in an ever-growing multilingual society where, in the case of the EU, 23 official languages coexist with more than 60 regional or minority languages, some of which have official status (Basque, Catalan and Sami, among others). Additionally, we need to include hundreds of other languages which immigrant communities provide. This multilingual diversity calls for an educational approach that can become an appropriate vehicle for intercultural communication. Consequently, CLIL can be understood as a truly European approach for the integration of language and content in the curriculum as part of the international mosaic of multilingualism.

In the following section, we will provide an overview of some of the models that sustain CLIL as a flexible and rich teaching approach in order to gain some insight into this area.

CLIL in education: the rationale behind the approach

CLIL has frequently been defined as a 'dual-focused' educational approach where content subjects are taught through the medium of the foreign language. This duality involves language learning and content learning, ideally with the integration of both of them as a unified approach (Coyle, Hood, and Marsh 2010; see also Lorenzo, this volume).

CLIL as a pedagogic tool has been implemented in a variety of forms in the curriculum since the 1990s, although teaching subject matter through a foreign language is not something new to recent decades: different bilingual communities and educational institutions have had a long tradition of teaching content through the second/foreign language in their curricula. What is probably new is the attempts made to create what can be considered a multidimensional approach, connecting different goals within the same conceptualization. One of the developments that better explain the rationale for introducing CLIL into the curriculum is the conceptual framework developed by Coyle (Coyle 2005, 2007; Coyle, Holmes, and King 2009), which consists of four dimensions (The 4C curriculum): content (subject matter), cognition (thinking processes), communication (language) and culture (intercultural awareness), with the benefits they may bring in the classroom (Coyle, Holmes, and King 2009, 12):

- integrating content from across the curriculum through high-quality language interaction (content),
- engaging learners through creativity, higher-order thinking, and knowledge processing (cognition),
- using language to learn and mediate ideas, thoughts and values (communication) and
- interpreting and understanding the significance of content and language and their contribution to identity and citizenship (culture).

By connecting these four dimensions, Coyle manages to place intercultural understanding at the core of the learning process.

Apart from this conceptualization, there have been other attempts to formulate integration perspectives about CLIL. For instance, the European Centre for Modern Languages, which is a Council of Europe institution based in Graz, Austria, assists stakeholders in Europe in bringing language education policies and practices together. However, it has proven hard to find conceptual guidelines that link and integrate the different dimensions of CLIL in the curriculum.

Despite this difficulty, CLIL as an educational approach makes underlying use of some of the theoretical models that have been pivotal in the last few decades. Although our aim in this section is not to provide a thorough account of all of them, these theoretical approaches include such models as the Monitor Model by Krashen (1985), moving on to the Interaction Hypothesis by Long (1996), Focus on Form (Doughty and Williams 1998) or the distinction between Basic Interpersonal Communication Skills (or BICS) and Cognitive Academic Language Proficiency (CALP) by Cummins (1984, 2003), among others. In some cases these theories will stress the need for comprehensible input, low affective filters or 'natural' contexts. In others, there will be a focus on interaction, whereby conversation becomes the means by which learning takes place, mainly when it comes to the negotiation of meaning. Focus on Form approaches bring together accuracy and fluency by drawing the attention to problematic linguistic features during communicative activities. Some of the classroom practices presented in this volume make use of some of the underlying assumptions of these theories (see, for instance, Grandinetti, Langellotti and Ting, also discussed in Cenoz, this volume). They are examples of good practices that can apply to CLIL settings, as they have already been used in second-language learning contexts.

Cummins' theories concerning bilingual education have been influential for CLIL pedagogies as well. The author makes the distinction between BICS, the language a student uses to communicate in everyday situations, and CALP, the language that students need to master for academic purposes. CLIL as a dynamic approach involves BICS and CALP: a social, communicative language acquired more easily (but probably inadequate for meeting the academic demands of the classroom), and an academic language which takes more time and effort to acquire in the teaching–learning process.

Another theoretical model that has probably more directly influenced some of the CLIL research of recent years is the framework of Systemic Functional Linguistics, a model which has been applied in education and educational research (Halliday 1989, 2004; Halliday and Hasan 2006). Halliday's hypothesis of the metafunctions (ideational, interpersonal and textual) and their role in the construction of register and genre have provided a model to study language in use.

> In our CLIL classrooms, we are studying the way language is used for learning, which involves spoken interaction to achieve pedagogic goals, and the comprehension and production of written texts as part of those objectives – that is, text and discourse production and reception in specific contexts. (Whittaker and Llinares 2009, 217)

Halliday's systemic grammar has been used for the analysis of discourse in classroom contexts and in work on literacy in English (see Lorenzo, this volume).

More recent theories, such as the Counterbalanced Approach by Lyster (2007) in the Canadian context, integrate language and content by observing instructional practices in content-based classrooms. Lyster justifies a counterbalanced approach that integrates both content- and form-focused instructional options as complementary ways of developing interlanguage competence. According to the author, this approach provides many opportunities for learners to process language through content by means of comprehension, awareness and production mechanisms, and to negotiate language through content by means of interactional strategies involving teacher scaffolding and feedback.

These theories, among others, have served as the background to implement CLIL methodologies in the classroom in order to enhance learner competence and learner autonomy as a blended learning approach. However, in order to reach a sound theoretical model of CLIL teaching, we still need to take research step by step to gain a clear insight of the complexity of the approach. What remains to be seen is whether the research findings in CLIL can actually help in the correct implementation of the approach in the classroom and in the attainment of this theoretical construct. In the next sections, we will review some of that research and will discuss the contributions of the chapters of this volume.

The classroom setting in CLIL contexts: research and implications

One of the strengths of CLIL is the opportunity the approach provides to learn the foreign language and content in an integrated way, taking the whole curriculum into consideration. Therefore, within the CLIL classroom, language and content have complementary value: content is expected to be the focus of the classroom, providing consistency to build linguistic progress. 'In non-CLIL classes, content is just a resource to teach and learn language, while content is expected to be an integral part of the process in CLIL classes' (Cenoz, this volume). The key issue of the approach is that the learner is gaining new knowledge about the content subject while using and learning the foreign language; the challenge remains of how to enable learners to make best use of both areas in the classroom (Coyle, Hood, and Marsh 2010; Dalton-Puffer 2011).

Much of what we know about CLIL comes from applied linguistic research and practitioner research (Dafouz and Guerrini 2009; Dalton-Puffer, Nikula, and Smit 2010a; Ruiz de Zarobe and Jiménez Catalán 2009; Ruiz de Zarobe, Sierra, and Gallardo del Puerto 2011, among others). Considering that 'CLIL could be interpreted as a foreign language enrichment measure packaged into content teaching' (Dalton-Puffer 2011, 184), most of that research has focused on learning outcomes, looking mainly at the different linguistic areas and competencies (Dalton-Puffer 2008; Ruiz de Zarobe 2011), at content-learning outcomes and also at pedagogical practice (see Dalton-Puffer 2011, for a comprehensive overview of these results).

CLIL as an educational approach focuses mainly on the classroom, which offers the appropriate setting for implementation, and it is the research undertaken in this setting that can help us share approaches that may benefit and potentially change educational practices: 'by covering actual classroom practices, (it) allows researchers to develop their descriptions and interpretations of the teaching and learning processes in a bottom-up rather than a top-down manner' (Smit and Dafouz 2012, 4). Most of the studies presented in this volume aim to provide examples of good pedagogical practices and effective teacher training programmes following this bottom-up approach.

As might be expected, the research undertaken in the classroom has sometimes offered contradictory results in its different dimensions, which involve such fields as students' attitudes and motivation, teachers' orientation, and the pedagogic design of lessons and material use, to mention but a few.

It is widely recognized that one of the most important challenges for teachers and educators is how to motivate students in language learning. CLIL has often been argued to be a powerful motivation factor, as students must put the language they are learning into practice from the very beginning in order to 'communicate'. Although some researchers claim that sometimes the need to communicate in another language may cause a challenge and therefore language anxiety (Gardner 2010, also discussed in Denman, Tanner and de Graff, this volume, but see Maillat 2010 and Nikula 2007 for different results), it has well been attested that CLIL classrooms can be motivating both for the teachers and for the students (Merisuo-Storm 2007; Lasagabaster and Sierra 2009; Lorenzo, Casal, and Moore 2010, but see Seikkula-Leino 2007, for some negative effects on self-esteem). Additional support comes from some of the contributions of this volume. One of them is the research undertaken by Denman, Tanner, and de Graff, who carried out a study in bilingual junior vocational secondary education in the Netherlands, focusing on the experiences and beliefs of teachers, students and school management both at the curriculum implementation and the classroom level. The results of the online surveys and interviews show how motivation increased in junior secondary vocational students, as CLIL gives them opportunities to work on their vocational literacy and vocational language proficiency, which becomes at the same time a 'positive' challenge for them.

Further support comes from Coyle, corroborating what she had already presented in the ITALIC Research Report (Coyle 2011), where she introduces a process model for interpreting motivation in CLIL classes. Her study in this volume investigates 'successful' learning across different CLIL contexts by analysing learner motivation and achievement from the learners' perspective, taking classroom practices as the context of investigation and the learners as mediators in the process (see also Ruiz de Zarobe and Coyle, 2015).

It needs to be remembered at this point that some research, notably in Asian contexts, have shown negative effects of the approach (Marsh, Hau, and Kong 2000; Yip, Cheung, and Tsang 2003, among others). These studies, undertaken mainly in Hong Kong, where English is considered a prestigious language, compared students following a programme in English as a medium of instruction and those following a Chinese programme, the first language (L1) of the students. In spite of the positive attitudes of parents toward English, these studies showed detrimental effects on content learning (subjects such as Mathematics, Geography, History or Science), and even poorer motivation results over a period of time in the case of English-medium instruction. The reasons behind these results may be, as the authors point out, the inadequate competence of English teachers, who may have had a low level of English, the oversimplification of materials or sometimes the fact that late immersion does not yield as positive results as early immersion.

It is evident that when integrating both content and language in the classroom, teachers become more aware of the importance of language as a fundamental tool in the dual approach (Dafouz 2011, see also Grandinetti, Langellotti, and Ting, in this volume). Therefore, the language proficiency of the teachers themselves becomes an important factor in the successful implementation of CLIL methodologies (see Denman, Tanner and de Graaff, and Escobar Urmeneta, both in this volume).

In other words, it seems that there are several factors that have to be taken into consideration when looking at pedagogical outcomes in CLIL settings. In that respect, another focus of interest has been the assumption that CLIL settings, where there is a focus on students' autonomy to learn in this combined approach, involve a change in the classroom pedagogy, moving from a more teacher-centred approach, typical of traditional teaching contexts, to a more student-centred approach (see Grandinetti, Langelotti and Ting, this volume). However, the research undertaken in some European contexts (Austria, with Dalton-Puffer et al. 2008 or Finland, with Nikula 2010, among others) has shown that in CLIL contexts the teachers' pragmatic use of the language is sometimes less varied than in the teaching of subjects in the L1, mainly in cases where teachers have a limited competence in the foreign language (FL) which forces them to restrict their interventions to more programmed and academic circumstances, rather than use them in a more relaxedcontext.

This finding would be in line with the research which states that student participation decreases in the CLIL classroom (Dalton-Puffer et al. 2008) and that they switch to their mother tongue whenever they are in peer-to-peer interactions (Coonan 2007; Tarone and Swain 1995). However, it is also true that in CLIL classrooms students and teachers' interactions seem to be more on a par when they both work in an FL, which implies that the fact that they need to communicate in a second language becomes a sort of pragmatic mask (the 'mask effect', Maillat

2010, 52), with students communicating more freely and in a more informal style, and even becoming confident enough to use the FL outside the classroom in social contexts (Nikula 2007).

Another important point in CLIL methodology is the design of lessons. Some studies (Badertscher and Bieri 2009; Dalton-Puffer 2007) have shown no clear differences in lesson design between CLIL and non-CLIL classrooms, but other studies (Llinares and Whittaker 2010; Whittaker and Llinares 2009), notably in the Spanish context, advocate the need for a scaffolded progression of tasks in CLIL methodologies, and the subsequent grading of what subject-specific language is to be learned. These authors support a genre-based pedagogy (see also Morton 2010 and Lorenzo, this volume), a pedagogy that seeks to increase students' awareness of the stages of school genres to guide them in the production of different text types. Students will produce a scaffolded use of genres involving many areas of language, which Lorenzo, this volume, calls a 'multilingual genre map across the curriculum'. What is important in CLIL contexts is that a 'genre-based approach provides a framework for the types of productive teacher-student (and student-student) spoken interaction which it is hoped will take place in CLIL or content-based instruction' (Morton 2010, 85).

Although more research is still required in the field, the discussion lines presented above allow for in-depth analyses that may be generalized across contexts. The contributions of this issue, which will be described below, aim to illustrate several points of access into classroom research and pedagogy.

Contributions of this volume

The chapters in this special edition of the *International Journal of Bilingual Education and Bilingualism* explore a wide range of evidence relevant to the issues mentioned above and present some of the recent research undertaken on CLIL. To contextualize developments in this field, the collection offers an overview of several European contexts, which describe experiences that could be extrapolated to many other communities worldwide. These countries include Austria, Italy, the Netherlands, Poland, Sweden, Spain and the United Kingdom, in addition to other countries mentioned throughout the contributions. These national initiatives are displayed across a wide range of educational perspectives, portraying the diversity that is a distinctive feature of CLIL in the European mosaic.

The chapters focus on issues related to language policy, moving from high-level policy-making to grassroots decisions, but all of them encompassing the major changes that can be recognized in education, which also evidence the shifts in society and economic life that have taken place in Europe in the last decades. These changes in language policy issues are coupled with changes in CLIL practice in the classroom, as some of the chapters of this volume foreground. Some of these concentrate on practice-based evidence of successful learning in CLIL on the part of both the students and the teachers, and others imply a shift from more teacher-centred pedagogies to more student-centred practices. All of them require a change in material development, as the last chapter puts forward.

The chapters collectively provide new insights into pedagogic, methodological and language policy issues in CLIL, and also cover some areas which have been insufficiently addressed in the literature, such as the implementation of CLIL in 'less successful' contexts, learner–teacher collaboration in the CLIL classroom or teachers' reflections in CLIL contexts.

In the first chapter 'Listening to learners: An investigation into perceptions of "successful" learning across CLIL contexts', Coyle provides practice-based evidence of students' perceptions of successful learning in a range of CLIL settings across 2 countries and 11 secondary schools. Data were gathered using the Learning-Oriented Critical Incident Technique process (Coyle 2010), a technique which analyses what is considered successful practice by learners as researchers, using a digital mediating tool. The results portray what is really perceived by learners as part of classroom-based evidence: the need to communicate, to engage actively in the learning process, and learner–teacher collaboration; in sum, how classroom dynamics should proceed for a successful integration of content and language learning.

The beliefs of teachers and learners involved in CLIL are also taken up in the following chapter. Hüttner, Dalton-Puffer, and Smit, in 'The power of beliefs: Lay theories and their influence on the implementation of CLIL programmes' present a study into the lay theories of teachers and learners involved in CLIL instruction in Austrian upper secondary colleges of technology. Their results show how language management, as in other geographical contexts, is weak in Austria, which gives a great deal of autonomy and responsibility to the individual teacher. Further discrepancies between policy-makers and stakeholders are discussed, which can cause some areas of conflict for CLIL implementation, although the potential opportunities are also presented.

The third chapter 'CLIL in junior vocational secondary education: challenges and opportunities for teaching and learning', by Denman, Tanner and de Graaff, is set in five bilingual junior vocational secondary schools in the Netherlands. Following the two previous contributions, the study analyses the experiences of stakeholders both at the curriculum implementation and the classroom level. The interviews and online surveys report how participants, though sometimes being considered 'lower achievers', are prepared for their future careers and cross-cultural communication through the vocational bilingual stream. The challenges the programme presents are met with optimism and motivation both by teachers and students for future professional development.

In another line of research, 'CLIL in Sweden. Why does it not work? A meta-perspective on CLIL across contexts in Europe' by Sylvén compares four European countries: Finland, Germany, Spain and Sweden. By using a coordinate system, which includes four quadrants, the policy framework factor, amount of research, the age factor and amount of input in CLIL, she compares nation-specific CLIL profiles. These profiles can facilitate policy-level discussions on CLIL implementation.

Policy-level implications are also discussed in the following chapter by Czura and Papaja, 'Curricular Models of CLIL education in Poland'. These authors provide a coherent account of four large-scale research studies that explore CLIL sections with several foreign languages. As in other European contexts presented in this volume, CLIL provision in the Polish context is characterized by a great deal of flexibility in the amount of content and foreign language in the curriculum, in teaching practices or instructional choices due to the lack of a coherent national initiative. But, as the authors argue, despite the fact that there is 'a gap between local grassroots activities and the supra-national level' (Dalton-Puffer 2007, 4), CLIL must be considered in a broader educational dimension, as an approach to promote European integration and multilingualism.

The next two chapters focus on classroom practice in CLIL contexts. In the first, 'Learning to become a CLIL teacher: Teaching, reflecting and professional development', Escobar Urmeneta presents the case study of a CLIL teacher-trainee in a Master's degree programme in Catalonia by means of a Classroom Interactional Competence analysis. This is an awareness-raising tool which helps teacher-trainees to analyse and reflect on their own teaching, progressing in the understanding of issues related to language acquisition and in the challenges posed by CLIL. By doing so, they can redirect their teaching, gain autonomy to lead their own teaching, and improve their professional skills.

The chapter by Grandinetti, Langellotti and Ting, 'How CLIL can provide a pragmatic means to renovate science-education- Even in a sub-optimally bilingual context', also addresses the issue of CLIL classrooms, this time in the Italian context, notably in Calabria, although it could once again be extrapolated to many international contexts. Through the collaboration of three teachers, a Science teacher, an English as a foreign-language teacher and a CLIL expert teacher, the authors devise the development of some scaffolded activities to move from more teacher-centred pedagogies to a more student-centred approach. Their study also demonstrates that through appropriate CLIL materials, the use of the foreign language may even facilitate science education and learning.

The following contribution of this volume, 'Genre-based curricula: Multilingual academic literacy in CLIL' by Lorenzo, addresses classroom discourse, highlighting the need to reorient language learning in CLIL. The author provides the necessary information for the practical implementation of CLIL programmes and materials development through multilingual genre-based, functional semiotic models.

The volume closes with the contribution by Jasone Cenoz, 'Towards an educational perspective in CLIL language policy and pedagogical practice', which digs deeper into the issues raised in this volume discussing some of the questions present in CLIL, and provides new food for thought on this educational approach.

Each contribution individually provides an examination of some of the questions present in relation to CLIL methodologies, highlighting the message that no single factor in CLIL classroom practice operates in isolation from the others. Collectively, the chapters provide a rich account of the work that needs to be done both empirically and conceptually across different contexts in CLIL classrooms in order to draw more general conclusions in the field. They also provide the very clear message that CLIL must be regarded as a rich and flexible teaching approach, with a range of research perspectives to be undertaken. This volume aims to add some insight into the complexity of the approach, which calls for further research in the area.

Acknowledgements

The author acknowledges the funding by the Spanish Ministry of Economy and Competitiveness FFI2009-10264 and FFI2012-31811 and the Basque Department of Education, Research and Universities IT311-10 (UFI 11/06).

References

Badertscher, H., and T. Bieri. 2009. *Wissenserwerbim Content and Language Integrated Learning.* Bern: Haupt.

Coonan, C. M. 2007. "Insider Views of the CLIL Class through Teacher Self-observation-introspection." *The International Journal of Bilingual Education and Bilingualism* 10: 625–646. http://dx.doi.org/10.2167/beb463.0.

Coyle, D. 2005. *Developing CLIL: Towards a Theory of Practice*, APAC Monograph 6. Barcelona: APAC.

Coyle, D. 2007. "Content and Language Integrated Learning: Towards a Connected Research Agenda for CLIL Pedagogies." *International Journal of Bilingual Education and Bilingualism* 10 (5): 543–562. http://dx.doi.org/10.2167/beb459.0.

Coyle, D. 2010. "Chapter 3, Language Pedagogies Revisited: Alternative Approaches for Integrating Language Learning, Language Using and Intercultural Understanding." In *Culturally and Linguistically Diverse Classrooms: New Dilemmas for Teachers*, edited by J. Miller, A. Kostogriz, and M. Gearon, 172–195. Ontario: Multilingual Matters.

Coyle, D. 2011. "The Italic Research Report." University of Aberdeen. http://www.abdn.ac.uk/italic

Coyle, D., B. Holmes, and L. King. 2009. *Towards an Integrated Curriculum. CLIL National Statements and Guidelines*. London: The Languages Company. http://www.rachelhawkes.com/PandT/CLIL/CLILnationalstatementandguidelines.pdf

Coyle, D., P. Hood, and D. Marsh. 2010. *CLIL: Content and Language Integrated Learning*. New York: Cambridge University Press.

Cummins, J. 1984. *Bilingualism and Special Education*. Clevedon: Multilingual Matters.

Cummins, J. 2003. "BICS and CALP." Clarifying the Distinction. Jim Cummins Bilingual Education Web. http://iteachilearn.org/cummins/bicscalp.html

Dafouz, E. 2011. "English as the Medium of Instruction in Spanish Contexts: A Look at Teachers' Discourses." In *Content and Foreign Language Integrated Learning: Contributions to Multilingualism in European Contexts*, edited by Y. Ruiz de Zarobe, J. M. Sierra, and F. Gallardo del Puerto, 189–210. Bern: Peter Lang.

Dafouz, E., and M. Guerrini, eds. 2009. *CLIL across Educational Levels: Experiences from Primary, Secondary and Tertiary Contexts*. Madrid: Santillana.

Dalton-Puffer, C. 2007. *Discourse in Content and Language Integrated Learning (CLIL) Classrooms*. Amsterdam: John Benjamins.

Dalton-Puffer, C. 2008. "Outcomes and Processes in Content and Language Integrated (CLIL) Learning: Current Research in Europe." In *Future Perspectives in English Language Teaching*, edited by W. Delanoy and L. Volkmann, 7–23. Heidelberg: Carl Winter.

Dalton-Puffer, C. 2011. "Content and Language Integrated Learning: From Practice to Principles." *Annual Review of Applied Linguistics* 31: 182–204. doi:10.1017/S0267190511000092

Dalton-Puffer, C., J. Hüttner, S. Jexenflicker, V. Schindelegger, and U. Smit. 2008. *Content and Language Integrated Learning* an ÖsterreichsHöherenTechnischenLehranstalten. Vienna: BundesministeriumfürUnterricht, Kultur und Kunst, Abt. II/2 (Austrian Ministry of Education, Culture and Art, Section II/2).

Dalton-Puffer, C., T. Nikula, and U. Smit, eds. 2010a. *Language Use* and *Language Learning* in *CLIL Classrooms*. Amsterdam: John Benjamins.

Dalton-Puffer, C., T. Nikula, and U. Smit. 2010b. "Charting Policies, Premises and Research on Content and Language Integrated Learning." In *Language Use and Language Learning in CLIL Classrooms*, edited by C. Dalton-Puffer, T. Nikula, and U. Smit, 1–23. Amsterdam: John Benjamins.

Doughty, C., and J. Williams, eds. 1998. *Focus on Form in Classroom Second Language Acquisition*. Cambridge: Cambridge University Press.

European Commission. 2010. "Learning Languages and Something Else." Accessed January 16, 2013. http://ec.europa.eu/languages/news/20100809-learning-languages-and-something-else_en.htm

European Commission. 2012. "Eurobarometer Survey, Europeans and Their Languages." http://ec.europa.eu/languages/languages-of-europe/eurobarometersurvey_en.htm

Eurydice. 2006. *Content and Language Integrated Learning (CLIL) at School in Europe*. Brussels: European Commission.

Eurydice Network. 2008. *Key Data on Teaching Languages at School in Europe*. Brussels: European Commission.

Eurydice Network. 2012. *Key Data on Teaching Languages at School in Europe*. Brussels: European Commission.

Gardner, R. C. 2010. *Motivation and Second Language Acquisition: The Socio-Educational Model*. New York: Peter Lang.

Halliday, M. A. K. 1989. *Spoken and Written Language*. Oxford: OUP.

Halliday, M. A. K. 2004. *An Introduction to Functional Grammar*. 3rd ed. Revised by C. Matthiessen. London: Edward Arnold (1st ed. 1985).

Halliday, M. A. K., and R. Hasan. 2006. "Retrospective on SFL and Literacy." In *Language and Literacy: Functional Approaches*, edited by R. Whittaker, M. O'Donnell, and A. McCabe, 15–44. London: Continuum.

Krashen, S. 1985. *The Input Hypothesis. Issues and Implications*. London: Longman.

Lasagabaster, D., and J. M. Sierra. 2009. "Language Attitudes in CLIL and Traditional EFL Classes." *International CLIL Research Journal* 1 (2): 4–17. http://www.icrj.eu/12/article1.html

Llinares, A., and R. Whittaker. 2010. "Writing and Speaking in the History Class: A Comparative Analysis of CLIL and First Language Contexts." In *Language Use and Language Learning in CLIL Classrooms*, edited by C. Dalton-Puffer, T. Nikula, and U. Smit, 125–144. Amsterdam: John Benjamins.

Long, M. 1996. "The Role of the Linguistic Environment in Second Language Acquisition." In *Handbook of Second Language Acquisition*, edited by W. Ritchie and T. Bhatia, 413–468. San Diego: Academic Press.

Lorenzo, F., S. Casal, and P. Moore. 2010. "The Effects of Content and Language Integrated Learning in European Education: Key Findings from the Andalusian Bilingual Sections Evaluation Project." *Applied Linguistics* 31 (3): 418–442. doi:10.1093/applin/amp041

Lyster, R. 2007. *Learning and Teaching Languages through Content: A Counterbalanced Approach*. Amsterdam: John Benjamins.

Maillat, D. 2010. "The Pragmatics of L2 in CLIL." In *Language Use and Language Learning in CLIL Classrooms*, edited by C. Dalton-Puffer, T. Nikula, and U. Smit, 39–58. Amsterdam: John Benjamins.

Marsh, H. W., K. T. Hau, and C. K. Kong. 2000. "Late Immersion and Language of Instruction in Hong Kong High Schools: Achievement Growth in Language and Non-language Subjects." *Harvard Educational Review* 70: 302–346. http://search.proquest.com/docview/212277787/fulltextPDF/13CA97C7EC53174E40C/1?accountid=17248

Merisuo-Storm, T. 2007. "Pupils' Attitudes Towards Foreign-language Learning and the Development of Literacy Skills in Bilingual Education." *Teaching and Teacher Education* 23 (2): 226–235. doi:10.1016/j.tate.2006.04.024.

Morton, T. 2010. "Using a Genre-based Approach to Integrating Content and Language in CLIL: The Example of Secondary History." In *Language Use and Language Learning in CLIL Classrooms*, edited by C. Dalton-Puffer, T. Nikula, and U. Smit, 81–104. Amsterdam: John Benjamins.

Nikula, T. 2007. "Speaking English in Finnish Content-based Classrooms." *World Englishes* 26 (2): 206–223. doi:10.1111/j.1467-971X.2007.00502.x.

Nikula, T. 2010. "Effects of CLIL on One Teacher's Classroom Language Use." In *Language Use and Language Learning in CLIL Classrooms*, edited by C. Dalton-Puffer, T. Nikula, and U. Smit, 105–124. Amsterdam: John Benjamins.

Ruiz de Zarobe, Y. 2011. "Which Language Competencies Benefit from CLIL? An Insight into Applied Linguistics Research." In *Content and Foreign Language Integrated Learning: Contributions to Multilingualism in European Contexts*, edited by Y. Ruiz de Zarobe, J. M. Sierra, and F. Gallardo del Puerto, 129–153. Bern: Peter Lang.

Ruiz de Zarobe, Y., and R. M. Jiménez Catalán, eds. 2009. Content and *Language Integrated Learning:* Evidence from *Research* in Europe. Bristol: Multilingual Matters.

Ruiz de Zarobe, Y., and D. Lasagabaster. 2010. "CLIL in a Bilingual Community: The Basque Autonomous Community." In CLIL in Spain: Implementation, *Results* and *Teacher Training*, edited by D. Lasagabaster and Y. Ruiz de Zarobe, 12–29. Newcastle: Cambridge Scholars Publishing.

Ruiz de Zarobe, Y., J. M. Sierra, and F. Gallardo del Puerto, eds. 2011. *Content and Foreign Language Integrated Learning: Contributions to Multilingualism in European Contexts*. Bern: Peter Lang.

Ruiz de Zarobe, Y. and D. Coyle, 2015. "Towards new learning partnerships in bilingual educational contexts - raising learner awareness and creating conditions for reciprocity and pedagogic attention". *The International Journal of Multilingualism*. 12 (4): 471–493. DOI:10.1080/14790718.2015.1071020

Seikkula-Leino, J. 2007. "CLIL Learning: Achievement Levels and Affective Factors." *Language and Education* 21 (4): 328–341. doi:10.2167/le635.0

Shohamy, E. 2006. *Language Policy. Hidden Agendas and New Approaches.* London: Routledge.

Smit, U., and E. Dafouz. 2012. "Integrating content and language in higher education: An introduction to English-medium policies, conceptual issues and research practices across Europe." *AILA Review*, 25: 1–12. http://dx.doi.org/10.1075/aila.25.01smi.

Tarone, E. and M. Swain. 1995. "A Sociolinguistic Perspective on Second-language Use in Immersion Classrooms." *The Modern Language Journal* 79 (2): 166–178. doi:10.1111/j.1540-4781.1995.tb05428.x

Whittaker, R., and A. Llinares. 2009. "CLIL in Social Science Classrooms." In *Content and Language Integrated Learning: Evidence from Research in Europe*, edited by Y. Ruiz de Zarobe and R. M. Jiménez Catalán, 215–234. Bristol: Multilingual Matters.

Yip, D. Y., W. K. Tsang, and S. P. Cheung. 2003. "Evaluation of the Effects of Medium of Instruction on the Science Learning of Hong Kong Secondary Students: Performance on the Science Achievement Test." *Bilingual Research Journal* 27 (2): 295–331. doi:10.1080/15235882.2003.10162808

Listening to learners: an investigation into 'successful learning' across CLIL contexts

Do Coyle

School of Education, University of Aberdeen, Aberdeen, UK

> This study is part of longitudinal research undertaken in 11 secondary schools across two countries, based in Content and Language Integrated Learning (CLIL) classrooms with 12–15 year olds. The aim was to listen to learners, provide them with a 'voice' to analyse their perceptions of 'successful learning' and to undertake participatory research not only to find evidence of successful learning but also to encourage greater ownership of CLIL classroom events. We believe that this study due to the innovative ways of involving learners has a unique contribution to make to our understanding of 'successful learning' using French, German and Spanish in CLIL classrooms where English is the usual medium for learning. For the purposes of this study, 'successful learning' was considered to have two components: motivation and achievement or pupil gains. Three distinct data-gathering methods were used: questionnaires, 'respectful discussions' and classroom video analysis using the LOCIT (Learning-Oriented Critical Incident Technique) process. The findings reveal that whilst discussing successful CLIL generates useful data to trigger further research by learners and teachers, classroom evidence selected by the learners is less aligned. This study suggests that these data could not only be used to support learners' understanding of 'successful learning' more deeply but also to create their own class-based research agendas and to be part of changing classroom practice.

1. Introduction

> Successful learning in CLIL lessons is learning which motivates us and where we know we have learned and understood new things. (ITALIC Learner Conference 2010)

Over the last two decades, the Content and Language Integrated Learning (CLIL) phenomenon has undergone significant developments across Europe and beyond. From its inception rooted in European contexts in the early 1990s, CLIL is evolving into a catalyst for conceptualising and re-conceptualising how languages can be used as both the medium and the object of learning in very different global contexts. Strongly influenced by an economic and social need to ensure that young people are equipped with a range of communication skills in more than two languages to enhance employability and mobility, CLIL is becoming increasingly positioned as a change agent i.e. to transform 'traditional' monolingual learning contexts into bilingual experiences; to contribute to the European vision for a plurilingual and pluricultural union; to connect with and learn from well-established global models of immersion and bilingual education such as in Canada; and to work towards a more equitable distribution of linguistic and social capital. Whilst such CLIL ideologies tend to focus on linguistic outcomes, the complexities of its growth and the demands of different contexts have led to wide-ranging questions as to how CLIL is put into practice, taking account of social, cultural, economic and political agendas.

The hybridity of CLIL as a learning phenomenon has both advantages and challenges. There are no fixed models which pre-determine how CLIL will develop. Hence its organic growth in different contexts is part of a changing educational paradigm. The concept of 'dual-focused approaches' to the learning and teaching of both content and language straddles theoretical boundaries linked to learning processes, second language acquisition, language learning, bilingualism, intercultural awareness, bi-literacies and so on, which in turn encourages cross-disciplinary engagement and debate from theoreticians and practitioners alike. As CLIL practice matures, there are increasing demands for evidence of classroom practices which demonstrate the effectiveness of learning experiences and outcomes for young people in terms of content (i.e. subject knowledge), linguistic and intercultural competence.

The context of this study is state secondary schools in England and Scotland. In both countries, foreign language learning is in decline. In England, 56% of 14 year olds do not continue with language studies, and Scotland has a steady decline to 69% of all 18 year olds studying a language. In 2012, the Scottish government launched a 10-year plan for an 'MT + 2' policy across primary and secondary schools which provides real opportunities for developing integrated approaches to language and content learning. Paradoxically, although Gaelic-medium education in Scotland is growing, this has not extended to learning through the medium of other languages. England, on the other hand, has no tradition of bilingual education in state schools – with the exception of some pioneering institutions. However, the situation is changing with regard to CLIL in both countries. Led mainly by language teachers, increasingly schools are trialling and piloting CLIL approaches in an attempt to motivate their learners to continue with language studies. In countries where English is the predominant language, there are assumptions made about Anglophones and their attitudes to using other languages (Lo Bianco 2006). However, more recent research confirms that whilst young people do recognise the value of communicating in other languages (Evans and Fisher 2009) they find their language classroom experiences neither motivating nor challenging enough to develop their skills to become competent users of other languages. Integrating language learning with thematic or subject learning is increasingly perceived as one possible route to motivating learners through *language using* at the same time as language learning so that more young people are given appropriate opportunities to become competent communicators in languages other than English. For the purposes of this study CLIL is defined as a developing, flexible concept where thematic or subject content and foreign languages are integrated in some mutually beneficial way to ensure more learners are motivated to learn and use other languages in the future.

This chapter argues that in order to make the language learning experience of young people more successful, the quality and nature of learning experiences have to be understood from the learners' perspective. This study therefore investigates 'successful' learning across different CLIL contexts by analysing learner motivation and achievement from the learners' perspective. It takes classroom practices as the locus of investigation and the learners as mediators in the process.

2. Defining 'successful' learning

Effective learning is usually measured by testing how far the desired learning outcomes of any programme have been achieved using specific criteria. Large-scale comparisons have led to exercises such as Pisa Tests (OECD 2007) influencing policy and practice on a global stage. In the UK, terms such as 'successful schools' and 'successful leaders' can be found in policy guidance and professional literature. These terms suggest that there is agreement about what constitutes 'successful learning' with little account taken of contextual variables and where empirical evidence such as test results is used to support such claims. This study does not visit the well-rehearsed arguments about the relative value attached to what is measurable in learning (Broadfoot 2008; Black and Wiliam 2009). Instead, underpinning this study is the following principle: measuring learner attainment provides only part of the picture of 'success' – not all aspects of 'successful learning' can be measured by tests. Instead it was decided to investigate 'successful learning' in CLIL settings through analysing what makes learners want to learn and how *they* perceived the value of the processes and outcomes of learning.

2.1. Learner motivation

Despite its fundamental role in the learning process and the extensive literature base, there remain differences of opinion about the nature of motivation and the necessary conditions for it to impact learning. It is clear that linking motivation and achievement is much more complex and dynamic than can be explained through attitudes to work and ensuing test results. Evidence emphasises the importance of pedagogic approaches to language learning which impact on learner attitudes and motivation (Lasagabaster and Huguet 2007; Pae 2008). In line with the current thinking and a move away from earlier work which foregrounded individual intrinsic and extrinsic drivers (Gardner 1985), this study was particularly interested in the role of the classroom as a socially situated locus of learning, the social relations within, participation in activities, personal goals set and learner-teacher reflections (Vandergrift 2005; Dörnyei and Ushioda 2011). As Dörnyei (2007, 719) notes:

> Long-term, sustained learning – such as the acquisition of an L2 – cannot take place unless the educational context provides, in addition to cognitively adequate instructional practice, sufficient *inspiration* and *enjoyment* to build up continuing motivation in the learners. Boring but systematic teaching can be effective in producing, for example, good test results but rarely does it inspire life-long commitment to the subject matter.

Moreover, according to Garcia (2009) learning which involves languages other than one's first, whether in the modern language classroom, immersion classroom or a dual-language setting, is closely related to learner identity and how an individual 'understands his or her relationship to the world, how that relationship is constructed across time and space and how the person understands possibilities for the future' (Norton 2000, 4). Bringing together learner identity and notions of self together with language learning experiences, Dörnyei and Ushioda's recent work (2011) proposes a *complex dynamic systems* model combining motivation, cognition and affect. They suggest that the way individuals feel about themselves and others and the ways in which they appraise their achievements in a specific L2 learning context will have a significant impact on their learning. This stance resonates with research into learner 'investment' where learning takes place in and through alternative languages (e.g. Cummins 2001; Pavelenko 2002) and which concludes that learner identity and the classroom environment together are crucial determinants of motivation.

As research into CLIL accrues so do reports on increased learner motivation in CLIL settings (e.g. Seikkula-Leino 2007; Dooley and Eastman 2008; Lorenzo, Casal, and Moore 2010; Coyle 2011b; Lasagabaster 2011). However, there is a need for caution when generalising from these studies (Bruton 2011) unless specific variables such as learner characteristics, teaching styles, age, composition of the class and pedagogic approaches are taken into account as well as contextual conditions impacting on ways in which CLIL is operationalised in different regions and countries. That noted, three aspects of learner motivation are consistently identified across different studies: the importance of the classroom environment (i.e. the pedagogies which are enacted); learner engagement (e.g. investment, challenge and interest); and the development of learner identities (values, attitudes and notions of self). Adapting Guilloteaux and Dörnyei's (2008, 50) construct of motivational teaching practice, the model shown in Figure 1 was constructed to guide our understanding of the processes inherent in learner motivation in the CLIL classes in this study.

2.2. Learner achievement

The second factor linked to successful learning is learner achievement. As has been discussed, learner achievement goes beyond attainment measures. Instead, the emphasis is on learning from a wider perspective including the effects of the classroom experience and individual roles within. There is tension, however, between what is achieved, what is gained from these experiences and what is tested – all of which impact on motivation especially learner engagement and sense of self as

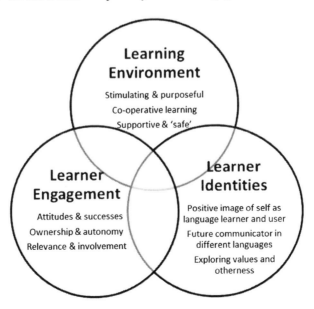

Figure 1. Process model for interpreting motivation in CLIL classes.

learner and language user. Having a sense of learning successfully, making progress and being in control of that learning are not necessarily reflected in the kind of learning outputs which schooling demands. In secondary schools in England and Scotland for example, CLIL outputs are usually situated in the language-learning domain. This is because CLIL is led by language teachers rather than by subject teachers – not necessarily the case in non-Anglophone countries. Expectations of language achievements are skills-based in terms of language competence. In England these include listening and responding, speaking, reading and responding and writing. In Scotland, the skill set goes beyond the four key skills and includes for example, organising and using information, using knowledge about the language, reading to appreciate other cultures. In schools where CLIL is associated with another subject domain rather than thematic study in language classes, especially when subject teachers as well as language teachers are involved, subject-related knowledge and skills are included – analysing sources for example in history and observational skills in science. However, an overemphasis on skills development, especially in language classrooms, tends not to take into account the role of content through which these skills develop, nor to build on the knowledge base which learners bring with them. CLIL, therefore, has a crucial role to play in shifting the prime position of skill development in the language learning setting, to its integration with cognitively appropriate content knowledge to engage learners more fully and engender a deeper sense of learning progression:

> ...educators know that students can't develop and use skills without a core body of knowledge. But they also know that they must emphasize higher order thinking and problem solving if their students are to ultimately learn for themselves... preparing teachers to effectively deliver both content and skills is a very real human capital challenge. (Silva 2009, 632)

Whilst a formal emphasis may be on skills development and language 'performance', learner achievement involves organic processes which cannot be exclusively captured through summative means. Alternative evidence is needed to understand 'successful learning' in the here and now.

> Any meaningful judgement of progress or attainment should be based on a range of activities, outcomes and contexts. This could include assessing the learning as it's happening through observation, discussion or focused questioning; involving pupils in the process through peer or self-assessment; or sampling a range of work over a period of time. (QCDA 2010)

Perhaps conceptualising learner achievement in terms of learner 'gains' in the context of this study is more appropriate since it seeks to capture and understand 'value-added' in terms of cognitive, social and personal gains of individuals within the school context. Understanding what motivates learners as individuals is determined by the learners themselves not predetermined by others. From this perspective, listening to learners is fundamental.

3. Designing a learner-oriented study

As the CLIL research agenda becomes more rigorous and demanding in terms of evidence for effective pedagogies, there is a move away from anecdotal evidence or evaluating small-scale and short-term 'projects' to more longitudinal and empirical studies, monitoring progression over time including linguistic as well as other learning gains or barriers. Due to divergent contextual variables associated with the range and interpretation of CLIL in practice, great care has to be exercised when making claims about the effectiveness of CLIL or otherwise. An emerging picture substantiated by empirical evidence suggests that CLIL raises as many issues as it solves (Ruiz de Zarobe, Sierra, and Puerto 2011). More critical findings of CLIL practice are limited (e.g. Vollmer 2008) or fiercely debated (Lorenzo, Casal, and Moore 2010; Bruton 2011). Mindful of these potential shortcomings, this study explores the synergies between empirical evidence generated by researchers (learner questionnaires), the narratives from learner discussion and reflection (individually and collectively across schools) and classroom practice-based evidence (Simons et al. 2003) generated by the learners. Developing this notion further, what constitutes evidence will be determined by the key players involved and not imposed – thus ensuring that learners will have a voice in the research process.

3.1. Learners as researchers

The phenomenon of learners as researchers was central to the research, concurring with Rudduck and Flutter's (2004, 2) proposition that we should 'take seriously what pupils can tell us about their experience of being a learner in school – about what gets in the way of their learning and what helps them to learn'. This resonates with Alderson's plea (2000, 43) for young people to be given more opportunities to contribute effectively to the quality of their education as *competent social actors*. Based on the work of prominent educational researchers (e.g. Stenhouse 1975; Elliott 1991) there is a growing substantial body of evidence (Holdsworth and Thomson 2002; Ruddock and McIntyre 2007) which suggests that when pupils, usually with their teachers, begin to engage in practitioner research a deeper understanding of conditions for learning evolves. When this understanding is shared and owned by the learners themselves, learner engagement in the learning process will be encouraged by a sense of being valued.

Research using pupil 'voice' has been described as creating opportunities for 'respectful discussions' (Giugni 2006, 106) involving teachers and learners. Young people have shown that they can articulate their own ways of knowing, and their own knowledge (Lewis and Porter 2007) as well as how they learn and under which conditions i.e. contributors and barriers to successful learning. Taking account of these opportunities led the research team to focus on two specific requirements of this study: supporting learners as researchers; and creating appropriate contexts for engaging learners in 'respectful discussions' about what they perceive as CLIL gains. It should be noted that whilst teacher involvement is fundamental in processes which enable learners to be researchers, the teacher role is not the focus of this chapter and is reported on in detail elsewhere (Coyle 2011a).

3.2. Dialogic spaces: respectful discussions

In order to identify the contributors to successful CLIL and engage learners in meaningful reflection and respectful discussions, it was decided to not only involve learners in focus group discussions which took place during researcher visits to schools, but to extend the scope of these discussion outside the classroom. A CLIL

Learner Conference was organised where learners from different schools could meet and exchange views and opinions. The conference provided a space for learners to be respected delegates; they taught each other what they had learned in their CLIL lessons mindful that they did not share the same target language; they discussed issues based on feedback from initial questionnaire data; they created a *Teacher Charter* to guide future classroom practice; they volunteered to go to the *Chill and Spill Room* to talk to a video camera about their CLIL experiences; they posted comments about CLIL; and, above all, they made use of opportunities for adults to listen respectfully to them. These events not only generated a rich narrative, but they also fostered a sense of agency and ownership of conditions for successful, and by inference unsuccessful, learning in a range of CLIL classrooms.

3.3. The LOCIT process

The LOCIT process (Learning-Oriented Critical Incident Technique) adopts a different approach to practitioner research than one which problematises classroom practice at the start (Dana and Yendol-Silva 2003). Instead, LOCIT takes as the *point de départ* an analysis of perceived successful practice by those involved, to understand why it is thought to be successful and how it can be sustained and developed by learners and teachers together. Building on the work of Wells (1999) and Wegerif (2006) which emphasises the need for dialogic classrooms, the CLIL learner-researchers in this study engaged in the LOCIT process (Coyle, Hood, and Marsh 2010; Coyle 2011b) to construct a shared understanding of successful learning amongst themselves and with their teachers.

Using a digital mediating tool (http://www.abdn.ac.uk/locit), the LOCIT process starts with CLIL lessons selected by those involved for filming, reviewing and editing using critical incident analysis (Coyle, Hood, and Marsh 2010; Coyle 2011a). A critical incident in this context is defined as the identification of a 'learning moment'. At a micro-level, learners independently from their teachers use the digital tool to analyse filmed lessons by identifying and justifying 'learning moments' (i.e. adding edit descriptors) before comparing video clips. This process acts as a prompt for a deep level of analysis, discussion and shared understandings using participant perceptions about when, how and why learning has taken place. These are substantiated by participant evidence (i.e. video clips of learning moments and justifications) stored in the LOCIT web-based repository. Analysing successful learning moments is less threatening for those involved than looking for less successful incidents. This analysis acts as the catalyst for reflection. Learners can share their findings with their own teacher, as well as across schools and across cultures using digital technologies.

Whilst critiques of the process may question the nature, validity and reliability of 'learning moments' drawing on a multiplicity of factors which may affect their identification, this misses the point. The learning moments themselves act as triggers for collaborative reflection and discussion between learners and between learners and their teachers. Such discussions can grow dialogic spaces which are based as much on the process of learning as the outcomes of it. These conversations do not stop at rationalising events but instead lead to the collaborative reframing of classroom practice. Moreover, when a group of schools, situated in very different CLIL contexts, engages in classroom inquiry with one shared objective i.e. identifying and analysing learning moments – there is a regulatory sense of a common goal. This has the potential to transform individual subjective judgements about learning into a more objective conceptualisation of CLIL processes which in turn can lead to learner-driven changes to classroom practice. Ultimately the LOCIT process aims to mediate teacher self-agency and learner engagement and to encourage further practitioner research shared with colleagues and learners within and across CLIL schools. In this study the LOCIT process was used as an accessible and supportive means to enable learners and teachers to engage in systematic and intentional inquiry – with an investigation into 'successful learning' based on classroom evidence as a positive induction into analysis, reflection and further action. Investigating the intricate and interrelated processes which generate shared evidence of successful learning requires multifaceted approaches to inquiry in the 'interpersonal space where minds meet and new understandings arise through collaborative interaction or inquiry' (Cummins 2005, 12) and where the sum of the parts is greater than the whole.

4. The study

This study was carried out over one year. Schools across the two countries were recruited to ensure a range of CLIL profiles in terms of experience, teacher orientation (language/language and subject), languages used (French, German and Spanish) and ability of the classes (mixed ability groups, high- and low-ability sets) within the 12–14 age range. The regular language of instruction is English. The majority of learners had limited language learning experience prior to secondary school at the age of 11. Eleven schools opted to participate divided between three categories: two 'experienced' schools with over five years of CLIL practice; four 'experimenting' schools with less than two years of piloting CLIL; and five 'introductory' schools with no former experience of CLIL. The total number of participants was distributed across 2 countries, 11 schools, 32 teachers and over 670 pupils. In nine schools CLIL was led by the language teachers and in five schools language and subject teachers collaborated.

The overarching question was how do learners perceive 'successful learning' in CLIL? There were three sub-questions: (1) What motivates learners in CLIL classrooms? (2) What do learners perceive as the contributors to successful CLIL? (3) What evidence is provided by learners of 'successful learning'?

Learner perceptions of 'successful learning' were analysed on two levels: the micro-level i.e. using context specific data to inform individual school CLIL practice and the macro-level i.e. building on shared understandings across schools to inform future class-based research and provide an impetus for participatory professional development. There were no intentions to make great claims by generalising from data, but instead to draw on collective experiences within and across contexts to inform future practice in the schools at the macro- and micro-levels of participation. This chapter focuses only on the macro-level, and in particular on the ways in which different data resonate in accordance with learner evidence of successful practice.

4.1. Methods

Whilst *Listening to Learners* is part of a larger research project (Coyle 2011a), the emphasis on learners required the use of both 'tried and tested' as well as innovative approaches to learner involvement in CLIL research. Three methods of data

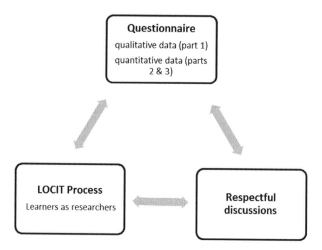

Figure 2. Data sources for understanding learner perceptions of successful learning in CLIL.

collection were identified (Figure 2) building on the theoretical stance previously discussed. Most of the data used in *Listening to Learners* is qualitative with only those data drawn from part 1 of the questionnaires subjected to statistical analysis. Data are anonymised but referenced according to the school and the pupil number e.g. T12.

4.1.1. Questionnaires

A pre- and post-study questionnaire was constructed using our process model of motivation – learner identity, learner investment and classroom ethos (Figure 1). An example of the post-questionnaire can be found in the Appendix – identical to the pre-questionnaire with an added sentence for learners to complete: *I would recommend/I would not recommend learning through another language because… (give reasons)*. Adapting instruments used in previous studies (Dorneyi and Otto 1998; Lasagabaster 2011), pupils responded to 22 statements scored on a 6-point Likert scale in Part 1. Responses were analysed using a range of statistical measures. Empirical data gathered were used as triggers for subsequent respectful discussions. Part 2 used open questions to elicit perceptions of successful learning. Part 3 required learners to select an adjective describing how they felt in their CLIL classes and why. Qualitative data from Parts 2 and 3 were interpreted using content analysis and were also used as catalysts for deeper investigation during 'respectful discussions'. An in-depth analysis of the quantitative and qualitative data can be found elsewhere (Coyle 2011a).

4.1.2. Respectful discussions

The locus for 'respectful discussions' was in school during researcher visits organised on a volunteer basis with individuals, pairs or small focus groups of pupils from seven schools. More discussions also took place during the Learner Conference organised for and by the learners from four schools. The transcripts were transcribed and analysed. Most of the data used in this study came from 'respectful discussions' and are presented in Figure 3. Data pertaining to motivation was analysed using the three themes embedded in the process-model framework. All other data were coded according to themes which emerged during content analysis.

4.1.3. LOCIT data

Video edits of examples of 'learning moments' in filmed CLIL lessons and selected by groups of learners were collated either using the digital space or from pen and paper analysis carried out by learners. Learners and teachers from six schools were able to access the digital tools and two other schools used pen and paper edits. These edits were used by learners to stimulate 'respectful discussions' in class with their teachers about what they believed to be examples of 'learning moments'. Learner justifications accompanying the edits were analysed by the researchers at the same time as reviewing the 'learning moment' clips to avoid misinterpretation of data. Themes emerged from repeated reviewing of the data and were supported by inter-coder reliability procedures where an outsider researcher coded the visual and textual evidence independently with an 80% agreement. The video clips which provided 'lived through' evidence were particularly important in supporting learner reasoning for what constituted 'learning moments' in CLIL classes. The LOCIT data can be subjected to further in-depth analysis, but for the purposes of this study capturing emergent themes across different contexts was sufficient to draw on what those pupils in the sample perceived as 'learning moments contributing to successful CLIL'.

5. Listening to learners

Taking account of the three research questions the findings are presented in terms of empirical data about what motivates learners in CLIL classrooms (Q1); qualitative data which focus on conceptualising and analysing perceived achievements or gains through identifying contributors to learning (Q2, Q3, RD and LC); and finally evidence provided by learners as to what they believe to be successful CLIL practice in their own classroom (LOCIT). These findings are summarised in Figure 3.

5.1. Learner motivation

A range of statistical measures were used to analyse the questionnaire data (Coyle 2011b). These data are useful in providing a general picture of learner perceptions and what motivates or de-motivates them. An overview of these data reveals that 85% of learners wished CLIL to continue in their schools; 15% disagreed, stating it was too difficult, boring and of no use. In some cases despite perceived 'downsides' of CLIL (e.g. 'boring' and 'difficult' being the most frequently cited), 93% of learners were able to see benefits either due to the nature of the experience itself *'CLIL develops my speaking skills'* [R28] or by comparing CLIL lessons favourably with their modern language lessons. 70% of learners saw themselves as someone using more than language for work and leisure in the future, thereby rejecting the idea of being monolingual. This challenges the commonly held view that our young people, many of whom are first language English speakers, have little interest in other languages. 79% of learners perceived language skills as being important. 80% commented that learning through the medium of a foreign language did not conflict with self-image nor did using the target language in front of classmates. Learner engagement in CLIL was very much linked to the progress learners

Contributors to Successful Learning – extracts from what the learners say

Motivation	Learning Environment	Tackling new things was good for our confidence[P13] We were bold – learning subjects in French [R24] I learned to listen more otherwise I wouldn't know what they were saying [C12] We used each other's ideas[F12] How to use different strategies to break things down [Z14] It helped me to improvise [P16] We were better at problem solving [R08]We didn't have to use the text books [T11] I improved my memory [X14] Its more gripping you have to listen so hard [Z19]
	Learner Identities	It puts me in mind of a French person in a French classroom [F19] We were bold – learning subjects in French [Z09] I think I developed a German frame of mind [D09] Got more confidence [P21] I think it gives you a hand in life [C21] It makes you feel like you've achieved something [T14] I am amazed about how people talk and write different [R21] I get a real sense I've done something well [A17]
	Learner Engagement	I think I learnt more probably because I had to listen much more- we got involved more [D20] In ITALIC lessons a lot more people got involved – it wasn't just the people that are confident [R4]
Learner Gains Achievements	Communication	I liked having conversations in groups and pairs in a different language [X08] I really do not like using baby sentences so we didn't have to [X42] It's important to get the confidence to talk to other people in Gerrman or other languages [D28]. We had conversations about the news, describing and explaining things [X21] We learnt how to agree and talk in detail [F10] We worked more in the target language and this was sometimes hard - sometimes OK [F09] I think we talked more in English and in German so that's both really[T12] When we could talk [P05]
	Content/subject	I'm not so sure it helped my language but it certainly helped my understanding of the topic [D55] I think you explore subjects further and understand them more [D32] Being able to pick up information from a text and agreeing or disagreeing with their opinions [F04]. I can back my opinions up [X17] Things turned out better than expected I learnt more than normal [A 24] I didn't always understand the History in my History class but I do now[Z03]
	Language	Learning new words and putting sentences together [Z12] I have developed the skill to talk in French-past present and future [R14] Learned how to speak more fluently by learning more French than the other classes [C06]
	Awareness (discourse, literacies)	Learning more about the language which you wouldn't normally learn [A18] I think I will now look at pieces of writing more carefully in English coz I'll be able to spot more things coz I'm used to working it out [F10] I have achieved and learnt that PHSE in French is no different from PHSE in English [C09] Using both languages made me think more about the way I use English when analysing History texts [C14] You use your brain for big challenges it helped me improvise [A50]

(Data from Questionnaires parts 2 and 3, and transcripts from Respectful Discussions)

Figure 3. Learners' perceptions of contributors to successful CLIL.

perceived they were making, with 85% reporting a sense of achievement when learning through another language. Where learners felt there were 'gains' they were prepared to invest in their learning. A significant difference between pre- and post-data suggests that 71% of learners felt it more natural to be using a language for learning new 'things' than in modern language lessons. Another significant difference between the pre- and post-data suggests that learners perceived CLIL lessons as *different* rather than more *difficult* when compared with modern language lessons.

In the open questions, there were clear references to developing confidence and a feeling of achievement through being engaged in 'hard' work. *'Once you have learned something new and difficult you have achieved something you feel proud'* [R30]. Learner satisfaction appeared to grow from increased understanding and a feeling of progression especially in subject-related skills, such as analysing source documents, empathising with past events from different perspectives, having 'for' and 'against' arguments about topical, controversial and relevant issues which came from 'within' rather than having been formulated and practised in advance. However, some learners reported that they found the lessons boring because the teacher talked too much and there was too much translation. Others felt that it was too much to learn both content and language and therefore 'gave up'. Interestingly several learners said they became bored because they already 'knew' the topic or that there was too much writing. In terms of the learning environment, many felt that they had more opportunities to learn collaboratively and less textbook work stimulated their engagement. Learners also made frequent reference to having 'fun' and playing games, referring to activities where the games focused on content rather than on language. Consequently such lessons were perceived as being more interesting, enjoyable and useful.

Whilst questionnaire data were used to provide an essential contextual backdrop, this study wanted to go deeper into learner perceptions and explore with them their experiences corroborated by class-based examples.

5.2. Learner achievements/gains

The data across all the schools have been summarised and in so doing are drawn from open questions in the questionnaire, but mainly from 'respectful discussions' both in their schools and at the Learner Conference. Three distinct themes emerged: communication, language gains and subject or learning gains (see Figure 3). As has already been stated, this chapter focuses on learners' perceived contributors to 'successful learning' rather than the barriers. Communication emerged as one of the greatest priorities with learners expressing an overwhelming wish to communicate and to develop their communication skills. They wanted to talk with each other and their teacher more and use their language skills. *'We communicate all the time so we need this skill above all others to do it in the foreign language'* [T17]. They believed that CLIL approaches could help them. There were many examples across different schools where learners reported having a discussion in the target language which they would not have had in language lessons – *'thinking quickly to answer questions about something you haven't prepared'* [A12]. Spontaneity was highlighted on many occasions. There was a strong message that the content of the CLIL lessons provides a better stimulus for discussion and communication than those topics associated with language textbooks, although there was a sense that more 'real' discussions were needed. There were also suggestions that the concept of becoming fluent by increasing vocabulary had developed more into an awareness of forming phrases and sentences, responding to questions that had not been pre-prepared, and engaging in authentic discussion. Interaction which impacted both on communication and on enhancing subject-related skills was noted by many learners.

5.2.1. Language gains

Learners generally felt that they had improved their speaking skills. At the Learner Conference they explained how they believed CLIL enables them to go beyond the word level in language learning – they had to 'put together' words into longer utterances (which of course relates to developing their communication skills) and giving them a sense of meaning construction. There was frequent reference to vocabulary and the extension of content-related lexis thus reflecting the widely adopted approach to language learning based on a literacy/learning model which emphasises 'word level' as the starting point. Whilst this approach is embedded in government policies and integrated into National Curricula, many learners, especially those with more limited language skills, perceived their CLIL classes pushed them beyond what could be interpreted as restrictive practice, and enabled them to construct more complex language which in turn facilitated what they defined as *genuine communication*. Learners from six schools made specific reference to how in CLIL lessons they had exceeded predicted levels of speaking output when matched against pre-defined national performance levels. Some data suggest that in particular schools learners relied on written scripts to support speaking e.g. in learner presentations. In others, learners were more confident spontaneous language users. This relates to specific classroom contexts and the ways in which the target language is *used* rather than learned.

Learners indicated that they found writing particularly difficult in CLIL. It was negatively perceived in many but not all of the schools. There is clearly a mismatch between types of writing and levels of language expected in language classes in comparison with those in other subjects, especially in the lower age range in secondary school. However, one school decided to focus on extended writing for Geography. Learners were taught and supported in academic writing, constructing texts which were longer than those produced in language lessons and which developed subject discourse. Learners in this school stated how proud they were of this achievement – which underlines the importance of transparent ownership of learning progression. '*I get a real sense I've done something well*' [A17]. There were few references to reading skills, and listening was often linked to concentration and comprehension. Many learners reported that comprehension was not an issue especially when supported through visual and drama techniques.

In two schools, learners felt that they had improved their translation skills. Translation in CLIL settings is rarely discussed as a pedagogic strategy – often dismissed as negative. Yet some learners believed that translation had helped their understanding both in their first language as well as in the second. According to these learners, it is timely to study the role of translation in practice and as a learning and comparative awareness-raising strategic tool in supporting CLIL.

A strong message emerged regarding the value of CLIL for understanding one's first language better on two levels. The first implies that when the CLIL language required attention (Lyster's 'noticing and awareness strategies' 2007) for 'making meaning' there was a greater emphasis not necessarily on direct translation but on using other clues to guess meaning which were subsequently checked. This checking process led some learners to compare how ideas are expressed in different languages. The second was associated with extending vocabulary in their first language. Through becoming more aware of linguistic features e.g. word families, prefixes and suffixes, increasing awareness of language was commented upon by learners especially where closer analysis of text had been a regular feature of their CLIL lessons. These findings have implications for language awareness and literacy across the curriculum.

5.2.2. Learning gains

At the Learner Conference participants were asked to define 'fun' and 'boring'. There was consensus that learners link these to the need for appropriate levels of cognitive challenge, supported interaction and a sense of involvement in shared learning, where individual learners have a role to play. '*If it's too hard you cannae really do it but if its normal hard and you teach it well, it's easy and hard at the same time*' [K21]. Learners appreciated a sense of discovering new things and having opportunities to discuss 'real' issues. In instances where content was already 'known', learners commented that this was boring. '*I think it's more interesting because before we were learning I have a pet dog and my hobbies are playing football*' [P8]. It was learning 'new things' which was important. Prior learning needs to be treated with caution. Many learners, and not only the more competent linguists, emphasised the importance of being involved in their learning. There was general agreement concerning the need to concentrate in CLIL lessons, that it is normal to make mistakes and 'having a go' is more important than being correct. Having to concentrate more in many cases was synonymous with learning 'better'. '*I think I learnt probably more because I had to listen much more and we got involved more*' [T12].

Crucially greater *involvement* emerged as a key driver for sustaining interest. Confidence in using the target language was repeatedly mentioned alongside a greater willingness to 'guess' meaning. There were many references to content skills and widening perspectives such as '*being aware of how I need to use French to talk History – I never thought about it before*' [P10]. Learners enjoyed researching the content themselves, believing that they had been given more choice and greater autonomy in following their own interests. Greater use of study skills including those needed for researching and analysing content suggested that there were more opportunities for independent learning. Learners felt that they were rising to the challenge of using the language for learning. Dictionary skills were frequently mentioned '*using more complicated words that you hadn't covered yet you could look up*' [P20].

Learners reported feeling CLIL offered different ways of doing things, and overwhelmingly of 'learning together' in contexts where the language teachers were teaching topics beyond the usual language curriculum – '*with this you get to learn more stuff and it's different*' [T11]. The demand for greater interaction and opportunities for richer discussion and collaborative learning were repeatedly referred to by learners across all schools and in particular those schools where CLIL was in its earliest stages of development. Less use of textbooks was also emphasised by learners across all schools as a positive.

6. Successful learning

The LOCIT data positions itself at the interface between motivation and perceptions of 'successful learning'. Having presented the data collected through questionnaires and 'respectful discussions' in the previous sections, the classroom video clips consist of the 'learning moments' identified and justified by the learners. These provide insights into the perceptions of the value of shared experiences within the classroom. The 'learning moments' selected by pupils in the eight schools participating in the LOCIT process and representing different practices and experiences in CLIL fall into three distinct categories: content-focused (knowledge construction and conceptual understanding), language-focused (usually but not exclusively dealing with vocabulary) and affect (Figure 4).

The largest category of 'learning moments' identified by learners across all participating schools was content-focused, highlighting the importance of teacher input for individual comprehension – especially teacher explanation and questioning. Many clips also emphasised how different types of learner engagement can lead to understanding of content and the development of content skills. Learner output was also exemplified especially where learners answered questions or presented their own work. The category containing the language-focused clips emphasised the learning of key content vocabulary which would not have been learned in language lessons. Across the schools, learners selected those moments where lexis was practised through language learning type activities (repetition, true/false, flashcards) and hence practising the language rather than using it was perceived as successful language learning in the CLIL classroom. Learners also identified the importance of affect and in particular satisfaction and achievement – such as when an individual 'got something right'. Interaction and having fun were also identified as well as helping each other.

Strong messages did emerge from the LOCIT data. There were anomalies; all evidence demonstrated an emphasis on learning content-related vocabulary – identified as having greater value perhaps because this would not have occurred in a language lesson. There were no clips of discussions and using the language for learning new content. Language-oriented moments focused almost exclusively on practising the language with an emphasis on new vocabulary, whereas content-focused moments revealed extensive comprehension activities, questions and answers as well as learner output.

In order to analyse the learning moments data, Coyle's Triptych (Coyle, Hood, and Marsh 2010) was used to frame language-oriented learning moments. Building on *content-obligatory* and *content-compatible* language suggested by Snow, Met, and Genesee's (1989, 205), the Triptych is a conceptual representation of the kinds of language CLIL learners need in order to learn both new language and new content and subsequently deepen their understanding. Language *of* learning is needed to access basic concepts and skills, language *for* learning is needed to operate effectively in tasks and activities in the classroom and language *through* learning is required to connect thinking and language to enable learners to articulate their learning and understanding as it evolves. The LOCIT clips showed many examples of *practising* language *of* learning but with very little evidence of language *for* and *through* learning. This may be because the learners perceive less importance attached to language other than keywords which is not as *transparently* linked to understanding content. Contextual variables which impact on the lessons analysed may include the

Learning Moments		Examples of learners reasons for selecting learning moments
Content-Focussed For knowledge construction & conceptual understanding	Teacher Input	I understood by the way she explained it [19] I did understand mostly what she said – key vocabulary [26] We were shown a PowerPoint and I think this helped out learning because we could read the French as well as listen to it [201] Using the IWB, explaining clearly gives us a better understanding of the language you are learning [92] Using the IWB helps teachers explain clearly [136] Explaining gives us a better understanding [74] Our teacher repeated the questions so we have more time [40] The teacher used pictures to help us [82] The teacher used simpler words so we could understand [36] The teachers asks us good questions [12] Our teacher asked us questions and when others answered it gives us a chance to develop our understanding [33]
	Learner Engagement	When we were matching the names of parts of the boat to the picture [25] When we sang the song it helped me to recap and link the pirate life to the slave life [28] The song helped us learn in a more fun way [51] Describing pictures helped me remember the key words such as sugar [39] We made a human diagram to help us understand what went to each continent using key words [79] We did a quiz and this help us learn our history in a fun way [68] She made us complete written work on types of historical proof [content skill] – it helped us learn new vocabulary and also the types of proof that historians accept at the same time [02] When Mrs R told us about their lives – we understood what it was like to be one [content skill] [07] When someone goes to the board and writes up an answer – we can decide [52] We learnt to discuss things in French [23] When we use words we know to learn new things but when we also learn new words to learn new things [03]
	Learner Output	We did a presentation about the topic and it showed what we had learnt [12] We explained what our group had done [06] We had to describe their lives – what it was like, what happened – this helped us expand our knowledge about their lives [empathy] and to combine our History and French [89]
Language-Focussed for lexical understanding	Repetition	We repeated vocabulary using flashcards – this helps us remember [73] Flashcards is an easy way to learn vocabulary [117] Our teacher told us to repeat it so we could learn [102] The teachers makes us repeat things so we get the pronunciation [04]
	Questions/answers	Answering questions – gives the chance to develop our French because we are answering questions in French [38] Questions help us practice our French [09] We learnt to answer questions in French using the right words [44] We learnt how to say landslide [key content word] in French [18] We played games to help us learn words [24]

Figure 4.   Identifying learning moments and emergent meaning-making strategies.

	Pronunciation	We revised French vocabulary and how to pronounce them We learned to say the sounds of words by repeating [93]
	Feedback	The teacher corrected our French so we could learn from our mistakes When we all said whether something was right or not [107]
	Practising new language (lexis)	We practised the play – it helps us learn French [57] Right or wrong tasks help us learn the French [139] We worked on worksheets so we learnt about the History whilst practising French [46] We learnt language words [31]
Affect	Achievement	Satisfaction/learning environment (Getting it right, interacting with others, fun – songs, humour) When he got it right [123] When K answered the question- because she got it right [151] C got stuck and we helped her and we all joined in [33] When A answered the first question [40] S answered and got it right [95]

'Meaning–Making' Strategies for Successful CLIL

Meaning-making **Cognitively–oriented**	Scaffolded input explanations	e.g. miming, known language, interactive activities – human diagrams, IWB, quizzes and explanations with visual support, written/reading support, miming; developing subject specific skills e.g. writing a report, using history sources. Putting two and two together [51] Flashcards provide pictures to help us understand without words [61] I guessed the rest [88] When we repeat words in our heads [111] We write things down to help us remember [36]
Meaning-making **Language–oriented**	Lexis	Word level: repetition, memorisation, practising, comparison with L1, recording vocabulary, body language, The human diagram helped me memorise the vocabulary we had been learning [124] Acting out helped us because the words and phrases were useful in other lessons [75] Comparing what things mean in different languages [28] Picking out what we know from a text then putting it together again [49] Using the words and sounds together to get meaning [109]
Meaning-making **Affect-oriented**	Learner investment	Peer support, feeling of making progress/celebration of correctness, interactive activities, feelings of enjoyment i.e. supportive yet challenging learning environment Listening to what others are saying [22] We showed what we knew [30] My friend explained it to me [115]

(Data from LOCIT process)

Figure 4. (Continued)

sequence of learning activities within a unit of work, the presence of a subject teacher and/or language teacher and so on. Interestingly, learners identified very clear *meaning strategies* which they believed led to successful learning. These divide into content-, language- and affect-oriented strategies, presented in more detail in Figure 4. Further monitoring of these learner-owned strategies could lead to deeper reflections on learning to learn.

Whilst it could be argued that some of findings are consistent with previous studies, these findings are unique in that they are 'owned' by the learners substantiated in part by classroom-based evidence through LOCIT. 'Ownership' of the data and indeed the processes which led to the findings at both the macro- and micro-levels change the research landscape. Not all the findings are positive by any means, but the feedback both positive and negative enables learners to work together with their teachers to create a shared learning environment. This shift in ownership marks a significant difference in the way an alternative lens can contribute to the CLIL field. The voices speak for themselves: *'Being listened to and* heard *helps us to go for it more'* [P72].

Whilst the learners in this study were clearly working in collaboration with their teachers, the potential for teacher development and further learner-teacher class-based inquiry stimulated by both 'respectful discussions' and LOCIT processes are summarised in one's teacher comments:

> You can't really ignore it and say it's Ok in theory because it's all about us and what we do, not some nameless schools in nameless places...something concrete to work on with our learners – we are sharing responsibilities and I never thought we could achieve that...we have created our own map.

In conclusion, this study revealed how learners perceive the need for changes to pedagogic practice through CLIL experiences. They detail the overwhelming need to communicate, to develop ways of using language and to engage in the learning process. They identify how literacy practices need to change and how expectations of achievement need to develop in order to sustain motivation. This is study is not, however, about finding the 'best approach' for CLIL, nor about claiming that CLIL practices will lead to successful learning. Instead it experiments an approach to classroom research where the data generated through listening to learners are 'owned' by them and their teachers. Selecting and combining data-gathering procedures from this repertoire – and in particular the LOCIT process – when used reflectively and collaboratively can provide a trigger to bring about changes to classroom practices, and those within their professional community. Arguably it is the process of data gathering and reflection which will influence classroom practice in any context where strategies for 'successful learning' emerge from what learners say and do, but at the same time *listening to learners* provides a frame of reference about how situated professional practice needs to change if successful content and language integrated learning is to be sustained across very different contexts.

References

Alderson, P. 2000. "School Students' Views on School Councils and Daily Life at School." *Children and Society* 14 (2): 121–134. doi:10.1111/j.1099-0860.2000.tb00160.x.

Black, P., and D. Wiliam. 2009. "Developing the Theory of Formative Assessment." *Educational Assessment, Evaluation and Accountability* 21 (1): 5–31. doi:10.1007/s11092-008-9068-5.

Broadfoot, P. 2008. *An Introduction to Assessment*. London: Continuum.

Bruton, A. 2011. "Are the Differences between CLIL and Non-CLIL Groups in Andalusia Due to CLIL? A Reply to Lorenzo, Casal and Moore. 2010." *Applied Linguistics* 32 (2): 236–241. http://applij.oxfordjournals.org/content/early/2011/03/01/applin.amr007.full. doi:10.1093/applin/amr007

Coyle, D. 2011a. *The Italic Research Report*. University of Aberdeen. http://www.abdn.ac.uk/italic

Coyle, D. 2011b. "Post-method Pedagogies: Using A Second or Other Language as A Learning Tool in CLIL Settings." In *Content and Foreign Language Integrated Learning: Contributions to Multilingualism in European Contexts*, edited by Y. R. Zarobe, J. M. Sierra, and F. G. Puerto, 49–73. Bern: Peter Lang.

Coyle, D., P. Hood, and D. Marsh. 2010. *Content and Language Integrated Learning*. Cambridge: Cambridge University Press.

Cummins, J. 2001. *Negotiating Identities: Education for Empowerment in a diverse society*. 2nd ed. Los Angeles: California Association for Bilingual Education.

Cummins, J. 2005. "Using Information Technology to Create A Zone of Proximal Development for Academic Language Learning." In *Information Technology and Innovation in Language Education*, edited by C. Davison, Chap 6, 105–126. Hong Kong: Hong Kong University Press.

Dana, N. F., and D. Yendol-Silva. 2003. *The Reflective Educator's Guide to Classroom Research: Learning to Teach and Teaching to Learn Through Practitioner Inquiry*. Thousand Oaks, CA: Corwin Press.

Dooley, M., and D. Eastman, eds. 2008. *How We're Going About It: Teachers' Voices on Innovative Approaches to Teaching and Learning Languages*. Newcastle: Cambridge Scholars Publishing.

Dörnyei, Z. 2007. *Research Methods in Applied Linguistics: Quantitative, Qualitative and Mixed Methodologies*. Oxford: Oxford University Press.

Dörnyei, Z., and I. Otto. 1998. Motivation in action: A process model of L2 motivation. *Working Papers in Applied Linguistics* 4: 43–69, Thames Valley University.

Dörnyei, Z., and E. Ushioda. 2011. *Teaching and Researching Motivation*. Harlow: Pearson Education.

Elliott, J. 1991. *Action Research for Educational Change*. London: Open University Press.

Evans, M., and L. Fisher. 2009. Language Learning at Key Stage 3: The Impact of the KS3 Modern Languages Framework and Changes to the Curriculum on Provision and Practice. HMSO: Final Research Report DCSF-RR127. https://www.education.gov.uk/publications//eOrderingDownload/DFE-RR052.pdf

Garcia, O. 2009. *Bilingual Education in the 21st Century: A Global Perspective*. Chichester: Wiley-Blackwell.

Gardner, R. C. 1985. *Social Psychology and Second Language Learning: The Role of Attitudes and Motivation*. Baltimore, MD: Edward Arnold.

Giugni, M. 2006. "Conceptualising Goodies and Baddies through Narratives of Jesus and Superman." *Contemporary Issues in Early Childhood* 7 (2): 97–108. doi:10.2304/ciec.2006.7.2.97.

Guilloteaux, M. J., and Z. Dörnyei. 2008. "Motivating Language Learners: A Classroom-oriented Investigation of the Effects of Motivational Strategies on Student Motivation." *TESOL Quarterly* 42 (1): 55–77. http://www.zoltandornyei.co.uk/uploads/2007-guilloteaux-dornyei-tq.pdf.

Holdsworth, R., and P. Thomson. 2002. "Options Within the Regulation and Containment of 'student voice'." Student Voice Symposium, American Educational Research Association. New Orleans, April 4, 2002.

Lasagabaster, D. 2011. "English Achievement and Student Motivation in CLIL and EFL Settings." *Innovation in Language Learning and Teaching* 5: 3–18. doi:10.1080/17501229.2010.519030.

Lasagabaster, D., and A. Huguet. 2007. *Multilingualism in European Bilingual Contexts. Language Use and Attitudes*. Clevedon: Multilingual Matters.

Lewis, A., and J. Porter. 2007. "Research and Pupil Voice." In *Handbook of Special Education*, edited by L. Florian, 222–232. London: Sage.
Lo Bianco, J. 2006. "Arguing for Perspective in LOTE." *Languages Victoria* [1328-7621] 10 (1): 16–24.
Lorenzo, F., S. Casal, and P. Moore. 2010. "The Effects of Content and Language Integrated Learning in European Education: Key Findings from the Andalusian Bilingual Sections Evaluation Project." *Applied Linguistics* 31 (3): 418–442. doi:10.1093/applin/amp041.
Lyster, R. 2007. *Learning and Teaching Languages Through Content: A Counterbalanced Approach*. Amsterdam, NLD: John Benjamin.
Norton, B. 2000. *Identity and Language Learning: Gender, Ethnicity and Educational Change*. Harlow: Longman.
OECD PISA Tests. 2007. Paris: OECD. http://www.oecd.org/dataoecd/54/12/46643496.pdf
Pae, T.-I. 2008. "Second Language Orientation and Self-Determination Theory. A Structural Analysis of the Factors Affecting Second Language Achievement." *Journal of Language and Social Psychology* 27 (1): 5–27. doi:10.1177/0261927X07309509.
Pavelenko, A. 2002. "Post-structuralist Approaches to the Study of Social Factors in Second Language Learning and Use." In *Portraits of the L2 User*, edited by V. Cook, 277–302. Clevedon: MultiLingual Matters.
Qualifications and Curriculum Development Agency (QCDA). 2010. Assessing pupils' progress: learners at the heart of assessment. http://curriculum.qcda.gov.uk/key-stages-3-and-4/subjects/key-stage-3/modern-foreign-languages/assessing-mfl/index.aspx
Ruddock, J., and D. McIntyre. 2007. *Improving Learning Through Consulting Pupils*. London: Routledge.
Ruddock, J., and J. Flutter. 2004. *Consulting Pupils: What's in It for Schools?* London: Routledge Falmer.
Ruiz de Zarobe, Y., J. M. Sierra, and F. G. Puerto, eds. 2011. *Content and Foreign Language Integrated Learning: Contributions to Multilingualism in European Contexts*. Bern: Peter Lang.
Seikkula-Leino, J. 2007. *CLIL Learning: Achievement Levels and Affective Factors*. http://www.scribd.com/doc/13539167/CLIL-Learning-Affective-Factors
Silva, E. 2009. "Measuring Skills for 21st Century Learning." *Kappan* 90 (09): 630–634. http://216.78.200.159/Documents/RandD/Phi%20Delta%20Kappan/Measuring%20Skills%20for%2021st%20Century%20-%20Silva.pdf
Simons, H., S. Kushner., K. Jones, and D. James. 2003. "From Evidence-based Practice to Practice-based Evidence: The Idea of Situated Generalisation." *Research Papers in Education* 18 (4): 347–364. doi:10.1080/0267152032000176855.
Snow, M., M. Met, and F. Genesee. 1989. "A conceptual framework for the integration of language and content in second/foreign language instruction." *TESOL Quarterly* 23: 201–217. doi:10.2307/3587333.
Stenhouse, L. 1975. *An Introduction to Curriculum Research and Development*. London: Heineman.
Vandergrift, L. 2005. "Relationships among Motivation Orientations, Meta-cognitive Awareness and Proficiency in L2 Listening." *Applied Linguistics* 26 (1): 70–89. doi:10.1093/applin/amh039.
Vollmer, H. 2008. "Constructing Tasks for Content and Language Integrated Assessment." In *Research on Task-based Language Learning and Teaching. Theoretical, Methodological and Pedagogical Perspectives*, edited by J. Eckerth and S. Siekmann, 227–290. New York: Peter Lang.
Wegerif, R. 2006. "A Dialogic Understanding of the Relationship between CSCL and Teaching Thinking Skills." *International Journal of Computer Supported Collaborative Learning* 1 (1): 143–157. doi:10.1007/s11412-006-6840-8.
Wells, G. 1999. *Dialogic Inquiry: Towards a Socio-cultural Practice and Theory of Education*. Cambridge: Cambridge University Press.

CONTENT AND LANGUAGE INTEGRATED LEARNING

Appendix

Student **POST** Questionnaire [2]

To be completed after the ITALIC lessons

School _____

Class _____   Initals _____

Date _____

Funded by Esmée Fairbairn Foundation

PART 1

Below you will find some statements. Decide how strongly you agree or disagree with each statement by ticking a box. There are no right or wrong answers. Just decide what YOU think.

	STATEMENT	strongly agree	agree	partly agree	slightly disagree	disagree	strongly disagree
1.	The 'future me' is someone who will use more than one language for work or leisure						
2.	Using more than one language helps my brain develop						
3.	I have strategies that I use to help me understand when the lesson is not in English						
4.	Using another language to learn new things, you need to be at a high level or have studied it for years						
5.	Learning and improving my language skills is important to me						
6.	Across the world, if most people (the majority) use more than one language then I want to be like them						
7.	Using a language other than my first language to learn new things is a challenge						
8.	In school and with my mates, it's not 'cool' to use a language other than English						
9.	When I think about the 'future me' I also think about using more than one language						
10.	In lessons which use a different language to learn new things, I have to concentrate more						
11.	Everyone makes mistakes when we use different languages – it's normal						
12.	It feels more natural to use a different language in lessons for learning new things than in Modern Language lessons						
13.	Monolinguals are people who only speak one language. The 'future me' will be monolingual						
14.	You don't need to be 'clever' to use another language- anyone can						

CONTENT AND LANGUAGE INTEGRATED LEARNING

15.	In lessons which use a different language to learn new things, having a 'go' at saying what I want to say is what matters - not whether or not it is 100% correct					
16.	I feel a sense of achievement when I learn in a language other than English					
17.	If I spend time **now** learning how to use a different language for learning new things, it will benefit the 'future me'					
18.	I feel silly talking in a different language in front of my class mates					
19.	Lessons where we use a different language to learn new things are not more difficult than those in English- they're just different					
20.	I don't really feel like 'me' when I use a different language to learn new things					
21.	I feel I learn as much about the subject in lessons which use a different language, than I would do if it were taught in English.					
22.	The way I am in lessons which use a different language to learn new things, is just the same as in other lessons on my timetable					

PART 2

Below you will find six questions. Answer each question in the box below. There are no right or wrong answers – just write what you feel.

1. What did you **most** look forward to in lessons when you used a different language to learn new things? Did it work out how you expected?

2. What did you **least** look forward to in lessons when you used a different language to learn new things? Did it work out how you expected?

3. What do YOU think you **achieved** through learning new things in a different language? What did you like doing best?

4. What kind of **skills** do you think you developed whilst learning new things through another language?

CONTENT AND LANGUAGE INTEGRATED LEARNING

5. Give an example of what you **LEARNT better in a different language in ITALIC lessons.**

6. Give an example of how you **USED language in ITALIC lessons**?

PART 3

Complete the sentence below by choosing a word or words from the box OR by putting in your own word/s. After 'because' give your reasons for choosing the word/s

In lessons where a different language is used, I was usually _____

choose one or more of these:
confident
fed-up
interested
achieving
the 'real' me
bored
Or
add your own word or words

because...[give your reasons]

_____

I would recommend/ I would not recommend learning through a different language because...[give your reasons]

_____

Thank you

The power of beliefs: lay theories and their influence on the implementation of CLIL programmes

Julia Hüttner[a], Christiane Dalton-Puffer[b] and Ute Smit[b]

[a]*Department of Modern Languages, University of Southampton, Southampton, UK;* [b]*Department of English, University of Vienna, Vienna, Austria*

Content and Language Integrated Learning (CLIL) is one of the most dynamic pedagogic trends in language teaching in Europe, and yet, the enthusiasm with which this innovation is implemented by stakeholders and 'made a success' is not fully understood. In this chapter we argue for an investigation of CLIL implementation as a form of extended language policy, which relates language management, practice and beliefs, and so expands the notion of policy well beyond a top-down legislation. In this contribution, the suggested centrality of beliefs to CLIL policy analysis will be shown by a detailed investigation into the lay theories of teachers and learners involved in CLIL instruction in Austrian upper secondary colleges of technology, which traditionally attract students considered as relatively unsuccessful foreign language learners. The data consist of 48 in-depth interviews with teachers and students in this setting, covering a range of teacher specialisations and of student abilities. The discursive and content analysis of these interviews shows clear clusters of beliefs relating to language learning, the effects and benefits of CLIL and to the construction of success regarding CLIL. Findings suggest that the strength of beliefs and the relative absence of language management result in a construction of CLIL and of CLIL success that is partly at odds with those of experts or policy-makers, but which is linked directly to local CLIL practices. Issues arising of these mismatches are discussed.

1. Introduction

When we consider the fate of pedagogic innovations in mainstream teaching, a complex situation can be observed with some changes being accepted quickly and enthusiastically by the stakeholders involved, without the apparent need or desire for scientific evidence supporting the benefits claimed, while other changes meet with reluctance or even open opposition, possibly despite good research evidence in their favour. In the Austrian context, Content and Language Integrated Learning (CLIL) as well as many other forms of, especially early, bilingual education fall into the first category of easy acceptance, while, for instance, standardised exams or external student competence evaluations generally come into the latter category of reluctance and opposition. CLIL has, indeed, experienced a quite remarkable adoption rate and positive attitudes by stakeholders, even with student groups stereotypically perceived as less motivated language learners, even before any research evidence or systematic assessment of CLIL students' language development was available to support such a view of CLIL.

This chapter sets out to argue that the beliefs held by stakeholders in education are able to shed more light onto this situation of diverse acceptance of pedagogic innovations, and especially onto the seemingly undiminished success of CLIL in Austria. Decisions on foreign language pedagogy at a national level, such as the adoption of CLIL in Austrian mainstream schooling, form a core aspect of language policy (LP), and there are a number of explicit language management statements on both national and EU levels on the use of CLIL. It would, however, be simplistic to view the perceived success of CLIL language practices in Austria as a direct result of these LP statements. As argued by Spolsky (2004), LP documents stand in a complex relationship with both language practice and, importantly, with language beliefs. Over the last few decades, research into teachers' beliefs has shown effects on classroom practices (cf., e.g. Borg 2003), on individuals' development as professionals (cf., e.g. Johnson 1994) and also on their adoption and acceptance of new teaching approaches (cf., e.g. Donaghue 2003). Despite a wealth of research conducted into learner beliefs and into teacher cognition, these have – to our knowledge – so far not been related explicitly to one specific educational approach in its trial phase. Here we shall discuss the construction of beliefs on CLIL by the stakeholders involved in relationship with relevant language practices and language management (cf. Spolsky 2004). We shall argue that especially the construction of this approach as 'successful', as well as the conceptualisation of learning by most stakeholders, relies heavily on beliefs and in the absence of CLIL management generally favours an unstructured adoption of CLIL. However, we shall also be pointing out contradictory trends as well as distinctions of opinion within the groups of stakeholders interviewed.

2. Theoretical background
The policy framework

Given our interest in beliefs as a central force in creating the success of CLIL, our concern lies with its design, implementation and social construction, and in showing how these three aspects are interrelated and codependent. The resultantly complex conceptualisation is best encapsulated by the tripartite model of LP, put forth by Spolsky (2004) and elaborated by Shohamy (2006) and Spolsky (2009) as 'expanded view of LP' (Shohamy 2006, 32).

Spolsky's tripartite model is an extension of original discussions on LP and planning, which largely focused on officially published policy documents and measures of policy implementation (cf., e.g. Ferguson 2006, 16–17). The model recognises that a community's LP, or 'language choices made by individual speakers on the basis of rule-governed patterns recognized by the speech community (or communities) of which they are members' (Spolsky 2009, 1), is complex and integrates three socio-linguistically rather disparate components: *language practices, language management* and *language beliefs* (Spolsky 2004, 5–14). Language practices refer to which varieties are used by whom, for which purposes and under which circumstances; language management covers the various statements and documents that attempt to influence the actual language practices; and language beliefs capture how the social players involved think about and construct their language choices.

Additionally, each of these components is complex in itself in that it relates to various political levels – from supra-national to institutional. Such a tri-componential and multilayered conceptualisation not only captures the complexity surrounding a community's 'language choices', but it also allows for a critical assessment of the contested nature of the societal mechanisms behind 'organizing, managing and manipulating language behaviours' (Shohamy 2006, 45). Given the diverse interests and language ideologies of various societal groups, language practices, managerial decisions and language beliefs usually do not fit neatly together, but often stand in covert or even overt contradiction, competing for more societal relevance and impact. Or, as Shohamy (2006, 54) puts it, there is a 'battle between ideology and practice', which is waged by societal mechanisms that research needs to identify, address and critically assess. In other words, when dealing with a specific LP, researchers need to pay attention to all three components – what is done, what should be done and what is believed to be done – as well as their complementary or conflicting interdependence.

When applied to CLIL, the 'expanded view of LP' (Shohamy 2006, 32) clarifies that CLIL policies are made up of management statements, actual practices as well as stakeholders' beliefs, and that all three components are relevant in their individual complexity and mutual, potentially contested inter-relatedness. Interestingly, the extant CLIL research literature has paid much more attention to CLIL practices and CLIL management, but sidelined the component of beliefs (see Section 1.3).

In an attempt to counter-balance the picture, our focus here is particularly on the last, i.e. stakeholder beliefs about language use and language learning in Austrian CLIL settings.

Language learner and teacher beliefs

Although the precise definitions of beliefs in the context of second language learning and teaching are a little elusive (cf. Pajares 1992), the quite inclusive view we shall be following in this chapter is that beliefs are lay theories of teachers and learners and constitute the complex cluster of intuitive, subjective knowledge about the nature of language, language use and language learning, taking into account both cognitive and social dimensions, as well as cultural assumptions (cf. Barcelos 2003a, 8ff). Within the growing body of research into learner and teacher beliefs, we find sound empirical evidence suggesting that beliefs are important in understanding learner motivation (cf. Csizér and Lukács 2010; Dörnyei and Ushioda 2009) and that beliefs affect how learners make sense of their experiences and organise their learning (Mercer and Ryan 2010; Wenden 1998, 1999). Also, they affect teachers' classroom behaviour, although contradictions between beliefs and actions are also observed (e.g. Borg 2006; Farrell and Kun 2008; Farrell and Ng 2003; Li and Walsh 2011; Phipps and Borg 2009). Research evidence clearly shows the relevance of beliefs in teacher education (e.g. Borg 2003; Donaghue 2003; Johnson 1994; Mansour 2009), suggesting that without addressing teachers' pre-existing beliefs, changes cannot successfully be implemented in teacher attitudes or behaviour.

In the *contextual* approach to studying lay theories (Barcelos 2003a, 19) the focus lies on specific contexts, which themselves are viewed as 'socially constituted' and 'interactively sustained' (cf. Goodwin and Duranti 1992, 5), and beliefs are viewed as inherently dynamic constructions of the learning and teaching endeavour. In line with this position, we view the beliefs held by our interviewees as social constructions of their reality and as changeable and possibly contradictory. Other characteristics we associate with beliefs are that they are dynamic rather than static mental representations (Amuzie and Winke 2009; Tanaka and Ellis 2003; Mercer 2011) and inherently complex (Mercer 2011; Mori 1999; Woods 2003). Thus, beliefs are to be investigated and understood in their own right, without an a priori agenda of which beliefs there might be, or, more extreme, of changing existing beliefs.

We adopt a view of discourse as a locus of (co-)construction of these beliefs and not merely as a way of making these beliefs visible (cf. Kalaja 2003; Kramsch 2003; Potter 1996). The means of investigating such beliefs is therefore the analysis of the discourse constructing these beliefs in a twofold way by focusing, firstly, on the content of the discourse and secondly, on the way in which this content is transmitted. Both such content and discourse analyses are in our case based on interviews, where participants could within a loose structure talk about and develop their own views on language, language learning and CLIL. As we consider the beliefs held by all stakeholders in education to be of value, we focus equally on CLIL learners and teachers (cf. Barcelos 2003b; Brown 2009; Dufva 2003; Woods 2003 on combined investigations of teacher and student beliefs).

In this way, studying beliefs will be of relevance as a springboard for stakeholders' reflection on the nexus between their beliefs, policy documents and specific educational practices. This is in line with findings on teacher cognition that show the importance of addressing core beliefs of teachers in order to raise awareness and enable practitioners to make more informed choices in their practices (cf. Borg 2003; Olson and Jimenez-Silva 2008).

The following section discusses, albeit briefly, the current state of CLIL policy and practices in Europe.

Policy and practices in CLIL

The implementation of CLIL in Europe has been fuelled from two ends: high-level policy-making and grass-roots actions. What we see above all is individuals reacting to what they rightly perceive as major shifts in society and economic life, so that many parents believe that CLIL promises their children an edge in the competition for employment (Li 2002); on the same account, teachers often take the initiative to teach through the medium of English. On the other end of the spectrum, high-level political agents at EU level have also started to steer language management activities in the direction of CLIL, notably through the publication of policy papers. In a declaration by the European Commission, CLIL was invested with 'a major contribution to make to the Union's language learning goals' (European Commission Communication 2003, 8). These language-learning goals consist not only in 'the ability to understand and communicate in more than one language (...) [as] a desirable life-skill' (European Commission 2008, chapter 14), but also that 'the EU's language policy promotes multilingualism and aims for a situation in which every EU citizen can speak at least two foreign languages in addition to their mother tongue' (European Commission 2009). It is thus evident that language-learning goals are the defining feature of CLIL in EU policy papers.

Despite this ostentatious importance of CLIL, few of the 27 national education systems in the European Union have actually responded with substantial management investments into CLIL implementation, teacher education and research, so that explicit goals and precise curricular objectives are largely missing and CLIL continues to be carried forward in most cases by grass-roots stakeholders' practices (cf. Eurydice 2006). Austria, the local context of this study, is no exception in this respect; in fact, it can serve as a typical European case: numerous schools in all sectors of the education system run CLIL modules or whole CLIL streams, developing them in response to local needs and resources. While the last official statistics were published in 2005 (Nezbeda 2005), the education authorities are favourably inclined towards CLIL initiatives and have sanctioned CLIL provision globally and rather unspecifically in the shape of a brief and very general article about medium of instruction in the national school law (cf. Nezbeda 2005); however, a ministerial directive also rules that students must always have the possibility to take exams in the constitutional majority language German. Apart from that, there are no CLIL-specific curricular guidelines or learning goals, neither are there any binding requirements in terms of quantity or quality of provision, including teacher qualification. CLIL thus continues to be a fully grass-roots endeavour even after 20 years, which effectively means that schools of all types and levels (general, academic and vocational, primary and secondary) can and do offer the kind and extent of CLIL programme that suits the school's resources and the students' or parents' needs.

In contrast to the managerial void at national levels (except in Spain and The Netherlands), a series of transnational European expert groups have translated the high-level policy claims mentioned above into conceptualisations, curricular guidelines and model materials which are accessible through international workshops and online (e.g. www.clilcompendium.com, www.ccn-clil.eu, www.clilconsortium.jyu.fi, www.ecml.at/activities/intro.asp).[1] The extent to which these activities and the suggestions resulting from them impact upon national and local practices is hard to fathom. With regard to the Austrian national CLIL scene in focus in this study, it can be said that these offerings have been received only by a small number of individuals (cf. Gierlinger et al. 2010), and have therefore had a very limited impact. The practice of CLIL is thus exclusively guided by experiential criteria and beliefs of the individuals involved. Alongside the work just mentioned on conceptual development, empirical research on CLIL has seen a lively development since about 2005. However, this research has so far dealt with the participants' perspective only to a very limited extent (cf. Moate 2011; Viebrock 2007). In contrast, the outcomes of CLIL programmes have been studied in a number of larger-scale projects (e.g. Admiraal, Westhoff, and de Bot 2006; Hüttner and Rieder-Bünemann 2010; Jexenflicker and Dalton-Puffer 2010; Lasagabaster 2008; Lasagabaster and Ruiz de Zarobe 2010; Llinares and Whittaker 2010; Lorenzo, Casal, and Moore 2005; Mewald 2007; Ruiz de Zarobe 2008; Zydatiß 2012; see Dalton-Puffer 2011 for a comprehensive survey). In general, the findings in different studies concur in that CLIL students have more highly developed language skills than had the mainstream comparison groups on a range of dimensions, but not on all (e.g. CLIL has not been shown to confer clear advantages for pronunciation or textual competence). With regard to content learning some studies report cognitive advantages (van de Craen et al. 2007) while others found reduced complexity of subject-specific concepts (Airey 2009; Walker 2010) and yet others adopt an intermediate position (Badertscher and Bieri 2009; Jäppinen 2005). Also, doubts are now being formulated regarding the implied causality between CLIL and the good learning results found by outcomes studies (cf. Bruton 2011); a fundamental problem affecting comparisons between CLIL- and mainstream learners being that participants in CLIL programmes (a) tend to come from socio-economically strong backgrounds, (b) tend to have a special interest in languages and (c) continue to receive the same EFL teaching as the mainstreamers on top of their CLIL.

Alongside outcome studies a growing research literature on the practices observable in CLIL classrooms offers interesting perspectives on issues relevant to this study. Several researchers report that active student participation is lower than in parallel groups instructed in L1 (e.g. Kiraz et al. 2010; Lim Falk 2008). The declaration that CLIL lessons are pedagogically more innovative and student-oriented or at least different from L1 lessons was not confirmed by Badertscher and Bieri's (2009) comparative observation of Swiss CLIL and non-CLIL content lessons; they found no differences in the overall pedagogical design of the two modes, an observation that can also be made on the basis of Dalton-Puffer's Austrian data (2007). What does seem to happen, though, is a subtle readjustment of roles in the sense that the L2 puts teachers and learners more on an equal footing (e.g. Nikula 2010; Smit 2010), a phenomenon on which our data add an interesting twist. In addition to the meaning orientation of L2 use in CLIL, such interpersonal effects may play a decisive role in explaining reduced L2 speaking anxiety of CLIL learners (e.g. Maillat 2010).

In this brief synopsis we have noted two gaps in the current research into CLIL: the perspective of students and teachers and the question of what CLIL does for people who are not specially inclined towards or interested in foreign language learning. Both of these are addressed in the present chapter.

3. Context and design of the study
Institutional context

As has become noticeable from our discussion in Section 1.3, Austrian educational culture is characterised by a relatively high degree of teacher autonomy with regard to curricular and methodological matters, including a certain amount of classroom time that can be devoted to subject-related project work. While this autonomy does not hold for administrative and organisational matters in general, assessment is one aspect typically performed by the class teacher, including for school-leaving exams. Only recently the introduction of a national diagnostic test at grade levels 4 and 8, as well as a partly standardised school-leaving exam at grade level 12 have started a possible cultural change in this respect. Another characteristic of the country's educational culture is the high degree of orality in the teaching and assessment of non-language subjects. Thus, setting writing tasks in content subjects such as History, Geography or Economics would constitute an unusual pedagogic decision in Austria, and written tests in these subjects are balanced by oral exams.

The teacher and student voices we draw on in this chapter come from Austrian colleges of technology and crafts, known by the abbreviation of *HTL*, which stands for *Höhere technische Lehranstalt*, a label that enjoys considerable prestige, so that in many cases an HTL will have the pick of the best technically interested students from lower secondary schools. This type of upper secondary schools is rather specific to the Austrian education system, as in many other countries the specialisations they offer are available only at tertiary level, ranging from mechanical engineering, construction, mining and textile product engineering to materials engineering, software development and many more. The HTL curricula also include general knowledge subjects as well as two obligatory *English as a foreign language* lessons per week. The HTL encompasses grades 9–13 and provides its students with full university entrance qualifications.

In 2008 CLIL was used in 65% of the Austrian HTLs (that is 49 of 75 HTL sites) and approximately half of these schools were planning to further increase their CLIL provision (see Dalton-Puffer et al. 2008). In every single case the first 'L' in CLIL stood for English. As for the schools without CLIL, 80% of them reported they were interested in introducing it, though the majority had no concrete plan to do so. In the HTLs with CLIL, the most frequently taught theoretical specialist subjects which involve CLIL are Computer Science, Foundations of Data Processing, Electronics and Programming. The general knowledge subjects most frequently taught through CLIL are Geography, History and Chemistry. Practical technical subjects, however, are rarely taught in English (at only 21% of all CLIL sites), even though participants view their potential as high. The majority of CLIL teachers are content subject specialists without formal qualifications in the target language and/or language pedagogy, although there are some teachers who have combined degrees in English language teaching and a general knowledge subject.

Research design and methodology

For the present chapter we draw on the student and teacher interviews. The 20 students interviewed were in year one to year five (grade 9 to grade 13), their ages ranging from 15 to 20 years. At each school, however, the interviewees were attending the same grade level. In conversation with form teachers care was taken that students of different academic capability levels were interviewed at each site. Except for one student, the interviewees were all male, reflecting the gender distribution in these schools. Compared to the populations examined in other CLIL studies situated in general education programmes it is safe to say that the HTL students do not represent a 'positive selection' with regard to affinity for modern languages, on the contrary. In some settings, students had little choice but to accept being in a CLIL strand, as their strand of technical specialisation was only offered as a CLIL strand. Findings have thus to be interpreted also with this additional dimension in mind.

The 28 teachers who were interviewed teach either English and a general education subject ($N=7$) or else a variety of technology, engineering and business subjects ($N=21$). Several of them had previous work experience outside education, which they later complemented with a brief teacher preparation course. At the time of the interviews they had all spent at least 5 years teaching at their respective schools. Most of the teachers had teaching experience of 10 years and over. Sixteen teachers were male and 12 female.

The interviews followed the model of the semi-structured guideline interview (cf., e.g. Kvale 1996), and were conducted on site by graduate research assistants who had undergone interviewer training. Two different guidelines were designed for students and teachers. The topics covered in the interviews included motivation, goals, design and conduct of lessons, and effects of CLIL on both groups, as well as difficulties/critique and future perspectives. The combined data-set analysed for the present chapter consists of 48 interviews which were fully transcribed (amounting to around 200,000 words in total).

The data analysed here were collected in the context of a larger study conducted in 2007/2008 (Dalton-Puffer et al. 2008), addressing all stakeholders in CLIL education at HTLs through a variety of research methods. In addition to a document analysis, web-based questionnaires were presented to school managers and alumni. The central agents, i.e. students and teachers, were interviewed in a multiple case study at six focus schools. The schools were selected on the basis of the responses to the head of school/department's questionnaire ($N = 106$) in order to ensure variance along parameters such as specialisation, size, rural/urban, transparency of CLIL programme. The focus schools thus cover both urban and rural settings and a range of specialisations, and implement CLIL to different degrees. A double case study comparing English language proficiency of CLIL and non-CLIL students was also carried out at two schools (Jexenflicker and Dalton-Puffer 2010). The latter was the first research study on language attainment in this context.

As implied in the previous paragraph, the present analysis was conducted independently of the content analysis of the main study (Dalton-Puffer et al. 2008). Starting from the research questions (see below), the first two authors of this chapter first coded three teacher and three student interviews; in an iterative process of repeated cross-codings of these base-line interviews, combining deductive (research questions) and inductive elements (Miles and Huberman 1994), a common coding manual for both datasets was developed. The code-set consisted of a total of 29 codes in six main categories: What is Language, Language Learning Theories, Language & Content, Individual Factors, Language Level Students, Language Level Teachers (see Appendix for codes and code definitions). Each data-set was then coded separately while repeated conversational back-checks among the two researchers took place in order to validate the coding (cf. Hüttner and Dalton-Puffer forthcoming for preliminary findings on these data).

A common code set for teacher and student interviews seemed appropriate as we are dealing with members of the same community of practice (cf. Lave andWenger 1991) albeit in different roles. Although the teacher interviews were generally longer and showed a higher degree of reflection on CLIL in their contexts, both teacher and student interviews will be discussed together, given our focus on the joint perspectives of both of these groups of stakeholders.

The six content areas coded were not conceived of as being of equal relevance to our research questions or, indeed as fully independent areas, and, unsurprisingly, revealed diverse degrees of insightand overlap. In the process of analysis, however, three clearly distinct areas emerged, which provided a clear focus for the discussion. The following areas were identified:

(1) Conceptualisation of language learning (English in CLIL) (cf. Section 4.1)
(2) CLIL aims in this setting (cf. Section 4.2)
(3) Emotional dimension of language learning (affect, talent, etc.) (cf. Section 4.3)

The question of conceptualising English within this CLIL programme is highly relevant, but was discussed by participants within other thematic contexts. Mostly, English was discussed in relation to language learning and especially the aims associated with learning a powerful global language, used in most technology contexts as default. Findings will be discussed under Sections 4.1 and 4.2 and drawn together in Section 5.

The coded areas relating to student and teacher competences became relevant for participants in relation to the three main areas quoted above and are best conceived of as overarching themes. Findings from feed into several discussions under Section 4, importantly in Section 4.1, but will not be treated separately.

4. Findings: beliefs on language and language learning in CLIL

As explained above, we assume that the beliefs of the participants involved in CLIL instruction in Austrian HTLs are 'social constructions of the world' (cf. Kalaja 1995, 196) and as such will not be linked normatively to research-based theories. Furthermore, in line with the understanding of LP expounded on in the introduction, we see the beliefs we report on in the following section as co-determining in very significant ways how CLIL is constructed and 'what CLIL is' in the context we describe.

Beliefs on language learning

In an innovative language-teaching programme, such as CLIL, arguably the main belief to investigate in stakeholders relates to their views of how language learning takes place in general and, more specifically, how learning happens in CLIL settings. Importantly, teachers have beliefs about both student language learning and their own language learning, which at times differ quite noticeably.

The strongest belief to be found in all groups is that student language learning is 'doing'. More precisely, learning is characterised as repeated practice, i.e. using the language as much as possible, and being exposed to it as much as possible. This is also often linked to notions of language use becoming more routine and automatised, shown for instance in these teacher quotes:

> so that you don't have to think about what to say when you just want to make yourself understood [...] but that this [...] becomes automatic[2]

> as you use the language more often [...] to my mind this is how the pupil learns English

The notion that language learning in CLIL is practice is echoed by the students, for instance in statements like 'you only learn English if you speak it yourself' or 'it's easier for me to learn a language if I use it myself'.

Such a conceptualisation of learning as practice-related is at times explicitly linked to the perceived and sometimes experienced 'natural' way of language learning, i.e. on the job, using English. This is voiced by content teachers, who usually have previous work experience outside education and compare CLIL teaching environments quite explicitly with learning on the job.

> We provide [the students] with a practice [opportunity], just like they will find later in 'the wild', in business, where you usually – thank God – don't meet only English teachers.

Again, this view is echoed by students who view CLIL as closer to the reality of their future professions. Their statements refer to learning 'what one will really need in real life'.

Apart from the frequent experience of content teachers of having themselves learnt English 'by doing it', a proportion of them (5 of 28) explicitly state that through teaching CLIL they continue to learn English, e.g. 'you learn something new every day' or 'in this way you bring your own English up to scratch'. This parallel view of teacher and student learning expressed by content teachers is linked also to a generally collaborative view of the language learning aspect in CLIL classes. Students noticed that the atmosphere in CLIL classes is 'more relaxed'.

One content teacher's comment summarises a frequently expressed view:

> It is a more equal basis. The student corrects the teacher's English. The teacher accepts this gratefully. What the teacher is still better at, are the content and theoretical issues and in this way it is complementary. And this is beautiful to observe [...] it is a mutual completion.

This contrasts in interesting ways with established views of the roles of teachers and learners in English for specific purposes (ESP), where the ESP teacher is seen as the language expert and the students as content experts. In this setting, teachers view themselves as content experts and the students as at least co-experts in the foreign language. Thus, language learning as well as the language of classroom interaction is co-constructed (cf. also Smit 2010), while the technical content expertise remains with the teacher.

This dynamic and collaborative view is, however, in clear contrast to the qualified English teachers, who see their own language competence as more static, and their own language learning as more or less complete and only extendable by native English input. The potential of the students' English is viewed as much more limited, with one English teacher stating, when asked about the effects of CLIL on herself, that her students' less proficient English did not cause her to lose her English.

Underlying the teachers' views on their own learning appear to be two different conceptualisations of English: English teachers refer to a construct of the target language as native, while the CLIL teachers of content subjects clearly view English as ESP and/or English as a Lingua Franca, i.e. as a means of communication where no other shared L1 is available. The latter do grant expertise to the English teachers and native speakers, but their actual ideal target and idealised co-teachers are engineers and the potential of English specialists and native English speakers is viewed more critically. Thus, one content teacher stated that 'it would not be sensible to work on these terms (for writing chemical reports) in the English class, as I fear – the English teacher would be out of his depth'. There is, however, one interesting exception with a content teacher who while constructing CLIL as a clear success in her statements went on to say 'but I also think that you can still learn this [a foreign language] best in the country [where it is spoken] and extremely fast [...] basically, everything else is a struggle'. This ideal position seems to be in contrast with the actual situations of foreign language learners, but might be seen as an indication that naturalistic language learning is considered the best and a pedagogic innovation that is constructed to resemble this more closely than the current teaching is thus viewed positively.

Alongside this overwhelming view of language learning as an incidental effect of using the target language in the study of content, explicit and focused learning does seem to take an important position as well. It is, however, mentioned almost exclusively in connection with content-specific vocabulary, and the overwhelming view of ESP in these contexts is terminological. Thus, teachers of all categories and students view such vocabulary as items to be learnt explicitly. In addition, glossaries, vocabulary lists, conventional and online dictionaries, as well as vocabulary quizzes, are seen as requirements for students to become competent in their respective ESP. It does remain a little unclear, however, where teachers draw the distinction between vocabulary learning and learning new concepts, as the students involved are novices in their specialisations. As the teachers repeatedly highlight the necessity for students to also learn the German technical terms of their chosen specialisations, the need to learn English vocabulary does not seem to be a feature of it being a foreign language, but rather, competence in both English and German technical terminology is constructed as being a part of professional development. On the whole, teachers appear to view vocabulary learning clearly as explicit and taught learning, but do not comment on the contradiction with their overarching view of student language learning in CLIL as incidental.

Students on the other hand seem to conceptualise learning less clearly as either incidental or explicit, thus expressing not only a more complex view of their experience but also one that is more commensurate with the complexity of expert positions on language learning. For instance, students do mention explicit vocabulary study (dictionaries, lists, etc.; see above) but also view terminology learning as part of learning by doing, viz. a student talking about the analytic chemical lab work and stating that 'it's almost impossible not to learn the [content specific] terms' and another who felt that 'if I need [vocab] and use it, then I remember it'. One student even formulates a participatory stance towards language learning: 'That you participate. That you take part. You learn a lot from that, I believe' and another appears to be an advocate of comprehensible output (cf. Swain 1995):

> you often have discussions in lessons and when you have to think about what you want to say and which words you can or should use for that, then they are imprinted on your mind and you can use them much more quickly next time.

Beliefs on the aims of CLIL

As some of the beliefs exemplified earlier show, CLIL is constructed by both teachers and students as complementary to EFL lessons, which remain the traditional language learning domain with focus on correctness. Students and teachers construct the difference between CLIL and EFL as one of professional vs. general language use, e.g.:

> [CLIL is] English as used for the job in technology, with EFL that's a bit difficult.

CLIL as a domain of more direct professional relevance is also emphasised by the need of engineers to access work-related literature, which is frequently available first in English, in order to remain up-to-date professionally. The overall view of EFL classes is, however, not negative and most students actually accord a crucial role to English lessons for their linguistic development: 'you don't actually learn a language in CLIL but in your English lessons'. This view is shared by all teachers interviewed, who construct CLIL clearly as additional to EFL instruction and not as a replacement.

Such a perceived distinction in learning aims is also reflected in the fact that concrete aims for improved language competence in CLIL lessons are rarely specified for the students (viz. content teachers' typical statement that 'I don't have language aims'), with the exception of some mentions of knowledge of content specific terminology. Interestingly, content teachers mention their own improved language competence more frequently as an aim than that of their students, whose improvement is taken as fairly self-evident or as one content teacher stated: 'If you expect that they [the students] develop a little, then this development happens'. Of all our interview partners, only one commented explicitly on the lack of evidence for the improved language competence of the students, which is, however, implicitly the main agenda of the education authorities, as evidenced in published policy papers (cf. Section 1.3). Thus, one content teacher stated 'let's say that is a gut feeling [...] that they have a better communicative competence, more fluency. We have never tested that and said, is this really true?'.

With regard to the CLIL literature, there is one core tenet held by researchers and policy-makers and clearly not shared by our stakeholders and that is the dual focus in CLIL on language and content, and the presumed balance in curricular aims between English and the subject taught through English. None of our respondents felt that any curricular aims in English were part of their CLIL classes and indeed seemed quite astonished at the question. Clearly, CLIL is not constructed as an alternative to EFL classes or, indeed, as a response to dissatisfaction with EFL provision.[3] CLIL is seen as an extra provision of English practice, made more enjoyable precisely by the absence of clear curricular aims and thus also forms of assessment for the language component of the class. An insistence by school authorities on an enactment of this official CLIL tenet would, we argue, have detrimental effects on the perception of CLIL as a success, as the relaxed atmosphere and positive affect would not realistically be maintained.

Beliefs on the affective dimension in the subjective construction of success in CLIL

Success in CLIL is linked strongly to learners becoming confident in using English and this notion of success equalling 'daring to do' is extended also to content teachers' language learning, by all groups interviewed. Recurring expressions in this connection are *security, feel (more) secure, more relaxed, more familiar, no inhibitions, more agreeable, no more fear* and these occur in the statements of all stakeholders. This conceptualisation of success as first and foremost a change in affective factors regarding English, and especially speaking English, can be related to the way CLIL itself is constructed as a success story. Strikingly, as all seem to be confident in using their English, there seems to be little impetus to evaluate their English systematically.

Success is constructed as relative by all participants, i.e. as 'better than' students without CLIL instruction, the same students before the onset of CLIL, or teachers' own experience of language learning. Thus, students view their English as better than other students', and as having become easier; one content teacher stated that students' English 'improves from month to month [...] due to practice', and an English teacher noted 'that they learn some more English, it has to be, perforce'. Especially the choice of *perforce* indicates what has been argued above, namely that teachers seem convinced of the success of CLIL with regard to English, without either clear language competence aims and goals or objective assessments of students' proficiency levels. Arguably, success in CLIL is not defined as being proven to be better at English, but to *feel* better about speaking English.

Importantly, this aim of gaining confidence is linked, like the difference constructed between CLIL and EFL, to the international aspect of engineers' working lives, where the dominant role of English is taken for granted. One content teacher's statement can be seen as summarising this view of CLIL: 'a vocational school trains for the job and with all this globalisation it is actually unthinkable to manage without English'. In this context, English is also usually viewed as English as a Lingua Franca, and its importance as a means of communication internationally with speakers of diverse L1s highlighted. The importance of English is seen as self-evident, or as one content teacher put it: 'even the stupidest person understands that he needs languages or that languages are important and so nobody asks "why do we need this [CLIL]?"'. Interestingly, this need for international expertise and language proficiency is implicitly linked only to CLIL and not seen as the domain of the subject English. To some extent this might be explained by the construction of CLIL as closer to 'real life' than English, or as one student put it 'the technical stuff is one thing, where you do technology in English, and the other thing is the English lessons where you talk about your hobbies'. This 'division of labour' between CLIL and EFL classes has interesting parallels with an observation made above, namely the different construction of English as 'native language (ENL)' on the part of the English teachers versus its construction as international lingua franca (ELF) on the part of the technology teachers.

5. Discussion and conclusion

In this chapter, through investigating stakeholders' beliefs of language learning as an integral part of extended LP, we have endeavoured to find explanations for the ease of acceptance of a specific pedagogic innovation, i.e. CLIL, by analysing discursive constructions of both learning in teacher and student interviews and in policy statements on CLIL. Relating our findings back to Spolsky's (2004) conceptualisation of LP, we find that language management is remarkably weak in the Austrian CLIL context. None of our participants make reference to official CLIL policy, either with regard to the one national policy document on CLIL in Austria or to the host of European Commission papers outlining CLIL in Europe. Arguably, this relative absence of official language management in Austrian CLIL policy leads to the other two factors in extended LP, i.e. language beliefs and language practice, to become the de-facto CLIL policy.

We suggest that the beliefs of CLIL stakeholders on language learning and the construction of success in this particular language pedagogic innovation resonate with the (reported) classroom practices and we would argue that without overt language management, an alignment between these two aspects takes place in stakeholders' conceptualisations. This alignment allows for a wide range of practices to be given the label CLIL, such as actual use of the L2 from 10% to 100% of class time, since as long as stakeholders are happy to view a certain practice as CLIL there is no controlling language management to question or critique this view. The lack of language management enables teachers to decide largely autonomously on their ability to teach CLIL and the materials and methods they wish to use, and thus places high levels of responsibility on the individual teacher.

We would suggest that it is also this absence of language management which allows for the construction of success that we found as essentially a learner-intrinsic change in affect towards English and increased self-confidence as a foreign language user. Clearly, this change is hard to measure in an educational context, where tests usually only measure performance and not emotion, and letting emotions of stakeholders take centre stage in evaluation is in contrast to the current educational trends of measuring language proficiency through standardised tests. Yet, one might argue that stakeholders can make CLIL into a success more easily by changing their or their learners' feelings as English speakers, than by changing the language proficiency of a large and mixed cohort of learners. Thus, success truly is 'believing', as it is constructed as essentially non-testable.

Yet, this mismatch as well as the non-testable nature of CLIL success seems to be fully accepted by Austrian school authorities, who in their own construction of 'success' focus on participating school numbers and – albeit anecdotal – accounts of feelings of success by the stakeholders. All this finds support in CLIL being a grass-roots initiative (at least in Austria); stakeholders have the possibility of creating an untested and untestable learning environment where measurable differences in proficiency are viewed as being of little account, especially when considering that CLIL is constructed as a 'free space' of extra L2 provision in a more egalitarian atmosphere. This also seems to be a reason why there is remarkable little call for research evidence in this area; the beliefs on what CLIL should do and does are unperturbed by verification, and so – with one exception (see final quote in Section 4.2) – the question about what is actually achieved is irrelevant. We would argue that this position leads to viewing research into CLIL very differently from the way researchers construct it, namely as providing formal proof of something already known, possibly for advertising reasons, versus searching for the pedagogical practice that achieves the most competent learners.

Another issue that emerges quite clearly is that CLIL for our stakeholders is about increased *English* provision, and not a general measure of increasing European multilingualism as proposed by EC policies. The position of English as *the* major global language for professional success in engineering and technology, as well as a means of communication in a multilingual work environment, is accepted without any challenge.

We have argued that understanding the driving forces behind the spread of CLIL across the globe, the pace of which 'has surprised even its most ardent advocates' (Maljers, Marsh, and Wolff 2007, 7), is best understood through the lay theories constructing it. So far in most contexts, CLIL is very much LP from below (cf. Shohamy 2006; Spolsky 2004); it emerges from the individual decisions and joint actions of stakeholders which are informed by their respective beliefs. Such a view of CLIL implementation as a kind of self-organising system also indicates potential areas of conflict. Policy statements on CLIL view it quite clearly as a means attaining improved language competence, even to the extreme of cutting foreign language instruction as CLIL takes over the role of EFL instruction, as is happening in numerous programmes in the tertiary sector. Once the political agents assert such goals explicitly the contradiction will become visible and the new 'policy from above' might not find support with practising teachers and students involved, despite the administrative appeal of 'two subjects for the price of one'. Additionally, the lack of language management allows for avoidance of some difficult overarching LP questions, such as the role of standard German in a professional context where

English is seen as the major language 'of the job'. That there is a direct comparison being created between English (for specific purposes) and Standard German was evident in one student comment (on being asked whether he felt shy about using English in CLIL classes) that he would speak 'rather English than Standard German'.

This chapter has addressed the role of beliefs in one specific CLIL context only, and so it would be important for future research in other contexts to establish whether similar belief structures are in place. Information on contexts where language management regarding CLIL is more clearly present, such as the Netherlands or some Spanish regions, would add valuable information on how the triangular relationship of management, policy and practice in extended LP (Spolsky 2004) plays out when language management takes on a more powerful position.

Notes

1. Book publications by members of these groups include: Meehisto, Frigols, and Marsh (2008); Coyle, Hood, and Marsh (2010).
2. Interviews were conducted in German and extracts have been translated by the authors.
3. This is in contradiction to what is suggested in some European policy papers and also seems to be different from the position in, e.g. Andalucia.

References

Admiraal, W., G. Westhoff, and K. De Bot. 2006. "Evaluation of Bilingual Secondary Education in the Netherlands: Students' Language Proficiency in English." *Educational Research and Evaluation* 12 (1): 75–93. doi:10.1080/13803610500392160.

Airey, J. 2009. "Estimating Undergraduate Bilingual Scientific Literacy in Sweden." *International CLIL Research Journal* 1 (2): 26–35. http://www.icrj.eu/12/article3.html

Amuzie, G. L., and P. Winke. 2009. "Changes in Language Learning Beliefs as A Result of Study Abroad." *System* 37 (3): 366–379. doi:10.1016/j.system.2009.02.011.

Badertscher, H., and T. Bieri. 2009. *Wissenserwerb im Content and Language Integrated Learning*. Bern and Wien: Haupt.

Barcelos, A. M. F. 2003a. "Researching Beliefs about SLA: A Critical Review." In *Beliefs about SLA. New Research Approaches*, edited by P. Kalaja and A. M. F. Barcelos, 7–33. New York: Springer.

Barcelos, A. M. F. 2003b. "Conflict and Influence." In *Beliefs about SLA. New Research Approaches*, edited by P. Kalaja and A. M. F. Barcelos, 171–199. New York: Springer.

Borg, S. 2003. "Teacher Cognition in Language Teaching: A Review of Research on What Language Teachers Think, Know, Believe, and Do." *Language Teaching* 36 (2): 81–109. doi:10.1017/S0261444803001903.

Borg, S. 2006. *Teacher Cognition and Language Education: Research and Practice*. London: Continuum.

Brown, A. V. 2009. "Students' and Teachers' Perceptions of Effective Foreign Language Teaching: A Comparison of Ideals." *The Modern Language Journal* 93 (1): 46–60. doi:10.1111/j.1540-4781.2009.00827.x.

Bruton, A. 2011. "Are the Differences between CLIL and Non-CLIL Groups in Andalusia Due to CLIL? A Reply to Lorenzo, Casal and Moore (2010)." *Applied Linguistics* 32 (2): 236–241. doi:10.1093/applin/amr007.

Coyle, D., P. Hood, and D. Marsh. 2010. *CLIL: Content and Language Integrated Learning*. New York: Cambridge University Press.

Csizér, K., and G. Lukács. 2010. "The Comparative Analysis of Motivation, Attitudes and Selves: The Case of English and German in Hungary." *System* 38 (1): 1–13. doi:10.1016/j.system.2009.12.001.

Dalton-Puffer, C. 2007. *Discourse in Content and Language Integrated Learning (CLIL) Classrooms*. Amsterdam: John Benjamins.

Dalton-Puffer, C. 2011. "Content and Language Integrated Learning: From Practice to Principles." *Annual Review of Applied Linguistics* 31: 182–204. doi:10.1017/S0267190511000092.

Dalton-Puffer, C., J. Hüttner, S. Jexenflicker, V. Schindelegger, and U. Smit. 2008. *Content and Language Integrated Learning an Österreichs Höheren Technischen Lehranstalten.* Vienna: Bundesministerium für Unterricht, Kultur und Kunst, Abt. II/2 (Austrian Ministery of Education, Culture and Art, Section II/2).

Donaghue, H. 2003. "An Instrument to Elicit Teachers' Beliefs and Assumptions." *ELT Journal* 57 (4): 344–351. doi:10.1093/elt/57.4.344.

Dörnyei, Z., and E. Ushioda, eds. 2009. *Motivation, Language Identity and the L2 Self.* Bristol: Multilingual Matters.

Dufva, H. 2003. "Beliefs in Dialogue: A Bakhtinian View." In *Beliefs about SLA. New Research Approaches,* edited by P. Kalaja and A. M. F. Barcelos, 131–151. New York: Springer.

European Commission. 2008. Languages and Europe: Language Learning. http://europa.eu/languages/en/chapter/14.

European Commission. 2009. EU Language Policy. http://ec.europa.eu/education/languages/eu-language-policy/index_en.htm.

European Commission Communication. 2003. Promoting Language Learning and Linguistic Diversity: An Action Plan 2004–2006. http://ec.europa.eu/education/doc/official/keydoc/actlang/act_lang_en.pdf.

Eurydice. 2006. *Content and Language Integrated Learning (CLIL) at School in Europe.* Brussels: Eurydice.

Farrell, T. S. C., and J. Ng. 2003. "Do Teachers' Beliefs of Grammar Teaching Match Their Classroom Practices? A Singapore Case Study." In *English in Singapore: Research on Grammar,* edited by A. V. Brown and E. L. Low, 128–137. Singapore: McGraw Hill.

Farrell, T. S. C., and S. T. K. Kun. 2008. "Language Policy, Language Teachers' Beliefs, and Classroom Practices." *Applied Linguistics* 29 (3): 381–403. doi:10.1093/applin/amm050.

Ferguson, G. 2006. *Language Planning and Education.* Edinburgh: Edinburgh University Press.

Gierlinger, E., C. Carré-Karlinger, E. Fuchs, and C. Lechner. 2010. Die CLIL-Matrix in der Unterrichtspraxis. Innovative Impulse aus dem Europäischen Fremdsprachenzentrum des Europarates [The CLIL-Matrix in Classroom Practice: Innovative Impulses from the Council of Europe's European Centre for Modern Languages]. Praxisreihe 13. Graz: ÖSZ-Österreichisches Sprachenzentrum. http://www.oesz.at/download/diss/Praxisreihe_13.pdf

Goodwin, C., and A. Duranti. 1992. "Rethinking Context: An Introduction." In *Rethining Context: Language As An Interactive Phenomenon,* edited by A. Duranti and C. Goodwin, 1–42. Cambridge: Cambridge University Press.

Hüttner, J., and C. Dalton-Puffer. 2013. "Der Einfluß subjektiver Sprachlerntheorien auf den Erfolg der Implementierung von CLIL-Programmen [The influence of subjective theories of language learning on the success of CLIL programmes]." In *Content and Language Integrated Learning: Research, Policy and Practice,* edited by J. Viebrock and S. Breidbach. Frankfurt (Main): Peter Lang.

Hüttner, J., and A. Rieder-Bünemann. 2010. "A Cross-sectional Analysis of Oral Narratives by Children with CLIL and Non-CLIL Instruction." In *Language Use and Language Learning in CLIL Classrooms,* edited by C. Dalton-Puffer, T. Nikula, and U. Smit, 61–80. Amsterdam: John Benjamins.

Jäppinen, A.-K. 2005. "Thinking and Content Learning of Mathematics and Science as Cognitional Development in Content and Language Integrated Learning (CLIL): Teaching Through A Foreign Language in Finland." *Language and Education* 19 (2): 147–168. doi:10.1080/09500780508668671.

Jexenflicker, S., and C. Dalton-Puffer. 2010. "The CLIL Differential: Comparing the Writing of CLIL and Non-CLIL Students in Higher Colleges of Technology." In *Language Use and Language Learning,* edited by C. Dalton-Puffer, T. Nikula, and U. Smit, 169–190. Amsterdam: John Benjamins.

Johnson, K. E. 1994. "The Emerging Beliefs and Instructional Practices of Preservice English As A Second Language Teachers." *Teaching and Teacher Education* 10 (4): 439–452. doi:10.1016/0742-051X(94)90024-8.

Kalaja, P. 1995. "Student Beliefs (or Metacognitive Knowledge) about SLA Reconsidered." *International Journal of Applied Linguistics* 5 (2): 191–204. doi:10.1111/j.1473-4192.1995.tb00080.x.

Kalaja, P. 2003. "Research on Student Beliefs about SLA Within A Discursive Approach." In *Beliefs about SLA: New Research Approaches*, edited by P. Kalaja and A. M. F. Barcelos, 87–108. New York: Springer.

Kiraz, A., A. Güneyli, E. Baysen, S. Gündüz, and F. Baysen. 2010. "Effect of Science and Technology Learning with Foreign Language on the Attitude and Success of Students." *Procedia Social and Behavioral Sciences* 2 (2): 4130–4136. doi:10.1016/j.sbspro.2010.03.652.

Kramsch, C. 2003. "Metaphor and the Subjective Construction of Beliefs." In *Beliefs about SLA: New Research Approaches*, edited by P. Kalaja and A. M. F. Barcelos, 109–128. New York: Springer.

Kvale, S. 1996. *Interviews. An Introduction to Qualitative Research Interviewing*. London: Sage Publications.

Lasagabaster, D. 2008. "Foreign Language Competence in Content and Language Integrated Learning." *The Open Applied Linguistics Journal* 1 (1): 30–41. doi:10.2174/1874913500801010030.

Lasagabaster, D., and Y. Ruiz De Zarobe, eds. 2010. *CLIL in Spain: Implementation, Results and Teacher Training*. Newcastle upon Tyne: Cambridge Scholars Publishing.

Lave, J., and E. Wenger. 1991. *Situated Learning. Legitimate Peripheral Participation*. Cambridge: Cambridge University Press.

Li, D. C. S. 2002. "Hong Kong Parents' Preference for English-medium Education: Passive Victims of Imperialism or Active Agents of Pragmatism." In *Englishes in Asia: Communication, Identity, Power and Education*, edited by A. Kirkpatrick, 29–62. Melbourne: Language Australia.

Li, L., and S. Walsh. 2011. "'Seeing is believing': Looking at EFL Teachers' Beliefs Through Classroom Interaction." *Classroom Discourse* 2 (1): 39–57. doi:10.1080/19463014.2011.562657.

Lim Falk, M. 2008. *Svenska i engelskspråkig skolmiljö. Ämnesrelaterat språkbruk i två gymnasieklasser* [Swedish in an English-speaking school environment. Subject-related language use in two high school classes]. Acta Universitatis Stockholmiensis. Stockholm Studies in Scandinavian Philology 46. Stockholm: Eddy.

Llinares, A., and R. Whittaker. 2010. "Writing and Speaking in the History Class: A Comparative Analysis of CLIL and First Language Contexts." In *Language Use and Language Learning in CLIL Classrooms*, edited by C. Dalton-Puffer, T. Nikula, and U. Smit, 125–144. Amsterdam: John Benjamins.

Lorenzo, F., S. Casal, and P. Moore. 2005. *Orientaciones para la elaboracion del curriculo integrado de las lenguas en los centros bilingües* [Orientations for the elaboration of the integrated language curriculum in the bilingual centres]. Sevilla: Consejería de Educación.

Maillat, D. 2010. "The Pragmatics of L2 in CLIL." In *Language Use and Language Learning in CLIL Classrooms*, edited by C. Dalton-Puffer, T. Nikula, and U. Smit, 39–58. Amsterdam: John Benjamins.

Maljers, A., D. Marsh, and D. Wolff, eds. 2007. *Windows on CLIL. Content and Language Integrated Learning in the spotlight*. The Hague: European Platform for Dutch Education.

Mansour, N. 2009. "Science Teachers' Beliefs and Practices: Issues, Implications and Research Agenda." *International Journal of Environmental and Science Education* 4 (1): 25–48. http://ijese.com/IJESE_v4n1_Mansour.pdf

Meehisto, P., M. J. Frigols, and D. Marsh. 2008. *Uncovering CLIL*. London: Macmillan.

Mercer, S. 2011. "Dispelling the Myth of the Natural-born Linguist." *ELT Journal* 66 (1): 22–29. doi:10.1093/elt/ccr022.

Mercer, S., and S. Ryan. 2010. "A Mindset for EFL: Learners' Beliefs about the Role of Natural Talent." *ELT Journal* 64 (4): 436–444. doi:10.1093/elt/ccp083.

Mewald, C. 2007. "A Comparison of Oral Language Performance of Learners in CLIL and Mainstream Classes at Lower Secondary Level in Lower Austria." In *Empirical Perspectives on CLIL Classroom Discourse*, edited by C. Dalton-Puffer, T. Nikula, and U. Smit, 139–178. Frankfurt a.M.: Peter Lang.

Miles, M. B., and A. M. Huberman. 1994. *Qualitative Data Analysis*. 2nd edn. Thousand Oaks, CA: Sage.

Moate, J. M. 2011. "The Impact of Foreign Language Mediated Teaching on Teachers' Sense of Professional Integrity in the CLIL Classroom." *European Journal of Teacher Education* 34 (3): 333–346. doi:10.1080/02619768.2011.585023.

Mori, Y. 1999. "Epistemological Beliefs and Language Learning Beliefs: What Do Language Learners Believe about Their Learning?" *Language Learning* 49 (3): 377–415. doi:10.1111/0023-8333.00094.

Nezbeda, M. 2005. *Überblicksdaten und Wissenswertes zu Fremdsprache als Arbeitssprache* [Foreign languages as media of instruction: Basic statistics and points of interest]. EAA Serviceheft 6. Graz: Österreichisches Sprachenkompetenzzentrum.

Nikula, T. 2010. "Effects of CLIL on One Teacher's Classroom Language Use." In *Language Use and Language Learning in CLIL Classrooms*, edited by C. Dalton-Puffer, T. Nikula, and U. Smit, 105–124. Amsterdam etc: Benjamins.

Olson, K., and M. Jimenez-Silva. 2008. "The Campfire Effect: A Preliminary Analysis of Preservice Teachers' Beliefs about Teaching English Language Learners after State-mandated Endorsement Courses." *Journal of Research in Childhood Education* 22 (3): 246–260. doi:10.1080/02568540809594625.

Pajares, M. F. 1992. "Teachers' Beliefs and Educational Research: Cleaning Up A Messy Construct." *Review of Educational Research* 62 (2): 307–332. doi:10.3102/00346543062003307.

Phipps, S., and S. Borg. 2009. "Exploring Tensions between Teachers' Grammar Teaching Beliefs and Practices." *System* 37 (3): 380–390. doi:10.1016/j.system.2009.03.002.

Potter, J. 1996. *Representing Reality: Discourse, Rhetoric and Social Construction*. London: Sage.

Ruiz De Zarobe, Y. 2008. "CLIL and Foreign Language Learning: A Longitudinal Study in the Basque Country." *International CLIL Research Journal* 1 (1): 60–73. http://www.icrj.eu/11/article5.html

Shohamy, E. 2006. *Language Policy. Hidden Agendas and New Approaches*. London: Routledge.

Smit, U. 2010. *English as A Lingua Franca in Higher Education. A Longitudinal Study of Classroom Discourse*. Berlin: Mouton de Gruyter.

Spolsky, B. 2004. *Language Policy*. Cambridge: Cambridge University Press.

Spolsky, B. 2009. *Language management*. Cambridge: Cambridge University Press.

Swain, M. 1995. "Three Functions of Output in Second Language Learning." In *Principle and Practice in Applied Linguistics*, edited by G. Cook and B. Seidlhofer, 125–144. Oxford: Oxford University Press.

Tanaka, K., and R. Ellis. 2003. "Study Abroad, Language Proficiency and Learner Beliefs about Language Learning." *JALT Journal* 25: 63–85. http://jalt-publications.org/jj/articles/2635-study-abroad-language-proficiency-and-learner-beliefs-about-language-learning

Van de Craen, P., E. Ceuleers, K. Lochtman, L. Allain, and K. Mondt. 2007. "An Interdisciplinary Research Approach to CLIL Learning in Primary Schools in Brussels." In *Empirical Perspectives on CLIL Classroom Discourse*, edited by C. Dalton-Puffer and U. Smit, 253–275. Frankfurt: Lang.

Viebrock, B. 2007. *Bilingualer Erdkundeunterricht. Subjektive didaktische Theorien von Lehrerinnen und Lehrern* [Bilingual geography. Teachers' subjective didactic theories]. Frankfurt/Main: Peter Lang.

Walker, E. 2010. "Evaluation of A Support Intervention for Senior Secondary School English Immersion." *System* 38 (1): 50–62. doi:10.1016/j.system.2009.12.005.

Wenden, A. L. 1998. "Metacognitive Knowledge and Language Learning." *Applied Linguistics* 19 (4): 515–537. doi:10.1093/applin/19.4.515.

Wenden, A. L. 1999. "An Introduction to Metacognitive Knowledge and Beliefs in Language Learning: Beyond the Basics." *System* 27 (4): 435–441. doi:10.1016/S0346-251X(99)00043-3.

Woods, D. 2003. "The Social Construction of Beliefs in the Language Classroom." In *Beliefs in SLA: New Research Approaches*, edited by P. Kalaja and A. M. F. Barcelos, 201–232. New York: Springer Science + Business Media, LLC.

Zydatiß, W. 2012. "Linguistic Thresholds in the CLIL Classroom? The Threshold Hypothesis Revisited." *International CLIL Research Journal* 1 (4): 17–28. http://www.icrj.eu/14/article2.html

CLIL in junior vocational secondary education: challenges and opportunities for teaching and learning

Jenny Denman[a], Rosie Tanner[b] and Rick de Graaff[c]

[a]Research Centre for Urban Talent, Rotterdam University of Applied Sciences, Rotterdam, the Netherlands; [b]Centre for Teaching and Learning, Utrecht University, Utrecht, the Netherlands; [c]Faculty of Humanities, Utrecht University, Utrecht, the Netherlands

> In many countries, Content and Language Integrated Learning (CLIL) in secondary education, whether by default or design, focuses primarily on high-achieving students. This chapter presents a study of CLIL programs for a different population: junior vocational students in the lower streams of secondary education in the Netherlands. On the basis of a context description of the highly streamed Dutch secondary education system and a literature review related to bilingual education for lower achievers and vocational CLIL, the chapter examines the implementation of bilingual education programs at school and task level. More specifically, it describes the perceptions and motivation of junior vocational students and their teachers with respect to the organization and practice of vocational CLIL. As a result, the chapter reports the successful linguistic, curricular, and pedagogical characteristics of bilingual education programs for this type of learner and summarizes the challenges and opportunities for CLIL in junior vocational education.

Introduction

Bilingual education at secondary level in the Netherlands – in Dutch called *TTO*, for *tweetalig onderwijs* – began as a small grass-roots initiative around 1990. Within 20 years there were about 120 secondary schools offering bilingual education (English/Dutch, with the exception of a few schools near the German border that offer German/Dutch). The introduction and implementation of bilingual education began in schools with the highest academic level and the highest entrance requirements, but it is slowly being established in other types of secondary schools as well. At the moment, the largest growth in secondary bilingual education is occurring in the lowest of the three streams of secondary education, in the form of additive bilingualism through partial immersion.

The purpose of the present study was to gain insight into the relevance for our target population of previous research related to bilingual education, and then explore the considerations, implementation, and appreciation of bilingual programs particularly focusing on junior vocational secondary education. This target population is special for a number of reasons: the programs are relatively new, students are definitely not part of an academic elite, junior vocational secondary streams are rare outside of the Netherlands, and bilingual education programs are growing despite a paucity of research in this specific field. Parallel practices in bilingual programs at this level in the Netherlands are compared and contrasted; the needs of learners and teachers are different, yet the grouping of results enables a broad general picture from several different angles. We will present and discuss studies of the context, participants, and methodology of bilingual or immersion education relevant for lower achievers at the (junior) vocational level. Conclusions will be discussed from related research in other, but still relevant contexts such as at-risk learners, lower academic levels, lower socioeconomic background, English language learners with different home languages, and bilingual education as a motivating factor. Though it is problematic to draw any direct parallels between these different national situations and educational contexts, the conclusions may be relevant for bilingual programs internationally, and particularly for a lower-achieving secondary population.

Bilingual junior secondary vocational education in the Netherlands

An understanding of the highly streamed Dutch educational system is necessary to understand the context of bilingual education at junior vocational level. At the end of primary school, at the age of about 12 years, Dutch students are given a formal recommendation regarding their options for secondary education. This recommendation is based on several types of assessment: their performance on national standardized tests (administered by CITO, the Central Institute for Test Development) and both summative and formative assessments at the primary schools themselves. The recommendation is generally binding. Students are streamed into three types of secondary schools: *vwo* or pre-university education (six years); *havo* or general secondary education (five years); or *vmbo* or junior vocational secondary education (four years). The *vmbo* stream is further sub-divided into four sub-streams, from more demanding to less demanding and from more theoretical to more practical. Approximately 40% of Dutch students attend a *vwo* or *havo* secondary school, and approximately 60% attend one of the four types of *vmbo* junior secondary education.

The *vmbo* population is thus not only the largest, but also the most diverse. In addition to the largest spread in the CITO test results and the existence of four different substreams to accommodate different cognitive abilities, the junior vocational secondary education in the Netherlands is characterized by a higher percentage of students with a home language other than Dutch or a different ethnic background. Many of these students are second-generation Turkish or Moroccan; there is also a considerable population of asylum seekers. A relatively high percentage of students have learning challenges, ranging from dyslexia and dyscalculia to behavioural disorders such as attention deficit hyperactivity disorder. Junior vocational secondary schools have a higher percentage of students from lower socioeconomic backgrounds than general secondary or pre-university stream schools. There is thus a substantial learner population, compared to other types of secondary education, which could be considered 'at risk'. This is relevant for the subsequent background literature discussion. Regarding the development of bilingual education programs at this level, in 2009 there were six *vmbo* schools offering bilingual education, joined by seven more in 2010 and three more in 2011.

An additional 12 schools have plans to implement a bilingual program in the near future – a four-fold increase in just a few years. It is important to stress that in the Netherlands parents are free to choose a specific school for their children, taking the level of education into account. That is, it is the parents' and students' choice to attend a bilingual or a nonbilingual stream.

Perhaps due to the rapidity of the growth of bilingual junior secondary vocational education, and the research focus on bilingual education in the higher streams, there is a dearth of research into the specific context of bilingual education for less-elite populations despite calls for more attention to this area (Marsh 2003; Baetens Beardsmore 2007; Dalton-Puffer et al. 2009; Coyle, Hood, and Marsh 2010; Bruton 2011).

Content and Language Integrated Learning (CLIL), broadly interpreted, is the fundamental principle underlying bilingual secondary education in the Netherlands. On the one hand, CLIL is a methodological principle, according to which foreign language development is facilitated in subject classes, and subject knowledge development is supported by content-based language learning strategies in language classes. On the other hand, CLIL is an organizational principle for bilingual school in the Netherlands, which is structured and monitored by the network of bilingual schools within the requirements of the Dutch educational system. In cooperation with the European Platform, the national network of bilingual schools drew up a set of standards to which CLIL programs should adhere. This Standard stipulates that CLIL programs at pre-university and general secondary levels should offer 50% of the curriculum in the target language, including at least one subject from each of the main knowledge domains Science, Social Sciences, and Arts & Sports. Further, CLIL programs must not result in a decline in Dutch language or content subject proficiency, but must focus on additive bilingualism. Specifically, the school assessment results for the subjects taught in the target language, and for Dutch as a subject, may not fall under the national average scores for the standardized tests in these subjects (tested in Dutch). In the Standard, target L2 attainment goals for CLIL secondary schools are described in terms of Common European Framework of Reference (CEFR) levels and requirements for a European and International Orientation (EIO) component are laid out. Research at bilingual pre-university secondary level (*TTOvwo*) has shown that students achieve a higher level of English proficiency than their non-TTO peers, while maintaining proficiency in Dutch and content subjects (Huibregtse 2001). More recent research has shown that students not only achieve a higher level of English, but their linguistic repertoire – even in the first few years – is characterized by more frequent use of language 'chunks', indicative of more authentic, idiomatic acquisition (Verspoor et al. 2010; Verspoor, de Bot, and van Rein 2011).

As in the higher streams, the junior vocational secondary level has its own (provisional) Standard[1] for CLIL, quite similar to the Standard for the higher streams, with certain adjustments. CLIL at junior vocational level (*tvmbo*) should offer a minimum of 30% of the curriculum in the target language. This percentage is not based upon research results, but on a balance of time for the target language and the main language of education, in order to assure a degree of additive bilingualism for this population. The 30% must be spread over different subjects and domains; within this stipulation each school has a great deal of freedom not only in selecting which subjects are given in the target language, but also in the choice of methodology and didactic activities, and the degree to which cross-curricular collaboration and projects are included in the CLIL curriculum. As in the higher streams, the EIO component is a vital part of the junior vocational Standard. Additionally, for the junior vocational level, the CEFR target attainments are lower than for the general and pre-university levels, but higher than for the nonbilingual junior vocational streams.

Related research relevant to bilingual junior secondary vocational education

Despite differences in national context, educational level, socioeconomic background, degree of immersion, or first language, there are a number of relevant links with previous research for CLIL in (junior) vocational education in the Netherlands or elsewhere. Within a variety of bilingual and immersion education settings, relevant parallels have been found concerning 'at risk' students, lower (or simply average) achievers, socioeconomic or sociocultural status, vocational education, CLIL as the learner's third language (rather than the second), English language learners (ELLs), motivation, and CLIL teaching skills. In order to obtain a broader and evidence-based perspective on the considerations, implementation, and appreciation of bilingual programs, we will subsequently address studies with respect to the context, participants and methodology relevant for (junior) vocational education. The studies listed here are for illustrative purposes and are by no means exhaustive, but represent a variety of national and program-specific contexts.

Lower ability and 'at risk' learners

Genesee's bilingual immersion study in Canada (2007) showed that below-average students in French immersion programs were apparently not disadvantaged in their development or academic achievement if they participated in immersion. Their first language proficiency and academic development were similar to those of below-average students in nonimmersion schools, while their second language proficiency levels were significantly higher. Neither were the 'at risk' students – those with language, literacy, and other academic difficulties – differentially handicapped. In general, 'students' first language development and academic achievement are similar to (or better than) those of non-immersion students' (Lyster 2007, 22). Studies of non-elite student populations in other countries show similar results: in Finland, Merisuo-Storm's investigation of foreign language reading skills in bilingual education (2006) demonstrated that even students who fell into the 'lowest level' group scored better in most reading skills than students in monolingual classes. Another Finnish study showed that there were no major differences in content learning between a CLIL and a non-CLIL group, even for students of different intelligence levels (Seikkula-Leino 2007). This is further confirmed by Dalton-Puffer in an overview of CLIL in German-speaking countries (2007); although students with a high level of linguistic competence tend to perform well regardless of the type of instruction, average students show more foreign language improvement through CLIL than through traditional foreign language instruction. Mewald (2007), in contrast, found that although CLIL students over a broad range of abilities benefited from CLIL, average and higher achievers in Austrian schools benefited more from CLIL classes than lower achievers, as lower achievers were found to lag behind their non-CLIL peers in some aspects of oral fluency. However, according to Mewald, this may be due to certain classroom communicative patterns which are considered 'typical of CLIL lessons' in the context of the study (2007, 160), such as students' L1 responses, code-switching, and very restricted target language responses, rather than due to CLIL as such.

The socioeconomic and sociocultural background of student populations has also been studied in relation to bilingual education, albeit sparsely. This is relevant to the Dutch context and several other national situations because of the generally lower parental occupational status and parental educational levels of (junior) vocational students. Genesee found that students from lower socioeconomic backgrounds in French immersion classes scored just as well as other students on both English language tests and in mathematics. He states that there was 'nothing in the results [...] to suggest that students from lower socioeconomic groups will experience difficulties in English language development in immersion programs or that they cannot benefit from immersion in terms of second language achievement' (2007, 95). Similarly, in the Basque CLIL context, where the CLIL language, English, was the students' third language, Lasagabaster's study (2008) showed that there was no significant difference in language skills performance amongst students with a parent who had finished primary school, secondary school, or university as their highest level of education. It should be noted, however, that in the latter study a majority of the parents had completed university.

Motivation

The ITALIC Research Report by Coyle (2011) examines, among other things, aspects of motivation in foreign language learning at school, including motivation in the learning environment, learner engagement, and learner identities. This study, which included 11 schools offering CLIL in foreign languages other than English and over 650 students, found that students generally considered CLIL motivating in all three of these dimensions of motivation. Additionally, learners reported feelings of achievement through being stimulated by challenging work; they further disagreed with the statement that CLIL is only for the most able learners, which indicates that the students themselves seem to consider CLIL appropriate and accessible to learners of varying abilities. Perhaps the most revealing motivational pronouncement from the learners themselves in this report is the simple declaration that learning through CLIL is 'more fun' (2011, 3, 95). These are all important results for early adolescent CLIL learners in other contexts. In the Andalusian study, Lorenzo, Casal, and Moore (2010) found that CLIL students' motivation and self-concept was higher than that of non-CLIL students. Merisuo-Storm (2006), as well, showed that CLIL students had a more positive attitude towards foreign language study than their non-CLIL peers, and Lasagabaster (2011) indicates increased motivation and learner self-esteem.

Several studies report results that seem to conflict with these. In a Hong Kong study comparing lower secondary level English medium of instruction (EMI) students to Chinese medium of instruction (CMI), Sallili and Tsui (2005, 142) found that, regarding English learning, the lower-ability EMI students' self-efficacy (expectancy of success) scores declined significantly over a period of three years compared to their CMI lower-ability peers. Seikkula-Leino's study (2007) of affective factors in early adolescent CLIL learners indicated that the CLIL students had a low self-concept in regarding their own foreign language learning compared with the non-CLIL students, despite strong motivation. This is striking because the CLIL selection was made partly on the basis of foreign language proficiency. A possible reason may be the fact that CLIL students become more aware of their own linguistic shortcomings; they 'are forced to face the difficulties involved in learning content in a foreign language' (2007, 337).

Hood (2006, 142) concludes from interviews with CLIL learners that 'in the early stages of a CLIL program, enjoyment, motivation, and self-esteem can be at risk as students come to terms with the initial challenges of adapting to a CLIL methodology'. Another construct, language anxiety, may be a factor in ambivalent motivation. Gardner (2010, 91) considers it likely that language anxiety develops as a function of exposure to learning and attempting to use the language. It seems reasonable to suggest that teachers of lower-achieving students should pay particular attention to a possible motivational dip and language anxiety, especially in the early stages of CLIL.

Different language backgrounds

As stated above, a relatively high percentage of (junior) vocational students in many countries have a different home language than the respective primary language of education. Here both research on second language learners and studies of third-language CLIL students are relevant. Genesee et al.'s research on ELLs in the USA (2009) showed that though the ELLs scored lower at the start of the program, by the end they had reached, and usually surpassed, the educational outcomes of their comparison peers. Granted, ELLs have a greater degree of immersion both in school and outside of school than a CLIL student, but Lasagabaster (2008) notes similar progress in CLIL groups learning content through English as a third language in the Basque Country, despite a very weak presence of English in daily life. Swain et al. (1990, 78) argued that 'bilingual education programs that promote first language literacy have an overall positive effect on the learning of other languages'.

CLIL teaching skills

A number of studies have pointed to the need for CLIL content teachers to be aware of various language-related aspects of teaching, such as the specifically linguistic requirements of their subject (Llinares and Whittaker 2009), including linguistic features in their subject teaching (Mewald 2007), or be able to accurately assess the linguistic level of materials and capably scaffold reading activities (García and Tyler 2010). Teachers must also be wary of pre-empting the problem of L2 comprehension by conceptually simplifying the content in advance, leading to reduced content competence (Hajer 2000).

In order to provide more effective integration of content and language, collaboration between language and subject teachers is recommended (de Graaff et al. 2007; García and Tyler 2010; Lorenzo, Casal, and Moore 2010). This is also true for general learning skills applied across the curriculum (Bentley 2010). One of the key findings of the ITALIC Report by Coyle is that the reconceptualization of language learning to include other curricular subjects, including planning and participation by CLIL and language teachers, 'is urgent and of paramount importance' (2011, 5).

CLIL teachers' own language proficiency in English seems to be universally acknowledged as a crucial factor for successful CLIL programs (Marsh 2003;

Lasagabaster 2008; Maljers and van Wilgenburg 2008; Hillyard 2011). Interestingly, in the investigation of Dalton-Puffer et al. (2009) – though vocational students suggest that a changed student-teacher role resulting from imperfect teacher mastery of the target language may have positive ramifications – the students themselves emphasize the need for teachers' target language proficiency.

Conclusions from the literature review

The literature review has dealt with studies related to the considerations, implementation, and appreciation with respect to context, participants, and methodology of bilingual or immersion education relevant for lower achievers at the (junior) vocational level. The review indicates there are a number of justifications for initiating and implementing CLIL at junior vocational level and for developing students' vocational literacy and vocational second language proficiency (Vollmer 2006). Junior vocational students should be able to successfully learn through a second language if curriculum and teaching requirements are met. CLIL and immersion settings have been reported to be motivating and beneficial for the self-concept and self-esteem of lower-achieving students. The review further indicates that in junior vocational CLIL contexts students should be able to achieve a language level in English that is better than their peers in regular junior vocational classes. There is no evidence that their skills in the main language of education or in the subjects taught in English are negatively affected, if sufficient attention is paid to language learning strategies, benefiting from an additive bilingualism approach. The findings reported on CLIL teaching skills are not specific for bilingual education at the junior secondary vocational level, but rather relate to bilingual education in general.

The present study focuses on the following research questions:

- How has bilingual education/CLIL been implemented in junior vocational secondary education in the Netherlands at school and task level?
- How is bilingual education/CLIL in junior vocational secondary education perceived by teachers and pupils?
- What are the successful characteristics of bilingual education/CLIL, according to teachers' and pupils' perceptions, which are relevant for junior vocational secondary education?

Research method

The present study was carried out in partnership with five schools for junior secondary vocational education (henceforth *tvmbo*) in the Netherlands, which were all starting or had recently started with bilingual education. The schools were contacted through the task group for *tvmbo* schools, which is part of the Dutch network of bilingual schools. Some of these schools already had previous experience with bilingual education at the general or pre-university education level. First, CLIL coordinators of the five schools (one for each school) completed a short factual online survey[2], which gathered information such as the reasons for starting bilingual education for this target level, the aims of their junior vocational bilingual education departments, and facts about numbers of students, classes, and subjects taught in English.

Second, teachers, students, coordinators, and management at the five participating schools were interviewed about what they considered to be good bilingual education practice in junior secondary vocational education. The interview protocols were created as a result of the literature study and the factual online survey. These protocols were improved and fine-tuned as a result of feedback from nonparticipating staff at one of the partner schools. The interview protocols (both in English and Dutch) consisted of a number of key questions and some prompts, which triggered the interviewees to elaborate on the key questions. One of the researchers visited all schools to carry out the interviews. An e-mail was sent to each school with suggested instructions and a model program for the day. The interviews were all recorded for further reference. A total of 7 CLIL coordinators and managers, 11 English teachers, 14 subject teachers, and 22 students were interviewed. During the interview days, informal classroom observations were carried out at each school. The aim of these observations was to gather examples of activities and good teacher practices, which appear to work with *tvmbo* students as input for a later online survey.

Third, in order to gather a greater amount of data about bilingual education experiences in junior vocational education, the interview results and observations from the five schools were used to create two online surveys: one for teachers working in junior vocational bilingual education and one for students. The surveys were piloted by nonparticipating teachers at one of the schools and improved according to their feedback. The surveys were distributed and administered online through the *tvmbo* network and completed by 66 students from five schools and 19 teachers from nine schools (including the five schools that had been involved throughout the study). Students completed the online questionnaire in school during class hours, which made it logistically impossible for any student to complete the survey more than once. The majority of the students are from the more practical (lower) level of junior vocational education and nearly three-quarters from the first year. The teacher respondents are experienced in both the more theoretical and the more practical type of junior vocational education, and teach English as well as a variety of subjects such as mathematics, art, administration, economics, drama, history, car mechanics, and physical education.

In the Results section, the findings from the interviews and the online survey will be presented together, as they cover the same issues.

Characteristics of the five participating schools for junior vocational secondary education

Two out of five schools had one year of experience with junior vocational bilingual education, one school had two years of experience, one school had three years, and one had five years of experience. That is, in only one school had the first cohort of students already completed four years of junior vocational bilingual education. All five schools offered bilingual education at the more theoretical levels of junior vocational education; only two schools offered bilingual education at the more practical levels. Two of the schools incorporate bilingual education in regular subjects, and three in a combination of subjects and in cross-curricular projects (e.g. English and Sciences, Social Sciences, Technical Studies, Arts, or Drama). All schools were involved in or preparing for international collaboration projects and exchange trips.

With respect to its implementation at school level, bilingual education programs (CLIL) at junior vocational level were organized according to the Dutch Standard for *tvmbo*. Schools offered the target language in at least a total of 30% of the curriculum, in a combination of subject courses and language courses. Where possible, at least one native speaker was employed. EIO was an integral part of the curriculum. The target language was offered in the required domains, and the schools paid explicit attention to the target language level of the nonnative speaker teachers. Within the standard requirements, different implementation modes were reported, varying from single subjects offered in English on the one hand, to projects on the other, in which language, theoretical subjects, and practical skills were integrated thematically.

The CLIL coordinators mentioned the following main reasons for implementing bilingual education in junior vocational education: Firstly, junior vocational students are likely to work in English, at least to some extent, in their future jobs – in hotels, international transport, or ICT, for instance. Secondly, despite the clear need for a certain level of English proficiency for their future vocations, these pupils' level of English is generally quite low, which points to an obvious need to strengthen this area. Third, more and more primary schools are giving content lessons in English. Finally, intermediate vocational schools are increasingly offering course materials and courses solely in English. CLIL at junior vocational level seems therefore to be a logical step between the start in English made at primary school and intermediate vocational studies in English.

Results from the interviews and the online survey

In the classroom

The kinds of lessons that were reported effective in *tvmbo* are practical and hands-on, with lots of variety, communication between students in English, and short activities. According to the teachers, the concentration span of *tvmbo* students is short. The teachers' advice is to get them working, to get them active quickly, and to provide enough variety and short activities. A further important finding is that *tvmbo* students like creative tasks, where they can make things or write and speak in English and put something of their own personalities into the results. Linked to the idea of personalization, students also appreciate an element of choice. The use of popular media such as television and the Internet is also motivating and effective. Surprises also help: students find predictable lessons boring and unhelpful. The link to real life is also important – to their own lives or to events in the news or traditions such as Christmas or Halloween; this also includes the use of authentic materials in English and activities related to the school's EIO curriculum. Furthermore, repeating and recycling material in different ways is important.

In the online survey the students were asked which classroom activities help them to best learn their subjects in English. The activities in the online survey were chosen from activities mentioned in the interviews; respondents were asked to indicate how useful they found each of the different activities. Here we mention the activities, which at least 40% of the students chose as 'extremely useful' (the highest category). The students clearly believe that they learn mostly from doing things (55%) (as opposed to listening, reading, or completing exercises in workbooks), working in groups (48%), and working in pairs (55%). Apparently, they learn from practical, hands-on activities, and from doing presentations (55%). The next most popular categories are creative speaking activities (48%), finding things out for themselves (46%), taking notes (45%) and projects (47%), listening to music and songs and doing related activities (43%), and watching video clips or DVDs and doing related activities (47%). It is clear from their responses that *tvmbo* students believe that they need to *do* something with the language and the subject: only listening or reading about it is apparently less effective.

The teachers were also asked which classroom activities help their students to learn the subject through English; again, respondents were asked to indicate the effectiveness of various activities. Here we mention the activities that at least 40% of the teachers found 'extremely helpful'. Like the students, group work (59%) and pair work (65%) are the most important, followed closely by creating PowerPoint or 'show and tell' presentations (59%). After that come mind maps (53%), projects in English (53%), talking about their own lives and real things (53%), and visuals (pictures or photographs) (53%). Also considered useful by teachers is the course book (47%), which actually contradicts what the smaller number of student interviewees said – that they did not feel they learned from their course book. Games and puzzles in class (e.g. crosswords, word puzzles) (47%) and making things (e.g. a poster, cookery, making a film) (47%) are also considered helpful. Finally, discovery activities (41%) and doing activities related to podcasts or audio recordings (41%) are also popular, together with music, songs, and videos on YouTube or DVDs (41%).

An open question was also on the teachers' survey: What is the most important aspect(s) of classroom activities which best help your tvmbo students to learn your subject in English and why? In their answers, the teachers often mentioned the importance of speaking: 'talking about the projects', 'discuss in small groups', 'interaction', ' communicating in English', 'activities that compel pupils to speak', 'speaking English a lot', and 'giving presentations'. They also mentioned that *tvmbo* students need multimodal input: they need to see, hear, and use input in several ways in order to process it: 'being able to see the words they are going to speak – this enables word recognition and builds confidence; pictures and words'. It was also considered important to allow students to make mistakes and to be creative: 'Learning by doing, so they learn that mistakes are allowed; create an atmosphere where children aren't scared to make mistakes'.

Outside the classroom

Many *tvmbo* students believed that they learn a lot of English in their daily lives, outside school, through the use of English in the popular media, especially the computer and Internet. This is not only receptive – listening to songs or reading texts – but also interactive, in terms of writing and speaking to other English-speakers on the Internet. A question in the surveys asked the students about what activities they do in English outside the class and another one about how useful they found these activities in learning English. It turns out that many of them do quite a lot in English outside the classroom, the most popular activities being watching films in English with Dutch subtitles (films and series on Dutch television are not dubbed), closely followed by watching television in English. The other most popular activities are watching music on YouTube or other sites, chatting online in English (for example with other people around the world about computer games), and playing computer games in English. Around 40% of the students indicated that they believe that they learn English when they do such activities outside class.

EIO was reported to be an important key to the success of *tvmbo*, both during the lessons and outside of them. Incorporating EIO into lessons and projects is very motivating for students, since they see the clear link between real life and what they are learning. Hosting native speakers in the classroom also proves a very motivating and realistic activity. Trips abroad or exchanges also give *tvmbo* students a concrete, immediate reason to communicate in English. Visiting English-speaking countries and communicating with native speaker teenagers is perhaps the most motivating aspect of EIO. However, most schools mentioned that their EIO curriculum still needs to be further developed, designed, and implemented.

Teacher skills

In the online survey, a list of characteristics of good *tvmbo* teachers was included, based on the findings from the literature and the interviews. Students as well as teachers indicated the following characteristics of good *tvmbo*: good *tvmbo* teachers know how to activate students and use variety of tasks to stimulate participation. They are able to design and carry out a variety of activities in English and know how to design lessons around different learning styles in order to deal with diversity. They are good at checking understanding effectively. Good *tvmbo* teachers are enthusiastic and positive: they include humour and lots of compliments for good work in their lessons. They create an atmosphere where students are allowed to make mistakes, so that students experiment with the language they are learning. They are particularly sensitive to the pupil's comprehension levels in English and are able to simplify language and scaffold content.

We particularly asked the students which teacher behavior they find useful to help them learn subjects in English. The most important teacher behaviour – scoring far above all the others – is that the teacher speaks English (nearly) all of the time. The second teaching strategy which is considered useful is that the teacher encourages the students to use English themselves. Further, their English is good and they correct the students' English.

According to the teachers, good *tvmbo* teachers provide lots of structure by talking slowly, asking questions, and giving good explanations. They can also adjust their own level of English to their students' level. Good *tvmbo* teachers can assess the ability of the students, both in terms of language as well as in terms of content. Good *tvmbo* teachers want to develop themselves further in terms of English and CLIL methodology.

In the survey, teachers were asked which teaching strategies they use and which work in *tvmbo*. The list for the survey was compiled from what students and teachers had mentioned during the interviews. The strategies are summarized in order from considered *most* useful to considered useful by at least 50% of the teachers, in Table 1.

The results in the table show that the strategies that teachers consider useful largely correspond with the students' and teachers' perception of good *tvmbo* teachers. They encourage their students to use English; they provide lots of input and structure by talking slowly, asking questions, and giving good explanations; they can adjust their own level of English to their students' level; they use a variety of activating tasks, including group and pair work.

Table 1. Teaching strategies that teachers consider useful in *tvmbo*.

Useful teaching strategies	I do it and it works well ($n = 15$)
If students make a mistake I encourage them to carry on.	15
If students find it too difficult in English, I use some Dutch.	14
I praise students for using English.	14
I don't let students laugh at one other.	14
I use simple words.	13
I repeat and recycle information and language.	13
I ignore students' mistakes some of the time.	13
I translate (words) into Dutch.	13
I write things on the board.	12
I talk slowly.	12
I give students a time limit for activities.	12
I let students know when I am proud of them.	11
I keep classroom activities short: 5 to 10 minutes per activity.	10
I give tips to my students to help them learn words.	10
I use variety – lots of different assignments in one lesson.	10
I encourage my students to be creative with language.	9
I talk in English, then in Dutch afterwards.	9
I use a lot of group work.	8
I use a lot of pair work.	7

Discussion

This study has focused on the following research questions:

- How has bilingual education/CLIL been implemented in junior vocational secondary education in the Netherlands at school and task level?
- How is bilingual education/CLIL in junior vocational secondary education perceived by teachers and pupils?
- What are the successful characteristics of bilingual education/CLIL, according to teachers' and pupils' perceptions, which are relevant for junior vocational secondary education?

With respect to its implementation at school level, bilingual education programs (CLIL) at the participating junior vocational secondary schools have, in general, been organized according to the Dutch Standard for *tvmbo*. Schools offer the target language in at least a total of 30% of the curriculum, in a combination of subject course and language course. EIO is an integral part of the curriculum. Within the standard requirements, we have seen different implementation modes, varying between single subjects offered in English on the one hand and content and language integrated projects on the other.

Compared to bilingual programs in the pre-university *vwo* and the general secondary *havo* streams, bilingual junior secondary vocational programs in the Netherlands are inclusive, not streamed. Students whose scores and primary school assessments qualify them for a particular junior vocational level automatically qualify for the bilingual program. Anecdotal evidence from one of the (bilingual-only) schools in the present study indicates that some students enroll at the school without even realizing that they will be joining a bilingual program. There is a clear lack of socioeconomic status distinctions or parental pressure to participate. This contrasts with Bruton's assessment (2011) of the Andalusian context, in which he points to a selection influenced by status, class, or parental preference, despite the programs' claims to egalitarianism.

At task level, teachers are clearly aware of the need to vary activities and keep the activities short. They aim at offering tasks that involve the use of language, knowledge, and skills and which stimulate the use of multiple intelligences. Focus on meaning and focus on fluency and adequacy are considered more important that focus on form and accuracy. Target language learning clearly takes place outside as well as within the classroom setting. In general, activities that involve speaking and those which involve real-life international contact are considered highly motivating.

Related to the second research question, both junior vocational students and their teachers perceive bilingual education (CLIL) as being very motivating; the former because of the combination of challenges and the latter because of the type of student and their response to the challenges of CLIL. Students perceive it as important and relevant to their future educational opportunities and/or careers, and teachers perceive it as meaningful for their students' vocational education. EIO activities are perceived as particularly meaningful and motivating, as these provide real-world contacts between peers in an international context and make the usefulness and authenticity of communication in the target language tangible.

Related to the third question, the study reveals the following successful characteristics for bilingual junior vocational education. It is clear from the research results that both students and teachers consider it important to speak in the target language as much as possible. This perception is also borne out by the results from the literature survey. The teachers' ideas about what works in the classroom are very similar to those of their students: *tvmbo* teachers realize that their students learn best when actively doing things and when they can be creative. They also believe that the structure of a book, or of making notes, is helpful; the students partly agree. Teachers find it important to adapt their own language level and register to the students' level, both linguistically and conceptually. This is probably a key factor in any teaching at the (junior) vocational education level, but it becomes even more essential in a bilingual education setting. This implies that junior vocational secondary teachers should be proficient in the target language, just as their colleagues in pre-university bilingual education. Particularly with lower-achieving students, teachers need the flexibility to use the target language in a variety of ways, in order to feel comfortable and confident. Especially at this level, CLIL teachers need to have an affinity with the type of student and to be able to express this affinity by means of the target language to students who learn by doing, who need to see the relevance and the purpose of the language and the task.

The study reported here involved a rather small number of participants from a small number of schools. As students and teachers were not selected randomly but participated voluntarily, generalization of the findings to junior secondary vocational education for the Netherlands and elsewhere can only be made with great caution. Future research should include a larger number of teachers and students from a larger number of schools. Future research may also compare more specifically the perceptions of bilingual junior vocational students and teachers to the perceptions of their regular nonbilingual junior vocational peers, or to the perceptions of bilingual pre-university students and teachers. In a follow-up study, we will focus on the effect of bilingual education on the junior vocational students' proficiency in English and

Dutch; on their subject matter knowledge; and on their motivation, self-confidence, and willingness to communicate.

Conclusion

Participants in this study have reported many advantages for bilingual junior secondary vocational education, such as the preparation of students for their future careers and cross-cultural communication with other English language users. This has been shown both in the literature study (see also Coyle, Hood, and Marsh 2010) as well as in the interviews and the responses to the online surveys. *Tvmbo* gives opportunities for students to work on their vocational literacy and vocational language proficiency. It also appears that motivation increases in junior secondary vocational students who enjoy a challenge.

Teachers and students are quite optimistic – and certainly enthusiastic – about the challenge of further developing a junior vocational bilingual stream. Many teachers point out that they enjoy teaching *tvmbo* students and are optimistic about future developments. Particularly important seems to be that bilingual *tvmbo* gives *vmbo* students a chance and a challenge, and that students' self-esteem and motivation may be increased through being in a *tvmbo* stream. Teachers realize that creating an effective *tvmbo* takes time, especially setting up a dynamic EIO curriculum and program. Creating a strong *tvmbo* team and working together on content and language integrated cross-curricular projects may have a substantial impact on the success of teaching and learning. To conclude, the study indicates that over 70% of the students would recommend *tvmbo* to a friend or family member, because they feel it is fun and motivating, and it helps them develop their skills in English. The challenges for *tvmbo* are being met with optimism, teamwork, and professional development, which in turn expand the opportunities for teachers and students alike.

Notes

1. This Standard and quality indicators for tvmbo schools are at present only published in Dutch (http://www.europeesplatform.nl/tto/het-netwerk-tto/tto-standaarden/), though they may appear in English in the near future. The Standards for general and pre-university secondary education have been published in English (http://education.cambridge.org/media/2598232/tool-8-final.pdf), as well as the quality indicators (http://education.cambridge.org/media/2598232/tool-8-final.pdf). See de Graaff & van Wilgenburg (2015) for further explanation.
2. See <http://www.surveymonkey.com/s/tvmboresearch> for access to the survey.

References

Baetens Beardsmore, H. 2007. "The Working Life Perspective." In *Diverse Contexts – Converging Goals: CLIL in Europe*, edited by D. Marsh and D. Wolff, 27–31. Frankfurt: Peter Lang.

Bentley, K. 2010. *The TKT Course CLIL Module*. Cambridge: Cambridge University Press.

Bruton, A. 2011. "Are the Differences between CLIL and Non-CLIL Groups in Andalusia Due to CLIL? A Response to Lorenzo, Casal and Moore (2010)." *Applied Linguistics* 32 (2): 236–241. doi:10.1093/applin/amr007.

Coyle, D. 2011. *ITALIC Research Report. Investigating Student Gains: Content and Language Integrated Learning*. University of Aberdeen. http://www.abdn.ac.uk/italic.

Coyle, D., P. Hood, and D. Marsh. 2010. *CLIL: Content and Language Integrated Learning*. Cambridge: Cambridge University Press.

Dalton-Puffer, C., J. Hüttner, V. Schindelegger, and U. Smit. 2009. "Technology-geeks Speak Out: What Students Think about Vocational CLIL." *International CLIL Research Journal* 1 (2): 18–25. http://www.icrj.eu/12-741.

García, S. B., and B.-J. Tyler. 2010. "Meeting the Needs of English Language Learners with Learning Disabilities in the General Curriculum." *Theory into Practice* 49 (2): 113–120. doi:10.1080/00405841003626585.

Gardner, R. C. 2010. *Motivation and Second Language Acquisition: The Socio-Educational Model*. New York: Peter Lang.

Geneseee, F. 2007. "French Immersion and At-Risk Students: A Review of Research Evidence." *The Canadian Modern Language Review* 63 (5): 655–687. doi:10.3138/cmlr.63.5.655.

Genesee, F., K. Lindholm-Leary, W. Saunders, and D. Christian. 2009. "English Language Learners in U.S. Schools: An Overview of Research findings." *Journal of Education for Students Placed at Risk (JESPAR)* 10 (4): 363–385. doi:10.1207/s15327671espr1004_2.

Graaff, R. de, G. J. Koopman, Y. Anikina, and G. Westhoff. 2007. "An Observation Tool for Effective L2 Pedagogy in CLIL." *International Journal of Bilingual Education and Bilingualism* 10 (5): 603–624. doi:10.2167/beb462.0.

Graaff, R. de, and Wilgenburg, O. van. 2015. The Netherlands: Quality control as a driving force in bilingual education. In P. Mehisto & F. Genesee (Eds.), *Building bilingual education systems: Forces, mechanisms and counterweights* (pp. 167–179). Cambridge: Cambridge University Press.

Hajer, M. 2000. "Creating A Language-Promoting Classroom: Content-Area Teachers At Work." In *Second and Foreign Language Learning Through Classroom Interaction*, edited by J. K. Hall and L. Stoops Verplaetse, 265–285. Mahwah, NJ: Erlbaum.

Hillyard, S. 2011. "First Steps in CLIL: Training the Teachers." *Latin American Journal of Content & Language Integrated Learning* 4 (2): 1–12. http://laclil.unisabana.edu.co/index.php/LACLIL/article/view/2631

Hood, P. 2006. "Unpublished Data from CLIL Research Interviews with Students at Tile Hill Wood Language College, Coventry, UK." In *CLIL: Content and Language Integrated Learning*, edited by D. Coyle, P. Hood, and D. Marsh, 142. 2010. Cambridge: Cambridge University Press.

Huibregtse, I. 2001. "*Effecten en didactiek van tweetalig voortgezet onderwijs in Nederland* [Effects and pedagogy of bilingual secondary education in the Netherlands]." PhD diss., Utrecht University, the Netherlands.

Lasagabaster, D. 2008. "Foreign Language Competence in Content and Language Integrated Courses." *The Open Applied Linguistics Journal* 1: 30–41. doi:10.2174/1874913500801010030.

Lasagabaster, D. 2011. "English Achievement and Student Motivation in CLIL and EFL Settings." *Innovation in Language Teaching and Learning* 5: 3–18. doi:10.1080/17501229.2010.519030.

Llinares, A., and R. Whittaker. 2009. "Teaching and Learning History in Secondary CLIL Classrooms: From Speaking to Writing." In *CLIL Across Educational Levels: Experiences from Primary, Secondary and Tertiary Contexts*, edited by E. Dafouz and M. Guerrini, 73–88. Madrid: Richmond.

Lorenzo, F., S. Casal, and P. Moore. 2010. "The Effects of Content and Language Integrated Learning in European Education: Key Findings from the Andalusian Bilingual Sections Evaluation Project." *Applied Linguistics* 31: 418–442. doi:10.1093/applin/amp041.

Lyster, R. 2007. *Learning and Teaching Languages Through Content; A Counterbalanced Approach*. Amsterdam/Philadelphia: John Benjamins.

Maljers, A., and O. van Wilgenburg. 2008. "CLIL – Bilingual Education – TTO: Here to Stay!" The XPat Journal. http://www.xpat.nl/xpat_journal/back_issues_xpat_journal/xpat_journal_issue_spring2008_Education.

Marsh, D. 2003. The Relevance and Potential of Content and Language Integrated Learning (CLIL) for Achieving MT+2 in Europe. *ELC Information Bulletin* (no. 9, April). http://userpage.fu-berlin.de/elc/bulletin/9/en/marsh.html.

Merisuo-Storm, T. 2006. "Pupils' Attitudes Towards Foreign-Language Learning and the Development of Literacy Skills in Bilingual Education." *Teaching and Teacher Education* 23: 226–235. doi:10.1016/j.tate.2006.04.024.

Mewald, C. 2007. "A Comparison of Oral Language Performance of Learners in CLIL and Mainstream Classes at Lower Secondary Level in Lower Austria." In *Empirical Perspectives on CLIL Classroom Discourse*, edited by C. Dalton-Puffer and U. Smit, 139–178. Frankfurt: Peter Lang.

Sallili, F., and A. B. M. Tsui. 2005. "The Effects of Medium of Instruction on Students' Motivation and Learning." In *Language in Multicultural Education*, edited by R. Hoosain and F. Salili, 135–156. Research in Multicultural Education and International Perspectives, Vol. 4. Greenwich, CT: Information Age Publishing (IAP).

Seikkula-Leino, J. 2007. "CLIL Learning: Achievement Levels and Affective Factors." *Language and Education* 21 (4): 328–341. doi:10.2167/le635.0.

Swain, M., S. Lapkin, N. Rowen, and D. Hart. 1990. "The Role of Mother Tongue Literacy in Third Language Learning." *Language, Culture and Curriculum* 3 (1): 65–81. doi:10.1080/07908319009525073.

Verspoor, M. H., K. de Bot, and E. M. J. van Rein. 2011. "English As A Foreign Language; the Role of Out-of-school Language Input." In *English in Europe Today; Sociocultural and Educational Perspectives*, edited by A. de Houwer and A. Wilton, 147–166. Amsterdam: John Benjamins.

Verspoor, M. H., J. Schuitemaker-King, E. M. J. van Rein, K. de Bot, and P. Edelenbos. 2010. *Tweetalig onderwijs: vormgeving en prestaties* (OTTO). [Bilingual education: design and achievements]. Research report, University of Groningen, the Netherlands.

Vollmer, H. 2006. *Language Across the Curriculum – A Way towards Plurilingualism. Expertise for the Council of Europe, Language policy division*. Strasbourg: Council of Europe. http://www.coe.int/t/dg4/linguistic/Source/Vollmer_LAC_EN.doc.

CLIL in Sweden – why does it not work? A metaperspective on CLIL across contexts in Europe

Liss Kerstin Sylvén

Department of Education and Special Education, University of Gothenburg, Gothenburg, Sweden

> Many studies show positive correlations between content and language integrated learning (CLIL) and the learning of English as a foreign language. However, findings from CLIL research in Sweden do not match those obtained elsewhere. The aim of this chapter is to show that some explanations for discrepancies in results obtained across CLIL contexts in Europe may be found in nation-specific contextual factors. Four such factors are focused on: policy framework, teacher education, age of implementation, and extramural exposure to English. The chapter gives an overview of these factors in four European countries: Finland, Germany, Spain, and Sweden. A coordinate system is created using four quadrants: the policy framework factor is paired with amount of research; the age factor is combined with amount of CLIL; the teacher education factor includes pre-service and in-service programs; and extramural English is considered in amount and range. From this coordinate system, nation-specific CLIL profiles emerge. It is argued that such national profiles will serve as an essential theoretical point of departure for comparisons of research results across nations. Furthermore, the profiles will facilitate policy-level discussions on CLIL implementation in individual countries.

Introduction

In the European context, research focusing on various perspectives of content and language integrated learning (CLIL) has grown rapidly in the last decade. Most studies concern CLIL where English is the language of instruction, which is also the case in the present chapter. In some countries, these investigations show very positive results (Dalton-Puffer 2007; Isidro 2010; Lasagabaster 2008). For instance, in the Spanish context Navés and Victori (2010) found not only that CLIL students outperform their non-CLIL peers on a number of language proficiency measures in several grades, but also that eighth grade CLIL students outperformed ninth grade non-CLIL students on all of the measures tested. In Finland, Nikula's (2005) report showed that CLIL students, in contrast to students learning English as a Foreign Language, are looked upon as competent language users by their teachers, also showing signs of being confident in their use of English. Germany is another country where benefits of CLIL have been demonstrated, for instance, on linguistic accuracy (Klippel 2003; Zydatiss 2007). In Sweden, results from CLIL research are not equally encouraging. Washburn (1997) found that CLIL students did not gain as good competence in the subjects studied as their non-CLIL peers. Sylvén (2004) investigated lexical proficiency and concluded that it was the amount of exposure to English outside of school that was of importance for students' vocabulary development rather than CLIL in school. Moreover, classroom interaction is more limited in CLIL classes than in non-CLIL classes (Lim Falk 2008).

These remarkable and significant differences in results call for explanations. The aim of this chapter is to discuss four possible reasons for this discrepancy in CLIL across European national contexts, highlighting the need to include contextual factors in cross-national comparison. The factors focused on are policy framework, teacher education, age of implementation, and extramural exposure to the target language (TL). The reasons for choosing these factors are that they are all decisive for the implementation of a TL learning program, such as CLIL. Needless to say, there are other influential variables, for example, historical perspectives, the number of people speaking a country's majority language, the level of motivation for learning a foreign language (FL) among students, to mention just a few. Although of obvious relevance, such factors will not be considered here.

The chapter starts with a brief background of CLIL in Sweden, and comparisons are made with three other European CLIL countries, Finland, Germany, and Spain. The four factors described above are then addressed, starting in Sweden with digressions to the other countries. Based on these factors in each individual country, a coordinate system designed to sketch nation-specific CLIL profiles is introduced. This forms the point of departure for the discussion and conclusion.

Background

The reason for selecting the specific countries dealt with here is that Sweden is one of the Nordic countries, and so a comparison with one of its neighboring countries, Finland, is of interest. The inclusion of Germany in central Europe and Spain in southern Europe will contribute to a general overview of CLIL in Europe. In the following, a brief background of CLIL in the four countries will be outlined in order to give the reader some understanding of the varying national histories at hand.

In Sweden, CLIL was introduced in 1977, as an experiment by an individual teacher (Åseskog 1982). This experiment was followed by a growing number of other schools implementing CLIL in English. In 2001, a total of 20% of all schools at upper secondary level and 4% of those at lower secondary level implemented CLIL, to varying degrees, in one way or another (Nixon 2000). It would be of great interest to have access to a more recent update of these figures, but to date there is no such information available.

In Finland, there is a long tradition of bilingualism dating back several centuries. Immersion schools using Swedish as the medium of instruction were introduced in 1987 (Björklund and Mård-Miettinen 2011), which is about the same time as CLIL-classes using English as the vehicular language started. Presently, CLIL is found mostly at upper secondary level, even though it is becoming increasingly common at lower levels.

The history of CLIL in Germany is radically different from the other countries dealt with in this chapter. In 1963, German-French bilingual sections were set up in schools in Germany as an integral part of the reconciliation process in the aftermath of World War II, in order to promote linguistic as well as cultural bonds between the two neighboring countries (Mäsch 1993; Zydatiss 2007). As pointed out by Zydatiss (2007), rather than being based on academic theory, the introduction of bilingual education was done on the basis of a political decision. In the 1990s, English was introduced as another TL in CLIL teaching in Germany, and at present, English is the most commonly used CLIL language, even though other languages, such as Italian, Russian, and Dutch are also found (Wolff 2007).

CLIL in Spain has virtually exploded during the last decade. Having a history of bilingualism in some of its autonomous regions, the teaching of content through another language than Spanish is fairly uncontroversial (but see Figueras 2009). The implementation of CLIL, though, differs from one region to another. In Andalusia, for instance, an ambitious plan to promote plurilingualism was launched in 2005, with the main objective of meeting the European Union recommendation of 1 + 2 languages, that is, the knowledge of one's mother tongue plus two other European languages (European Commission 1995). This plan is comprehensive and seeks to address the need for an advancement of students' FL abilities in conjunction with a widened cultural understanding (for more details, see Casal and Moore 2009). In other parts of Spain, similar efforts at promoting FL learning are being made (cf. e.g. Navés and Victori 2010; Ruiz de Zarobe and Lasagabaster 2010).

After this brief overview of the background of CLIL in the four countries, let us turn to the four factors that I believe may be helpful in explaining some of the discrepancies in research results.

The four factors

In the following, the meaning of each of the four factors dealt with in this chapter will be accounted for and their theoretical impact in the CLIL context will be discussed. An account of each factor in the four countries will result in four quadrants merged into a coordinate system. For such a system, there need to be two axes per quadrant. Therefore, the policy framework factor is combined with the amount of research; the teacher education factor is looked at from the pre- and in-service perspectives; the age of implementation factor is combined with the amount of CLIL; and finally the extramural English (EE) factor includes types and amount. At the end of each section, an illustration of the quadrant at issue with details of each country is supplied. It should be pointed out that the illustrations are crude and generalizing; they are intended to serve as indicators rather than exact facts. The countries are represented by their flags, as illustrated in Figure 1.

Policy framework and research

Policy documents are the building blocks of any school activity. They provide guidance to schools and teachers involved, and, further, they are a necessary tool to ensure equity in a national school system. As pointed out by, for example, Alderson (2009), language policies are important as they determine how the languages are to be taught, learned, and assessed. Consequently, without a policy document at national level stating what CLIL is, and is not, CLIL may, and does, take any form or shape at the individual school. According to Marsh (2002), CLIL is an umbrella term, which refers to a dual-focused educational context in which an additional language, thus not usually the first FL of the learners, is used as a medium in the teaching and learning of non-language content. This is a broad definition,

The four countries

Figure 1. The four countries and their respective flags.

contrasting with Do Coyle's 4C's Framework as a definition of CLIL. According to the 4C's Framework, CLIL entails content, communication, cognition, and culture (Coyle 2008). In order to know what CLIL is in the individual national context, a specification is needed at policy level.

The intention of the European Union for its citizens to master their mother tongue plus two other European languages was stated by the European Commission in its White Paper of 1995. It was further stated that secondary school students should study certain subjects in the first FL learned (European Commission 1995). These aims, however, were accompanied neither by stated forms of implementation nor by specific funding. Thus, the capability and/or willingness of individual member states to convert these words into action may vary considerably (see also Dalton-Puffer, Nikula, and Smit 2010; Lasagabaster and Sierra 2010). The resulting discrepancies in, for instance, the implementation of CLIL between countries do not facilitate comparisons in the larger European context. In implementing a policy framework for CLIL, the national governing bodies not only ensure that certain requirements are fulfilled, but also enable and empower individual schools to make informed decisions about the enactment of CLIL.

The term CLIL is interpreted in several different ways in Sweden. As an example, one school, which received a European quality award in languages in 2010, defines it as 'teaching several subjects in the TL, promoting contacts and exchanges with schools in other countries and having a global perspective on teaching' (Skolverket http://www.skolverket.se/sb/d/2166/a/23007, my translation). Another example is the definition used by the Swedish National Agency for Education: 'CLIL is the teaching of a subject in another language than the student's first language' (Skolverket 2010). These two definitions differ in several respects. In the first one, *several subjects* are mentioned, whereas the second states that *a subject* should be involved. Where the definition used by the Swedish National Agency for Education is limited only to the use of another language, the definition used by the school includes 'contacts and exchanges' as well as an overall 'global perspective on teaching'. These two examples illustrate fundamentally different approaches to CLIL. Apart from the short definition provided by the Swedish National Agency for Education, there is no mention of CLIL in any official documents at a national policy level.

Given the relative spread of CLIL, the amount of research into CLIL in Sweden up until a few years ago has been surprisingly scarce. Recently, however, several studies have been published (Airey 2009; Lim Falk 2008; Sylvén 2004, 2007). Two major studies investigating the effect of CLIL on school results and vocabulary acquisition, respectively, suggest that there is indeed room for improvement. In Washburn (1997), the results corroborate the findings of Spada and Lightbown (1989:24), who found that most students in intensive programs have developed fluency skills in English as well as confidence and ease in using their second language, but also, more surprisingly, that CLIL and non-CLIL students were indistinguishable (Washburn 1997). In another major study (Sylvén 2004), where vocabulary acquisition was focused on, it was shown that the most influential factors on vocabulary acquisition is the amount of students' overall exposure to the TL, rather than CLIL per se. In a study focusing on classroom interaction, Lim Falk (2008) investigated language use in CLIL and non-CLIL classrooms. Her findings revealed that there was less interaction in the CLIL classroom compared to the non-CLIL classroom, and the interaction that took place was primarily conducted through Swedish. Airey (2009) investigated the use of English as the medium of communication at tertiary level and concluded that even though there were no apparent signs that students learned less from lectures in English than from those in Swedish, it is important for lecturers to rethink the organization of their lectures.

In the Finnish national curriculum for compulsory school from 2004 (Utbildningsstyrelsen 2004), CLIL and immersion teaching are outlined in a chapter of their own, dealing with aspects such as goals and ways of implementation. This forms a solid basis from which local schools can form their CLIL or immersion teaching. The research carried out in Finland on CLIL-related issues is prominent (cf. e.g. Järvinen 1999, 2010; Marsh 2002; Nikula 2005, 2007; Ringbom 2012). Also worth mentioning is the fact that the *International CLIL Research Journal* (http://www.icrj.eu/) is published at the University of Jyväskylä, Finland, which is one of the more prominent centers for CLIL research in Europe.

In Germany, the 16 fairly autonomous *Bundesländer* decide on their own educational policies; thus no single model of CLIL in the German context exists. However, there seems to be a consensus across the country pertaining to some general principles to be adopted. For instance, even though it is important for students to be able to account for their content knowledge in German, the promotion of language skills is regarded as a key objective of bilingual teaching of specialized subjects (Wolff 2007). Another central objective of CLIL in Germany is intercultural learning, dating back to the origins of bilingual teaching in Germany, nicely tying in with the CLIL 4 C's Framework (Coyle 2009). Great emphasis in German CLIL is placed on textual work, primarily focusing on the linguistic skills of reading and writing (Wolff 2007).

CLIL in Spain is fairly well defined, at least at the level of the autonomous communities. According to Ruiz de Zarobe and Lasagabaster (2010), the Spanish approaches to CLIL can be categorized into two main areas, namely those in monolingual areas, where CLIL adds a second/foreign language to the instruction, and those in bilingual ones, where the implementation of CLIL in reality means that the students are taught through their third language (L3). As mentioned above,

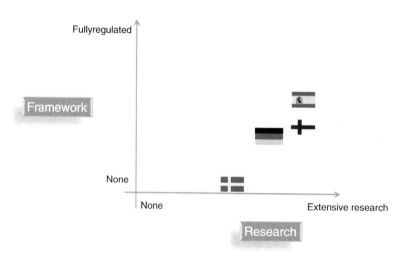

Figure 2. Degree of regulation and amount of research in the four countries.

CLIL research abounds in Spain (cf. e.g. Casal and Moore 2009; Lasagabaster and Ruiz de Zarobe 2010; Ruiz de Zarobe, Sierra, and Gallardo Del Puerto 2011).

Based on the above, the first of the four quadrants taking framework and research into consideration can be established. Figure 2 depicts the constellation of the four countries in this quadrant.

In Figure 2, we see that Spain and Finland are positioned farthest out on both the framework and research axes, with Germany and Sweden closer to the origo.

Teacher education – pre- and in-service

The inclusion, or exclusion, of areas or domains in teacher training programs, sets the agenda for a nation's future teachers. Teacher education influences future teachers as to what is regarded as important and what is not. Thus, in countries without any specific training for CLIL teachers, the general view might be that teaching content through another language is simply doing it in another language, when the truth is that there is a range of other key factors to take into account (De Graaff et al. 2007). Even though it is commonly suggested that teachers teach the way they were taught in school (Medgyes and Malderez 1996), the importance of teacher education should not be underestimated. It is during pre-service education that future teachers form their professional vision. One study found that teacher training courses addressing teaching and learning from an interdisciplinary perspective can enhance professional vision (Blomberg, Stürmer, and Seidel 2011). CLIL being interdisciplinary by definition, this is an important finding. Also, as pointed out by Maskit (2011), a teacher's attitude toward, and willingness to adapt to, pedagogical changes is not stable over time but varies. As in any other type of development, pedagogical development among individual teachers is an ongoing process (Fullan 1995; Guskey and Huberman 1995), lending support to the importance of in-service training.

When using an FL to communicate the content of a subject, the level of proficiency in that language needs to be fairly high. Teachers' command of the FL in CLIL is an area commonly commented upon by Swedish students (Sylvén 2004). Teaching through another language than one's L1 is challenging, and this challenge needs to be addressed in teacher education in order for CLIL teachers to be well prepared. The European Commission (Eurydice Network 2008) states that few countries require their CLIL teachers to have specific CLIL training. However, it is also emphasized that the lack of qualified teachers is often a hindrance for CLIL to develop and that amplified teacher qualifications would indeed help promote it.

In Sweden, teacher education was reorganized in 1999 and more recently in 2011. The 1999 remake allowed students to combine subjects as they saw fit. This enabled students studying to become teachers to combine non-language subjects with languages, for instance history and English. These types of combination are a good starting point for future CLIL-teachers. It turned out, though, that this plethora of subject combinations rendered some newly graduated teachers practically unemployable. For this reason, along with others, the teacher training program was radically changed in 2011, with a return, among other things, to fixed subject combinations. However, CLIL is not specifically addressed in the new pre-service program. Presently, the availability of in-service CLIL training is severely limited.

Finland has a long tradition of incorporating immersion and CLIL in teacher education, and there are certain requirements regarding teachers' level of language proficiency. CLIL teachers who are not native speakers of the TL are required to perform language tests (https://www.jyu.fi/hum/laitokset/solki/yki/svenska) and obtain results that correspond to the C1 level in the Common European Framework of Reference for Languages (CEFR) scale (Council of Europe 2001). Teachers who have studied the TL for at least two years at university level also qualify as CLIL teachers. Other than proven language proficiency, there are no further specific requirements for CLIL teachers in Finland.

Even though there is virtually no specific CLIL pre-service teacher education offered in Germany, there are in-service courses. CLIL teachers in schools with a CLIL strand are always expected to have one language and one content subject in their degree. Teachers with content subjects only, however, can prove their level of competence in the TL, which is required to be at the C1 level of the CEFR scale (Rumlich, personal communication January 13, 2013).

In a volume on CLIL in Spain, edited by Lasagabaster and Ruiz de Zarobe (2010), several examples are given of teacher training courses specifically aimed at CLIL teachers. In some areas, focus is on in-service training (Salaberri Ramiro 2010), whereas in others it is on pre-service training (Escobar Urmeneta 2010). In general, there appears to exist a high level of awareness of the need for CLIL teacher training, not only as regards competences in the FL, but also in other areas, such as how to teach the content of the subject and at the same time work on improving students' language skills (Ball and Lindsay 2010).

Figure 3 illustrates that the existence and amount of teacher education differ radically between the five countries, with Sweden in close proximity to the origo, Finland, and Spain at the outer edges of both axes and Germany in-between.

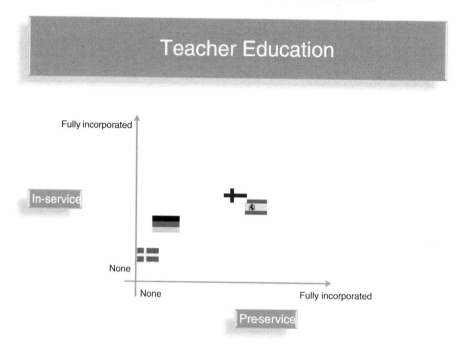

Figure 3. Amount of pre- and in-service CLIL teacher training in the four countries.

Age – year of implementation and amount of CLIL exposure

The age factor is interesting from a number of perspectives (Abrahamsson and Hyltenstam 2009; Birdsong 2006; DeKeyser 2000; Long 1981; Muñoz 2008, 2011), and decisions on when to implement a CLIL program need to be taken based on thorough discussions of, for instance, what the aim of the program is. Research shows conflicting results on effects on language acquisition based on the starting age of the individual second language (L2) learner. Whereas younger learners who are exposed to large amounts of exposure to the TL (which decidedly is one of the key features of CLIL) benefit from their implicit learning ability, older learners are at a cognitive advantage, showing a faster learning rate (DeKeyser and Larson-Hall 2005; Muñoz 2008, 2011).

The typical Swedish CLIL school is found at upper secondary level, but it is becoming increasingly popular also at lower levels (Skolverket 2010). However, the amount of instruction allowed through another language in school years one to nine is in Sweden limited to a maximum of 50%. At upper secondary level, no such restriction applies.

Finland offers a great variety of CLIL, being found at all age levels, from primary to tertiary level. Most commonly, though, CLIL with English as the TL is introduced in secondary education. The amount varies extensively, from a few subjects to all but language arts. A recent report (Kangasvieri et al. 2012) indicates that the popularity of CLIL in Finland seems to have leveled out, since the great expansion of the number of schools offering CLIL in the late 1990s.

In Germany, CLIL is typically introduced in year seven (age 12–13). In order for these students to be properly prepared, extra lessons in the TL are offered from year five or six, giving the students up to seven hours per week training in theTL, which is normally the students' first FL (Wolff 2007).

Spain introduces CLIL at various age levels in the different regions. In Andalusia, for instance, CLIL is implemented already in primary school and up to 40% of the teaching time is conducted through an FL (Lorenzo 2010). In the bilingual Basque region, some schools at secondary level implement the *Plurilingual Experience*, which states that a minimum of seven hours per week should be taught in the FL, and at post-compulsory level a minimum of 20–25% of the school subjects is required to be taught through CLIL (Ruiz de Zarobe and Lasagabaster 2010). Llinares and Dafouz (2010) report from the Madrid area, where CLIL is introduced in many schools already at primary level. The amount of CLIL ranges between 30 and 50% of the school syllabus.

In conclusion to this section on the age and amount factors, some diversity is found among the four countries. As illustrated in Figure 4, Spain and Finland are the two countries with the earliest implementation and largest amount of CLIL, followed by Germany and Sweden.

Extramural English – types and amount

Extramural exposure to English is an important source of TL input (Olsson 2011; Oscarson and Apelgren 2005; Sylvén 2004). Extramural English (EE) (Sundqvist 2009) can take many forms. TV programs or films produced in English with subtitles instead of dubbing are common sources of input in northern Europe. On the

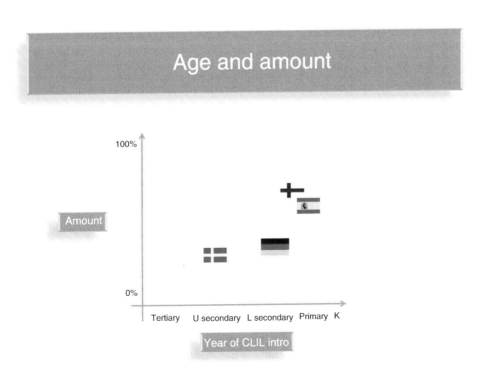

Figure 4. Age of implementation and amount of CLIL in the four countries.

Internet, English abounds and the increasing number of people traveling the world leads to amplified opportunities for using English as a lingua franca. The amount of exposure to the TL outside of school has been shown to correlate with a number of language skills (Cobb and Horst 2011; Kuppens 2010; Reinders 2012; Sundqvist 2009; Sylvén and Sundqvist 2012a).

Opportunities to encounter English in Swedish society are plentiful. English is encountered daily by citizens. The influx of American and British music is enormous, as are films, TV shows, and other media productions in English. All foreign-produced films and TV programs are subtitled. In fact, Swedish students get most of their English contacts outside of school. Studies have shown that students at upper-secondary level have some kind of EE for up to 40 hours per week (Sundqvist and Sylvén 2012; Sylvén and Sundqvist 2012a, 2012b).

Opportunities for exposure to English in Finland are likewise omnipresent. Like the other Nordic countries, Finnish television broadcasts programs and films in English with subtitles. In a number of domains, for example, youth culture, tourism, and commerce, English is now the dominant language (Björklund 2008).The availability of computers and the Internet are other sources of English input (Moncrief 2011).

The amount of EE in Germany is not as extensive as in the Nordic countries. One explanation is the fact that TV programs and films are dubbed, instead of subtitled. However, as in Finland, English is becoming the dominant language in several domains (Hilgendorf 2007; Hüllen 2007) and, again, the Internet and digital games are unlimited sources of English in Germany, too.

In Spain, opportunities to be exposed to English outside of school are relatively scarce. Movies and TV programs in English are dubbed into Spanish. Moreover, the number of movies and TV programs, as well as the amount of music produced in Spanish, is very large, by virtue of Spanish being a world language. Just as in Germany, though, for anyone seeking English input it is only a click away on the Internet.

In Figure 5, the great diversity in amount of exposure to English outside of school is clearly seen. The Nordic countries are at one end of the quadrant and Spain close to the origo.

National CLIL profiles

With the descriptions of the four factors in the four countries, it is possible to construct a coordinate system, where the four quadrants represent the factors discussed above. In this coordinate system, the teacher education quadrant has been turned mirrorwise, the age/amount quadrant has been turned mirrorwise and upside down, and the EE quadrant has been turned upside down.

The coordinate system illustrated in Figure 6 can be used to create specific CLIL profiles for each individual country. In Figures 7–10, the CLIL profiles for the four countries at issue here are illustrated.

These CLIL profiles indicate where some national differences are to be found. Finland is covered in all four quadrants and so is Germany, but to a lesser extent. Spain is well covered in three of the quadrants: framework/research, teacher education, and age/amount but hardly at all in the quadrant for extramural English. Finally, Sweden is only partially covered in the age/amount quadrant, very little in

CONTENT AND LANGUAGE INTEGRATED LEARNING

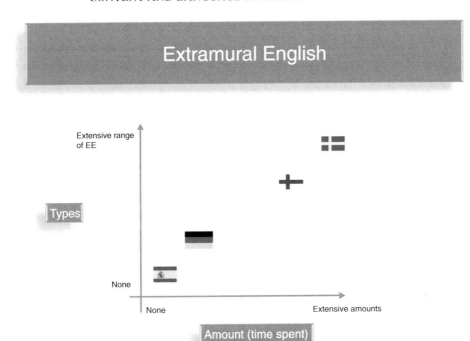

Figure 5. The amount and types of EE in the four countries.

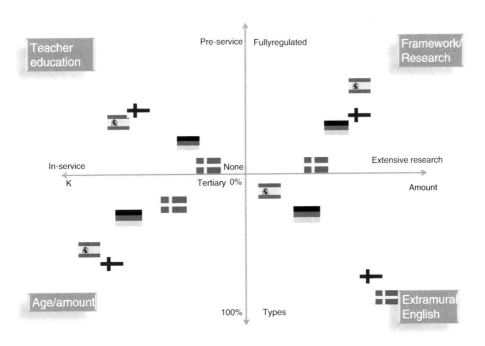

Figure 6. The coordinate system of the four quadrants.

CONTENT AND LANGUAGE INTEGRATED LEARNING

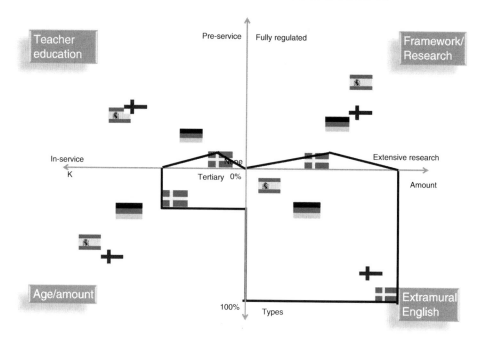

Figure 7. The Swedish CLIL profile.

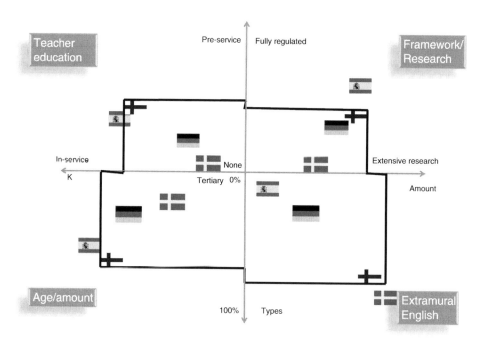

Figure 8. The Finnish CLIL profile.

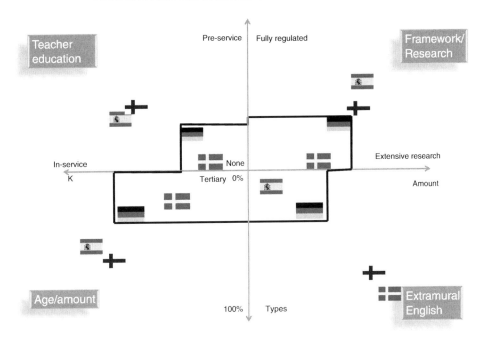

Figure 9. The German CLIL profile.

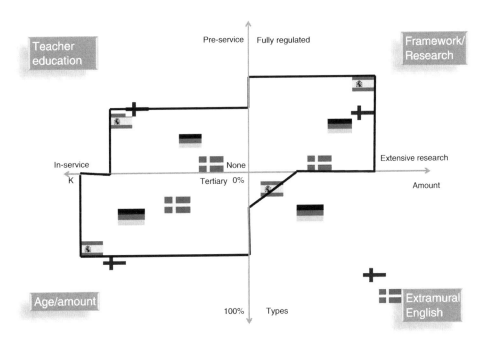

Figure 10. The Spanish CLIL profile.

both the framework/research and teacher education quadrants but very much in the extramural English quadrant.

Discussion

This chapter has described some fundamental contextual differences in four European countries relevant to the outcome and interpretation of CLIL research. There will always be differences between educational systems, and it is important that they be put on the table and discussed. In open dialog we can learn from one another. Examples of good practice in one context can be shared and tried in another, as can examples of unsuccessful implementations. New methods can be encouraged, tried, evaluated, and improved.

The factors brought up in this chapter appear necessary to bring into any analysis of results from CLIL research. Let us start with policy framework. Even though none of these countries has a thorough policy that prescribes in detail what CLIL is and is not, the presence of some policy document in combination with research seems to be a fruitful path. Spain is a case in point, where different regions have made large investments in CLIL education, and at the same time we see large amounts of high-quality research from those areas (cf., e.g., Casal and Moore 2009; Lasagabaster and Ruiz de Zarobe 2010). The situation in Spain seems to mirror that in Canada, when immersion was introduced in the mid-1960s, being accompanied by a host of various studies on attitudes, beliefs, and outcomes (cf., e.g., Spada and Lightbown 1989; Swain and Lapkin 1981). Also in Finland, CLIL is dealt with in the national curriculum for compulsory school. While the outline is made with a broad brush and no specific details are mentioned, the mere fact that CLIL is recognized makes it stand out as a teaching model worth implementing. Furthermore, Finnish CLIL is followed up by research (cf., e.g., Järvinen 2010; Nikula 2005). By researching new initiatives as they are being implemented, opportunities are provided to immediately remedy unexpected and unwanted outcomes. Sweden stands in stark contrast to these countries, with no framework and, thus far, very little CLIL research.

Furthermore, it seems that countries where CLIL teachers are offered specific training profit in terms of student results. As pointed out above, being a CLIL teacher necessitates awareness of how to deal with content in a language-enhancing manner (Ball and Lindsay 2010), not only qualifications in the language used. Again, Spain seems to be a country where this issue is taken seriously and initiatives are taken to secure the availability of knowledgeable CLIL teachers. In both Germany and Finland, teachers using another language than their own L1 are required to have a certain level of proficiency in that language. Sweden is the only country in the present comparison where no specific level of language proficiency is required.

Regarding the optimal level at which to introduce CLIL, there is no consensus. However, looking at the general level of L2 English proficiency, a comparison across eight European countries reveal differences (Erickson 2004). Sweden, together with Norway, scores high in all measurements in this comparison and there are several reasons for this. One is the early focus on English in Swedish schools. It is the first FL introduced and no later than in third grade (age nine). Another explanation is the multitude of potential exposure to English in Swedish society. This means that the level of English among Swedish students already at upper secondary level is relatively high. It is possible, then, that the introduction of English as the medium of instruction in two or more school subjects does not make a great deal of difference. Furthermore, if teachers of non-language subjects are not specifically trained in how to deal with language, it is difficult for learners to make progress in a language they already feel fairly confident in using.

The age factor has not been looked at specifically in relation to CLIL, so some hypothesizing is called for. Research on L2 learning shows that late starters benefit from their greater cognitive capacity (Cummins 1979; Muñoz 2008, 2011) and perform better on, for instance, grammar (Muñoz 2011). Early starters show greater proficiency in communicative abilities, above all in listening comprehension (Muñoz 2008), even though older learners seem to catch up after the same amount of exposure (Muñoz 2006). As is noted by Muñoz (2011), however, the limited scope of the research carried out so far should be kept in mind. We know very little about the age factor in relation to, for instance, productive vocabulary or pronunciation. If the extant findings were to be applied in a discussion of CLIL, a hypothesis could be that if CLIL were introduced at an early age, thus exposing the students to large amounts of the TL, they would achieve higher levels of communicative proficiency in that language. As these communicatively proficient students progress in their CLIL studies, it could be easier for them also to acquire higher-order skills needed for mastery of more academically oriented language.

It may be that the introduction of CLIL at secondary level does not provide sufficient input for any greater gains to be made. This may primarily be true in countries where the TL is an obligatory school subject from primary level and upward, and where the TL is present and readily available in the surrounding environment. A relevant issue in this discussion is what the ultimate aim of CLIL is. If the aim is for the learner to become a functional bilingual, then early introduction is probably the most effective (cf., e.g., Birdsong 2006). If, on the other hand, the goal is for learners to acquire subject-specific proficiency in vocabulary and terminology, then perhaps a late introduction will work better. This, then, has serious implications for the question of policy framework, where the goal of CLIL should be among the most prominent aspects to be articulated. This, in turn, has repercussions on the teacher training agenda.

Regarding the amount of exposure to English outside of school, there are huge differences in this respect throughout Europe. Even though English is present all over Europe, not least as a lingua franca, the great divide seems to be between countries where films and TV programs are dubbed versus subtitled (Berns et al. 2007), and as was shown above, the exposure to a TL outside the classroom correlates to several dimensions of the proficiency in that language. Sweden, being at the top of the countries compared here as regards the amount of extramural English, also shows top-results in a European survey of students' English language skills. Spain, on the other hand, does not offer such ample opportunities for exposure to English and, perhaps in part as a result, did not score equally well in that survey (Erickson 2004).

To summarize, several features on a national level need to be taken into account when looking at outcomes of CLIL. However, whether or not there is a perfect match of such features for CLIL to be optimal still remains to be seen. It seems, though, that in countries where the level of EE is high, as in the Nordic countries, the introduction of CLIL in English at upper secondary is too late. At that time, student proficiency in English is already high, with English classes in school combined with consistent exposure to English outside of school. Further, demands on CLIL teachers to be able to deal with language-specific issues with the aim of improving students' English skills increase the older the students are. This, in turn, would be facilitated by a policy framework stating requirements for CLIL teachers as regards pedagogical aspects and language proficiency level, as well as the expected outcomes of such teaching.

Conclusion

In this chapter four factors have been targeted as decisive for explaining variation in CLIL research findings. These factors have been discussed from four different national perspectives and a diversified picture of CLIL contexts across Europe has emerged. This diversification can be taken as evidence that CLIL in one country is not necessarily the same thing as in another, implying that CLIL as the object of research may differ a great deal from one country to another. It is thus imperative that, when discussing various results obtained within a CLIL framework, these factors are controlled and accounted for in order to be able to properly compare and draw on studies and results from different national contexts. At policy level, it is important that these factors are taken into account and that there is an ongoing discussion weighing contextual factors against the results obtained. One issue in need of addressing, for instance, is whether it is worthwhile for a country such as Sweden, where English abounds and where the level of proficiency among citizens in general and among adolescents in particular is already fairly high, to even arrange CLIL where English is the TL. Perhaps CLIL efforts should concentrate on other FLs, e.g. German, where positive results indeed have been obtained (Terlevic Johansson 2011).

The comparison across national contexts accounted for here will hopefully serve as a tool in making policy level decisions on when, how, and why to implement CLIL as well as how to improve and monitor progress by targeted research.

The most important part of this discussion is, of course, the students and their development. They spend time and effort in school in order to acquire skills in specific subjects. Decisions on the methods of performing and measuring the success of CLIL teaching always need to keep this important fact in focus. Introducing CLIL as a method of language teaching should not be based on guesswork, fashionable political ideas, or potential gains for a particular school. It should all be for the benefit of the student. This chapter has indicated four key factors that should each be taken into account for optimal results. In addition, I believe that the answer to the question posed in the title of this chapter can, to a large extent, be found in the interplay of these four factors.

Acknowledgments

I would like to express my gratitude to the two anonymous reviewers who added valuable input on both the content and the structure of this chapter. I am also grateful for the important input Heini-Marja Järvinen, Dominik Rumlich, and Sölve Ohlander so generously have supplied.

References

Abrahamsson, N., and K. Hyltenstam. 2009. "Age of Onset and Nativelikeness in a Second Language: Listener Perception versus Linguistic Scrutiny." *Language Learning* 59 (2): w249–306. doi:10.1111/j.1467-9922.2009.00507.x.

Airey, J. 2009. "Science, Language and Literacy: Case Studies of Learning in Swedish University Physics." PhD diss., Uppsala University.

Alderson, J. C. 2009. *The Politics of Language Education: Individuals and Institutions*. Bristol: Multilingual Matters.

Åseskog, T. 1982. *Att undervisa el-lära på engelska* [Teaching electrical theory in English]. Göteborg: University of Gothenburg.

Ball, P., and D. Lindsay. 2010. "Teacher Training for CLIL in the Basque Country: The Case of the Ikastolas – In Search of Parameters." In *CLIL in Spain. Implementation, Results and Teacher Training*, edited by D. Lasagabaster and Y. Ruiz De Zarobe, 162–187. Newcastle upon Tyne: Cambridge Scholars Publishing.

Berns, M., M. Claes, K. De Bot, R. Evers, U. Hasebrink, I. Huigtbregtse, C. Truchot, and P. Van Der Wijst. 2007. "English in Europe." In *In the presence of English. Media and European Youth*, edited by M. Berns, K. De Bot, and U. Hasebrink, 5–42. Berlin: Springer.

Birdsong, D. 2006. "Age and Second Language Acquisition and Processing: A Selective Overview." *Language Learning* 56 (S1): 9–49. doi:10.1111/j.1467-9922.2006.00353.x.

Björklund, M. 2008. *Conditions for EFL Learning and Professional Development*. Åbo: Åbo Akademi University Press.

Björklund, S., and K. Mård-Miettinen. 2011. "Integrating Multiple Languages in Immersion: Swedish Immersion in Finland." In *Immersion Education. Practices, Policies, Possibilities*, edited by D. J. Tedick, D. Christian, and T. Williams Fortune, 13–35. Bristol: Multilingual Matters.

Blomberg, G., K. Stürmer, and T. Seidel. 2011. "How Pre-Service Teachers Observe Teaching on Video: Effects of Viewers' Teaching Subjects and the Subject of the Video." *Teaching and Teacher Education* 27 (7): 1131–1140. doi:10.1016/j.tate.2011.04.008.

Casal, S., and P. Moore. 2009. "The Andalusian Bilingual Sections Scheme: Evaluation and Consultancy." *International CLIL Research Journal* 1 (2): 36–46. http://www.icrj.eu/12/article4.html.

Cobb, T., and M. Horst. 2011. "Does Word Coach Coach Words?" *CALICO Journal* 28 (3): 639–661. https://calico.org/memberBrowse.php?action=article&id=881.

Council of Europe. 2001. *Common European Framework of Reference for Languages: Learning, Teaching, Assessment*. Cambridge: Cambridge University Press.

Coyle, D. 2008. CLIL – "A Pedagogical Approach from the European Perspective." In *Encyclopedia of Language and Education*, edited by N. Van Dusen-Scholl and N. H. Hornberger, 97–111. New York: Springer Science + Business Media LLc.

Coyle, D. 2009. "Promoting Cultural Diversity Through Intercultural Understanding: A Case Study of CLIL Professional Development at In-Service and Pre-Service Levels in Carrio-Pastor." In *Linguistic Insights: Studies in Language and Communication*, edited by D. Coyle, 105–124. Bern: Peter Lang.

Cummins, J. 1979. "Cognitive/Academic Language Proficiency, Linguistic Interdependence, the Optimum Age Question and Some Other Matters." *Working Papers on Bilingualism* 19: 198–203.

Dalton-Puffer, C. 2007. *Discourse in Content and Language Integrated Learning (CLIL) Classrooms Language Learning and Language teaching*. Amsterdam: John Benjamins.

Dalton-Puffer, C., T. Nikula, and U. Smit, eds., 2010. *Language Use and Language Learning in CLIL Classrooms*. Amsterdam: John Benjamins.

De Graaff, R., G. J. Koopman, Y. Anikina, and G. Westhoff. 2007. "An Observation Tool for Effective L2 Pedagogy in Content and Language Integrated Learning (CLIL)." *International Journal of Bilingual Education and Bilingualism* 10 (5): 603–624. http://dx.doi.org/10.2167/beb462.0.

DeKeyser, R. M. 2000. "The Robustness of Critical Period Effects in Second Language Acquisition." *Studies in Second Language Acquisition* 22 (4): 499–533. http://journals.cambridge.org/article_S0272263100004022.

DeKeyser, R. M., and J. Larson-Hall. 2005. "What Does the Critical Period Really Mean?" In *Handbook of Bilingualism: Psycholinguistic Approaches*, edited by J. F. Kroll and A. M. D. De Groot, 88–108. Oxford: Oxford University Press.

Erickson, G. 2004. *Engelska i åtta europeiska länder* [English in eight European countries]. Stockholm: Skolverket.

Escobar Urmeneta, C. 2010. "Pre-Service CLIL Teacher-Education in Catalonia: Expert and Novice Practitioners Teaching and Reflecting Together." In *CLIL in Spain. Implementa-*

tion, Results and Teacher Training, edited by D. Lasagabaster and Y. Ruiz De Zarobe, 188–218. Newcastle upon Tyne: Cambridge Scholars Publishing.

European Commission. 1995. *White Paper on Education and Training. Teaching and Learning: Towards the Learning Society.* Brussels: European Commission.

Eurydice Network. 2008. *Key Data on Teaching Languages at School in Europe.* Brussels: European Commission.

Figueras, N. 2009. "Language Educational Policies within a European Framework." In *The Politics of Language Education*, edited by J. C. Alderson, 203–221. Bristol: Multilingual Matters.

Fullan, M. 1995. "The School as a Learning Organization: Distant Dreams." *Theory into Practice* 34 (4): 230–235. doi:10.1080/00405849509543685.

Guskey, T. R., and M. Huberman. 1995. *Professional Development in Education: New Paradigms and Practices.* New York: Teachers College Press.

Hilgendorf, S. 2007. "English in Germany: Contact, Spread and Attitudes." *World Englishes* 26 (2): 131–148. doi:10.1111/j.1467-971X.2007.00498.x.

Hüllen, W. 2007. "The Presence of English in Germany." *Zeitschrift für Fremdsprachenforschung* 18 (1): 3–26. http://www.dgff.de/de/zff/zff-artikel-index/zff-artikel-detail/artikel/the-presence-of-english-in-germany.html?tx_ttnews%5Bpointer%5D=3&tx_ttnews%5BbackPid%5D=709&cHash=d1230c2c0504100d84a8b6ca45dbd14d.

Isidro, S. 2010. "An Insight into Galician CLIL: Provision and Results." In *CLIL in Spain. Implementation, Results and Teacher Training*, edited by D. Lasagabaster and Y. Ruiz De Zarobe, 55–78. Newcastle upon Tyne: Cambridge Scholars Publishing.

Järvinen, H.-M. 1999. "Second Language Acquisition through CLIL at Primary School Level." In *Learning through a Foreign Language: Models, Methods and Outcomes*, edited by J. Masih, 72–80. London: Centre for Information on Language Teaching and Research.

Järvinen, H.-M. 2010. "Language as a Meaning Making Resource in Learning and Teaching Content: Analysing Historical Writing in Content and Language Integrated Learning." In *Language Use and Language Learning in CLIL Classrooms*, edited by C. Dalton-Puffer, T. Nikula, and U. Smit, 145–168. Amsterdam: John Benjamins.

Kangasvieri, T., E. Miettinen, H. Palviainen, T. Saarinen, and T. Ala-Vähälä. 2012. *Selvitys kotimaisten kielten kielikylpyopetuksen ja vieraskielisen opetuksen tilanteesta suomessa: Kuntatason tarkastelu* [A report on the situation for domestic languages: an analysis per municipality]. Jyväskylä: University of Jyväskylä.

Klippel, F. 2003. "New Prospects or Imminent Danger? – The Impact of English Medium Instruction on Education in Germany." *Prospect* 18 (1): 68–81. http://www.ameprc.mq.edu.au/docs/prospect_journal/volume_18_no_1/18_1_6_Klippel.pdf.

Kuppens, A. H. 2010. "Incidental Foreign Language Acquisition from Media Exposure." *Learning, Media and Technology* 35 (1): 65–85. doi:10.1080/17439880903561876.

Lasagabaster, D. 2008. "Foreign Language Competence in Content and Language Integrated Courses." *The Open Applied Linguistics Journal* 1: 31–42. doi:10.2174/1874913500801010030

Lasagabaster, D., and Y. Ruiz De Zarobe, eds., 2010. *CLIL in Spain: Implementation, Results and Teacher Training.* Newcastle upon Tyne: Cambridge Scholars Publishing.

Lasagabaster, D., and J. M. Sierra. 2010. "Immersion and CLIL in English: More Differences than Similarities." *ELT Journal* 64 (4): 367–375. doi:10.1093/elt/ccp082.

Lim Falk, M. 2008. "Svenska i engelskspråkig skolmiljö: Ämnesrelaterat språkbruk i två gymnasieklasser [Swedish in an English-speaking school context: Subject-related language use in two upper secondary classes]." PhD diss., Stockholm University.

Llinares, A., and E. Dafouz. 2010. "Content and Language Integrated Programmes in the Madrid Region: Overview and Research Findings." In *CLIL in Spain. Implementation, Results and Teacher Training*, edited by D. Lasagabaster and Y. Ruiz De Zarobe, 95–114. Newcastle upon Tyne: Cambridge Scholars Publishing.

Long, M. H. 1981. "Input, Interaction and Second Language Acquisition." In *Native Language and Foreign Language Acquisition*, edited by H. Winitz, 259–278. New York: Annals of the New York Academy of Sciences.

Lorenzo, F. 2010. "CLIL in Andalusia." In *CLIL in Spain. Implementation, Results and Teacher Training*, edited by D. Lasagabaster and Y. Ruiz De Zarobe, 2–11. Newcastle upon Tyne: Cambridge Scholars Publishing.

Marsh, D., ed. 2002. *CLIL/EMILE the European Dimension*. Jyväskylä: University of Jyväskylä.
Mäsch, N. 1993. "The German Model of Bilingual Education: An Administrator's Perspective." In *European Models of Bilingual Education*, edited by H. B. Beardsmore, 155–172. Clevedon: Multilingual Matters.
Maskit, D. 2011. "Teachers' Attitudes toward Pedagogical Changes During Various Stages of Professional Development." *Teaching and Teacher Education: An International Journal of Research and Studies* 27 (5): 851–860. doi:10.1016/j.tate.2011.01.009.
Medgyes, P., and A. Malderez, eds., 1996. *Changing Perspectives in Teacher Education*. Oxford: MacMillan.
Moncrief, R. 2011. "Out-of-classroom Language Learning: A Case Study of Students of Advanced English Language Courses at Helsinki University Language Centre." In *Out-of-classroom Language Learning*, edited by K. K. Pitkänen, J. Jokinen, S. Karjalainen, L. Karlsson, T. Lehtonen, M. Matilainen, C. Niedling, and R. Siddall, 107–118. Helsinki: Helsinki University.
Muñoz, C. 2006. "The Effects of Age on Foreign Language Learning." In *Age and the Rate of Foreign Language Learning*, edited by C. Muñoz, 1–40. Clevedon: Multilingual Matters.
Muñoz, C. 2008. "Age-Related Differences in Foreign Language Learning." Revisiting the empirical evidence." *IRAL* 46: 197–220. http://dx.doi.org.ezproxy.ub.gu.se/10.1515/IRAL.2008.009.
Muñoz, C. 2011. "Input and Long-Term Effects of Starting Age in Foreign Language Learning." *IRAL* 49: 113–133. http://dx.doi.org.ezproxy.ub.gu.se/10.1515/iral.2011.006.
Navés, T., and M. Victori. 2010. "CLIL in Catalonia: An Overview of Research Studies." In *CLIL in Spain. Implementation, Results and Teacher Training*, edited by D. Lasagabaster and Y. Ruiz De Zarobe, 30–54. Newcastle upon Tyne: Cambridge Scholars Publishing.
Nikula, T. 2005. "English as an Object and Tool of Study in Classrooms: Interactional Effects and Pragmatic Implications." *Linguistics and Education* 16 (1): 27–58. doi:10.1016/j.linged.2005.10.001.
Nikula, T. 2007. "Speaking English in Finnish Content-Based Cclassrooms." *World Englishes* 26 (2): 206–223. doi:10.1111/j.1467-971X.2007.00502.x.
Nixon, J. 2000. *Content and Language Integrated Learning and Teaching in Sweden*. Stockholm: Swedish National Agency for Education.
Olsson, E. 2011. "Everything I Read on the Internet is in English – On the Impact of Extramural English on Swedish 16-Year-Old Pupils' Writing Proficiency." Licentiate diss., University of Gothenburg.
Oscarson, M., and B. M. Apelgren. 2005. *Nationella utvärderingen av grundskolan 2003 (NU-03). Engelska* [The national evaluation of compulsory school 2003. English]. Ämnesrapport till rapport 251. Stockholm: Skolverket.
Reinders, H., ed., 2012. *Digital Games in Language Learning and Teaching*. Basingstoke: Palgrave Macmillan.
Ringbom, H. 2012. "Review of Recent Applied Linguistics Research in Finland and Sweden, with Specific Reference to Foreign Language Learning and Teaching." *Language Teaching* 45 (4): 490–514. doi:10.1017/S0261444812000225.
Ruiz De Zarobe, Y., and D. Lasagabaster. 2010. "CLIL in a Bilingual Community: The Basque Autonomous Community." In *CLIL in Spain. Implementation, Results and Teacher Training*, edited by D. Lasagabaster and Y. Ruiz De Zarobe, 12–29. Newcastle upon Tyne: Cambridge Scholars Publishing.
Ruiz De Zarobe, Y., J. M. Sierra, and F. Gallardo Del Puerto, eds., 2011. *Content and Foreign Language Integrated Learning*. Bern: Peter Lang.
Salaberri Ramiro, S. 2010. "Teacher Training Programmes for CLIL in Andalusia." In *CLIL in Spain. Implementation, Results and Teacher Training*, edited by D. Lasagabaster and Y. Ruiz De Zarobe, 140–161. Newcastle upon Tyne: Cambridge Scholars Publishing.
Skolverket. 2010. *Undervisning på engelska* [Teaching in English]. Rapport 351. Stockholm: Skolverket.
Spada, N., and P. M. Lightbown. 1989. "Intensive ESL Programmes in Québec Primary Schools." *TESL Canada Journal* 7: 11–32. http://www.teslcanadajournal.ca/index.php/tesl/article/view/557.

Sundqvist, P. 2009. "Extramural English Matters: Out-of-school English and its Impact on Swedish Ninth Graders' Oral Proficiency and Vocabulary." PhD diss., Karlstad University.

Sundqvist, P., and L. K. Sylvén. 2012. "World of VocCraft: Computer Games and Swedish Learners' L2 Vocabulary." In *Digital Games in Language Learning and Teaching*, edited by H. Reinders, 189–208. Basingstoke: Palgrave Macmillan.

Swain, M., and S. Lapkin. 1981. *Bilingual Education in Ontario. A Decade of Research.* Toronto, ON: Ontario Institute of Studies in Education.

Sylvén, L. K. 2004. "Teaching in English or English Teaching? On the Effects of Content and Language Integrated Learning on Swedish Learners' Incidental Vocabulary Acquisition." PhD diss., University of Gothenburg.

Sylvén, L. K. 2007. "'Swedish CLIL Students' Extracurricular Contact with English and its Relation to Classroom Activities." In *Diverse Contexts – Converging Goals. CLIL in Europe*, edited by D. Marsh and D. Wolff, 237–252. Frankfurt: Peter Lang.

Sylvén, L. K., and P. Sundqvist. 2012a. "Gaming as Extramural English L2 Learning and L2 Proficiency among Young Learners." *ReCALL* 24 (3): 302–321. doi:10.1017/S095834401200016X.

Sylvén, L. K., and P. Sundqvist. 2012b. "Similarities between Playing *World of Warcraft* and CLIL." *Apples – Journal of Applied Language Studies* 6 (2): 113–130.

Terlevic Johansson, K. 2011. "Erfolgreiches Deutschlernen durch CLIL?" PhD diss., University of Gothenburg.

Utbildningsstyrelsen. 2004. *Grunderna för läroplanen för den grundläggande utbildningen* [The preliminaries of the compulsory school curriculum]. Vammala: Utbildningsstyrelsen.

Washburn, L. 1997. "English Immersion in Sweden: A Case Study of Röllingby High School, 1987–1989." PhD diss., Stockholm University.

Wolff, D. 2007. "CLIL in Europe." Accessed October 17. http://www.goethe.de/ges/spa/dos/ifs/ceu/en2751287.htm.

Zydatiss, W. 2007. *Deutsch-Englische Züge in Berlin (dezibel). Eine Evaluation des Bilingualen Sachfachunterrichts in Gymnasien: Kontext, Kompetenzen, Konsequenzen* [German-English education in Berlin. An evaluation of bilingual education in upper secondary school: Context, competences, consequences]. Frankfurt am Main: Peter Lang.

Curricular models of CLIL education in Poland

Anna Czura[a] and Katarzyna Papaja[b]

[a]Institute of English Studies, University of Wrocław, Wrocław, Poland; [b]Institute of English, University of Silesia, Sosnowiec, Poland

> Bilingual education in Poland gained in popularity after the political changes in 1989 when Polish society started noticing the importance of foreign language learning. With the emergence of content and language integrated learning (CLIL) in the 1990s, which in the Polish context is still termed as 'bilingual education', foreign languages other than English were introduced as a medium of instruction. To provide a comprehensive overview of practices and help to identify operational features of this type of education, four large-scale research studies were conducted, exploring CLIL sections with English, German, Spanish and French as languages of instruction. The data collected on the basis of classroom observations and interviews with CLIL teachers and students revealed a number of regularities recurring in the schools that were studied. It enabled the researchers to formulate four curricular models of CLIL education at secondary level. This chapter aims to present the models of content subjects teaching. The models depend on the proportions of L2 use, the perceived focal point of the teaching/learning process and the educational level at which CLIL is introduced. The adoption of a particular model entails different instructional choices, teaching practices and learning objectives in terms of both content and language learning.

Introduction

Although teaching content subjects through the medium of a foreign language has been present in Europe for several decades, different terms have been used to describe the educational approaches that link content and language. Similarly, there is no uniform teaching methodology that could be applied in all European educational contexts. Baetens-Beardsmore (1993) observes that teaching subjects through the medium of a foreign language is determined not only by the educational traditions of a given country but also by the prevailing linguistic needs. Underlining the role of sociocultural traditions and educational regulations, Nikula (1997) notes that there is no universal pattern that could be applied in different countries. Kees de Bot (2001,12) enumerates the factors that exert the strongest effect on the adoption of a specific model of content and language integrated learning (CLIL) in different educational backgrounds: 'sociolinguistic environment, exposure, target language, teachers, discourse type, translanguaging, subject appropriacy and content-language ratio.' Wolff and Otwinowska-Kasztelanic (2010) indicate that approaches to CLIL vary in particular countries as a result of administrative decisions taken on a national level. Such top-down regulations often determine the choice of the content subjects, the proportion of CLIL and non-CLIL classes, the recruitment process, or the type of school in which CLIL is introduced. Depending on the educational contexts, CLIL is introduced at all stages of education, ranging from pre-school to tertiary education, while in other contexts it is limited to secondary education only. Moreover, the shape of CLIL provision is to a large extent determined by the teachers: their competence in L2, their qualifications in the field of CLIL as well as their ability to cooperate with their colleagues in order to facilitate the integration of language and content. Ongoing teaching practice and different initiatives undertaken by teachers are also affected by individual approaches and beliefs (Coyle, Hood, and Marsh 2010; Marsh, Maljers, and Hartiala 2001; Mehisto, Marsh, and Frigols 2008). A large number of the aforementioned factors as well as the multiple interpretations of the term itself triggered the emergence of diverse curricular objectives and teaching methodologies as well as approaches to the assessment process. The lack of a uniform teaching methodology that would integrate language and content has resulted in the development of multiple models of CLIL in different educational contexts.

Diverse approaches to CLIL methodology can also be observed in Poland, where CLIL-related pedagogies have been used for many years in secondary education. With the aim of providing a comprehensive overview of both the administrative and methodological foundations of CLIL provision in Poland, four large-scale research studies were conducted in the years 2005–2010 exploring CLIL sections with English, German, Spanish and French as a medium of instruction. The data collected by four independent research teams helped to pinpoint a number of regularities recurring in the schools in which bilingual education was adopted. The observations on approaches to CLIL methodology employed in the schools taking part in the studies enabled the researchers to formulate four main curricular models of CLIL education on the secondary level. This chapter intends to present the models that were observed as well as to discuss their immediate impact on everyday teaching practice. The models refer to the content subjects and depend on the proportions of L2 use, the perceived focal point of the teaching/learning process and the educational level at which CLIL is introduced. The adoption of a particular model additionally entails different instructional choices, teaching practices and learning objectives in terms of both content and language learning.

CLIL education in Poland

As the shape of CLIL education depends on a number of factors, it seems important to present the roots and further attempts to adopt CLIL within the Polish educational tradition in order to account for the emergence of the curricular models.

Poland is a linguistically uniform country in which Polish is the official language used to communicate in all spheres of public and social life. After years of political and economic isolation, starting from the 1980s, an urgent need to improve foreign language education emerged. The dominant position of Russian as the foreign language taught at all school levels was gradually challenged, and English has become the most widely taught foreign language in Poland. Other languages frequently offered by public schools include German, Spanish, French and Italian.

In compliance with the European Council's recommendation that every European citizen should be able to use at least two other languages apart from their mother tongue (European Council 2002), the Core Curriculum implemented in Poland in 2009 brought about a number of fundamental changes in language education, which should lead to an increased competence in foreign language among learners. Nowadays, foreign language education needs to be introduced from the beginning of primary education, and the second foreign language starts to be taught in the first class of lower secondary school, that is, when learners are at the age of 12 years. CLIL education, therefore, constitutes an interesting alternative to traditional approaches to foreign language teaching.

CLIL-related pedagogies were introduced in Poland in the 70s when one of the secondary schools in Gdynia offered selected classes with English as the medium of instruction (Zielonka 2007). In the early stages only English was used as the language of instruction to teach the whole or part of a content subject lesson. At present, public schools offer CLIL streams using English, German, French, Spanish and Italian as the languages of instruction. Recently there has also been an attempt to introduce Russian-medium class units.

It should be pointed out that the implementation of CLIL practice in education has been adopted in Poland under the name of bilingual education (Dzięgielewska 2008; Roda 2007). CLIL pedagogy is not applied in the entire school, but is restricted to selected class units only. Initially, CLIL classes existed only in upper secondary schools (age 16–19). In some schools, CLIL education was preceded by an additional 'zero class' in which the learners underwent an intensive course aiming at developing their second language skills, especially writing and reading (Multańska 2002, 90). Apart from the schools with Spanish as the language of instruction, where the 'zero class' is still in use, the preparatory year was discontinued as a result of the new Educational Reform in 1999. At that point, lower secondary schools (age 13–16) were created. Within a few years, CLIL streams started to emerge in some of these schools, and three years of this schooling were treated as a good preparation time for helping pupils participate in CLIL classes on a higher level in upper secondary school. Some forms of CLIL can be observed only in primary schools in private institutions where parents pay for their children's tuition (Eurydice 2008).

Polish educational regulations provide a clear definition of a CLIL stream: (1) education needs to be conducted in two languages – the mother tongue and one foreign language; (2) a minimum of two content subjects, with the exception of Polish, the history of Poland, the geography of Poland and an additional foreign language, need to be taught through these two languages. The most common subjects that are taught through the medium of a second language are mathematics, physics with astronomy, chemistry, biology, history, geography and computer science (Czura, Papaja, and Urbaniak 2009). The integration of content and a language different than Polish can also be observed in schools offering education in regional or minority languages, such as Kashubian, Russian, Lithuanian, or Belarusian. Still, minority education is subject to different regulations[1] and curricular requirements than CLIL. Moreover, this type of education was not investigated as part of Bilingual Education Research Project, which produced the Profile Reports. Consequently, education involving the integration of content and minority languages will not be included in the discussion of the curricular models.

Both lower and upper secondary schools offering any type of CLIL are of a selective type, that is, there is a recruitment procedure for the candidates specified by each particular school. As the number of available places is limited, applicants for entry need to possess a very good command of the second language and pass a diagnostic test, consisting in a language competence and/or a language aptitude test. Due to such tight enrolment regulations, the attributed prestige and tangible gains the pupils may obtain, such as a high level of L2 competence and knowledge of specialised vocabulary, CLIL streams tend to attract the most ambitious students who are likely to succeed in mastering the curricular requirements both in Polish and the language of instruction. Located in big cities, schools offering CLIL class units are perceived as elitist.

The main aims and at the same time benefits of CLIL in Poland enumerated in Eurydice Report on content and language integrated education (Eurydice 2006) are as follows: sociocultural, language-related and educational (learning ability). Still, in practice it appears that, unlike in other countries where the emphasis is placed on the content subjects or on both content and language, in Poland CLIL is primarily seen as a means of enhancing the level of competence in L2 (Wolff and Otwinowska-Kasztelanic 2010). In the case of language-related and educational aims, CLIL learners benefit from the greater number of contact hours with the foreign language, which is of a better quality on account of the deeper processing (Wolff 1997). Learners are motivated to involve themselves in an educational approach necessitating a heavy time commitment and workload as they realise it will help them enhance their competence in foreign languages. Due to the fact that Poland has joined the European Union, more and more students are deciding to take part in student exchange programmes or continue their education at universities in other countries. Additionally, a very good knowledge of foreign languages constitutes an important requirement in the job recruitment process both in Poland and abroad. Participation in CLIL education constitutes a preparatory stage for entering the labour market as 'teaching and learning in a CLIL classroom is comparable to real-life work' (Wolff 2007, 22).

The teaching of any subject in Poland needs to be congruent with the core curriculum imposed by the Ministry of Education for each subject. There is a separate core curriculum for foreign language teaching in CLIL streams in upper secondary school: the learning content together with the general and specific learning objectives are adjusted to this type of instruction. Still, there are no core curricula designed specifically for content subjects taught through the medium of a foreign language or L2 education for CLIL class units in lower secondary school. Due to the curricular requirements and the necessity of taking the school leaving examinations also in Polish, learners attending CLIL classes need to learn the same content material both in their mother tongue and the second language of instruction. Consequently, in comparison with other learners, those attending CLIL streams often have a larger number of classes per week and need to make a double effort to cover the same teaching material in both languages (Marsh et al. 2008).

Data collection methodology

The National Centre for Teacher Training (CODN), now renamed the Centre for Education Development (ORE), in Warsaw initiated a national research study aiming to provide an overview of practices in schools offering CLIL-type provisions in different foreign languages. The Bilingual Education Research Project produced four independent reports coordinated by CODN and other external organisations related to education in a given L2:

- French sections: Gajo 2005.
- English sections: Marsh et al. 2008.
- German sections: Wolski et al. 2010.
- Spanish sections: Tatoj et al. 2008.

The aim of the reports was not to evaluate but to provide an overview of practices with respect to teaching as well as the organisation of CLIL education, teacher training, cooperation with other teachers and general attitudes to this type of education. The reports revealed a number of strengths, which might serve as examples of good practice, as well as areas in need of improvement.

The Project focused on publicly funded lower and upper secondary schools that practised some form of CLIL-related education. Although there are secondary schools offering International Baccalaureate programmes, they were excluded from the research as they adopt a curriculum, student assessment, professional development for teachers and a process of school authorisation and evaluation established by the International Baccalaureate Organization.

On the onset of the Project, all CLIL schools were addressed and invited to take part in the research. Although participation was not obligatory, most of the schools offering CLIL education agreed to allow the researchers to conduct observations and interviews with the staff and students. When it comes to upper secondary schools, 34 schools took part in the research (12 schools with English, 9 with German, 7 with French and 6 with Spanish as languages of instruction). The representation of lower secondary schools appeared to be smaller, amounting to 13 schools offering English, 5 German, 7 French and 1 Spanish in CLIL class units.

The curricular models presented in this chapter were formulated on the basis of the reports prepared by the research teams investigating bilingual education with English, German, French and Spanish as the languages of instruction. The data obtained are qualitative in nature and were collected by means of classroom observation and focus group interviews with the teaching staff and learners attending CLIL streams.

The observations were carried out in each school that was involved, in at least one language class and one content subject class taught through the medium of L2. Some of the lessons were recorded and transcribed. As the observation sheets applied by the researchers in the four reports varied slightly in form and content, it is difficult to present one uniform instrument. However, it must be emphasised that all the observations focused on the same aspects of the teaching process both in the language and CLIL classes. Apart from attending to physical conditions, such as the setting and the size of the classroom in which learning takes place, the observers paid attention to the use of language and the teaching methodology used both in the L2 and content classes. The observation focused on the extent to which English was used an effective tool of communication and how learners' output was stimulated. The teachers' techniques of providing corrective feedback, handling pupils' language problems and raising their awareness of specific language aspects of the subject were also noted. The researchers also reported different teaching techniques and interaction patterns as well as the variety of teaching resources used in both types of classrooms. Observation of English language lessons additionally aimed at identifying examples of formal instruction and language learning strategy training.

The interviews took a semistructured form and were conducted on the basis of predesigned scenarios. The interviews with head teachers or coordinators of CLIL streams as well as focus group interviews with teachers of languages and content subjects aimed to collect the teaching staff's opinions about their work in CLIL class units as well as to obtain more insightful information concerning teaching techniques and materials used in the classroom. The learners who were interviewed were asked to give their subjective opinion about the advantages and disadvantages of attending this type of school, their learning strategies and attitudes to different aspects of CLIL education. The data collected on the basis of the interviews helped in analysing the classroom observations from a wider perspective. The combination of these two instruments allowed the researchers to obtain more insightful data about the practical implementation of this type of education and consequently to distinguish certain patterns in schools offering different languages of instruction.

Curricular models

The effectiveness of this type of education is largely determined by the ongoing teaching both in the language and content classrooms. The applied methodology, teaching techniques, types of discourse used, selection of teaching resources or attitudes to learner autonomy and learning strategies have a significant effect on the quality of integrating content and language subjects (Wolff and Otwinowska-Kasztelanic 2010). For this reason, it seems important to discuss how these aspects of teaching are interpreted and adopted in CLIL class units in Poland. The differences in the methodology used helped to distinguish a number of curricular models occurring to a greater or lesser extent in schools using different languages of instruction. It is important to single out and explain the existing models as they result in a range of learning outcomes in terms of both language and content (Marsh et al. 2008).

With a view to discerning regularities in CLIL education in Poland, an analysis of the Bilingual Education Research Project outcomes helped to distinguish four operating curricular models, which derive from the adoption of differing approaches to teaching content subjects through L2. Although the names of the models were articulated in the Profile Report devoted to CLIL with English as the language of instruction (Marsh et al. 2008), similar patterns of implementing CLIL pedagogy can also be observed in CLIL streams with German and French. Spanish-medium streams were excluded from this analysis as, due to significant disparities of an organisational and administrative nature, these schools adopted CLIL provisions different than schools using other languages of instruction. When establishing particular models, the following aspects have been taken into consideration: the amount of target language used during the CLIL lesson, content/language orientation, in other words, the amount of time spent on content and language and finally the learner's/teacher's role in the classroom (whether the lessons are teacher- or learner-oriented).

English and German sections

As far as *English* and *German* are concerned, there are four curricular models of CLIL education in Poland, which are further divided into subcategories depending on the adopted educational approach (Marsh et al. 2008, 13–16; Wolski et al. 2010, 48). In Figure 1 all curricular models in CLIL education in Poland are provided.

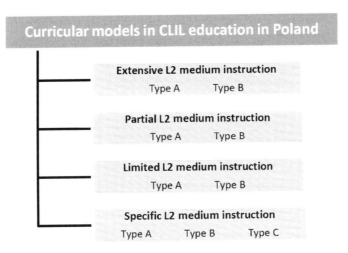

Figure 1. Curricular models in CLIL education in Poland.

Model A – extensive L2 medium instruction

In *Model A* the realisation of content subject objectives depends on a high level of competence in L2. In Model A, it is mainly English or German that is used during the content classes. It can be said that around 80% of the content classes are conducted in a foreign language, which leaves only 20% to the mother tongue. Polish is only used for the translation of terminology and a summary of the main concepts previously presented in L2. This model is divided into two types. In Type A, the main focus is on content with only occasional reference to the pronunciation and spelling of newly introduced content terminology. It can be said that these classes are content oriented. Type B, on the other hand, assumes a dual focus in a lesson – both the content and the linguistic features of L2 are paid attention to. The focus on the linguistic elements is adjusted to the ongoing needs; still, the content elements appear to be of utmost importance in the course of the lesson.

Most of the teachers using this model in their CLIL classroom employ a range of teaching methods that stimulate the pupils' language output: brainstorming, asking opinion and referential questions, dialogues in pairs, group work etc. Active engagement in the teaching process helps the CLIL learners to acquire content in a foreign language.

In both Type A and Type B, it is the learner who is in the centre. The lessons are learner oriented, and the teachers' aim is to 'guide' their learners.

As some of the interviewed learners reported, when content subjects are learnt in a foreign language they have a feeling that the teacher pays more attention to them, which may have a huge influence on their motivation or evoke positive attitudes to the learning mode.

In the case of the German Model A, it is important to mention that some of the teachers are of German nationality and do not speak Polish. This may lead to misunderstandings as some content terminology is very complex and may be better introduced in the mother tongue. However, most of the learners express their satisfaction when being asked about the CLIL lessons only in German, for example, 'Being in a bilingual classroom with German language helps me to communicate with foreigners,' or 'I acquire the content knowledge easily and I'm able to communicate in two languages due to our teacher whose teaching methods are very good' (Wolski et al. 2010, 48).

Model B – partial L2 medium instruction

In *Model B* considerable code-switching can be observed as both an L1 and L2 are used in a CLIL classroom. It can be said that around 50% of the content is taught in English or German and the other 50% in Polish. In this model we can also distinguish two types. In Type A, the main focus is only on content and switching between languages can be done according to a variety of functions, whereas in Type B the focus is both on language and content and the degree of code-switching varies from lesson to lesson. However, in most cases code-switching is constantly present during the lessons, especially when new terminology is introduced. The teachers also make effective use of English or German, but when they need to explain more difficult concepts, they immediately start using Polish. The learners tend to communicate in Polish, especially when they are asked to work in pairs or groups.

As teachers reported, the content was affected by the language so they had to use both languages and also some experiments in order to explain everything to the pupils. In general, physics is considered to be a very difficult subject even when taught in Polish, so learning this subject only in English poses additional difficulty that learners need to deal with. Being afraid that the learners may not understand the content properly, the teachers frequently tend to switch into Polish.

It is also worth mentioning that even though the teachers switch to Polish during the content lessons, the approach that they use is still learner centred. The learners have a lot of possibilities of using the language in various communicative activities. The learners, when asked about this mode of teaching, are aware of the fact that being bilingual means using two languages at the same level. 'We aren't bilingual yet, we need a lot of time to learn a second language. In fact, we learn for the whole of our life,' or 'being bilingual means using two languages so it's good that we use two languages during our lessons' (Wolski et al. 2010, 49).

Model C – limited L2 medium instruction

In *Model C* both English and German are used from time to time (10–50%). In most cases, the teachers adopt a teacher-centred approach with a limited amount of communicative activities. The foreign languages are only used to introduce some terminology. There are also two types present: Type A, in which the focus is mainly on the content (there is hardly any English or German present) and Type B, in which both content and language are treated equally, but the degree of focus varies from lesson to lesson. In most cases, it is the teacher who gives a lecture on a particular concept in a foreign language and the learners are asked to make notes.

This model does not seem to be very effective because the instruction is mostly teacher based. There are no communicative activities that would help the learners to acquire content in a foreign language. What is more, the teachers very often use specialised written texts in English or German but analyse them in Polish. When the learners from German CLIL classes were asked about their second language competence, they admitted that they knew a lot of specialised German vocabulary but they still had problems with speaking (Wolski et al. 2010); therefore, it might be assumed that this model does not facilitate the development of communicative language competence.

Model D – specific L2 medium instruction

Model D is divided into four different types. In Type A, all the content lessons are taught in Polish, and after a certain sequence of lessons there is one lesson in English or in German that aims at summarising the content material taught in Polish. The teachers usually provide learners with basic terminology in a foreign language and give them some exercises in which they are required to use the newly introduced terms. Most of the learners interviewed did not see any sense in this kind of teaching pattern. They do not like the idea of being given vocabulary that they are asked to practise only in exercises. They would like to be given an opportunity to be able to use it in natural situations, for example, in a conversation. In Type B, one lesson is conducted in Polish and another lesson is conducted in English or in German. The aim of the lesson conducted in the foreign language is to revise the content material previously covered in Polish. This type of teaching appears to be more beneficial than the previous one as the learners have more opportunities to practice the newly acquired vocabulary (e.g. every second lesson). In Type C, the content lessons are conducted in Polish but the teaching materials are in a foreign language (either in English or in German), for example, the teacher makes a presentation on various rock types in Polish (geography lesson) but provides the learners with handouts where specialised terminology is written in the foreign language. While listening to the teacher the learners can also read information from the handouts and familiarise themselves with the terminology in the foreign language. Most of the learners when asked about this type of teaching expressed their strong dissatisfaction. They said that they had to put a lot of effort into dealing with the content in a foreign language on their own. In Type D, the content lessons are taught in Polish and the learners are usually put into groups, where they are asked to work on different projects, which are prepared in the foreign language. Most of the learners expressed a positive attitude to this form of acquiring content knowledge in a foreign language. They said that they liked working in groups because it was less tiring and they did not have to spend so much time on studying at home.

French sections

The authors of the French report (Gajo et al. 2005) do not distinguish four different models, but stress the fact that in CLIL lessons with French the teachers pay more attention to the didactic process than to the final effect. However, when referring to curricular models, it can be said that most teachers use *Model B* in which both languages are used: French and Polish. Polish is used when new terminology is introduced by the teacher and when the teacher wants to make sure that the learners understand the concepts in the foreign language. What has been also noticed in CLIL classes with French is that the older the learners are the more the teachers try to use French. As a result, *Model A* was present in most final secondary school classes. For most learners 'being bilingual does not mean being perfect in a foreign language but being able to switch from one language into another' (Gajo et al. 2005, 13) and therefore most of the learners do not mind being taught content in both languages: French and Polish. What is more, being able to learn a subject in both languages gives the learners the possibility of looking at a particular case from two different perspectives. One of the learners says 'it's very interesting to be able to learn history by reading Polish and French books' (Gajo et al. 2005, 13).

Spanish sections

The authors of the Spanish bilingual report (Tatoj et al. 2008) point out the distinctiveness of CLIL provision with Spanish as the language of instruction. The main assumptions in the English, German and French models are not connected with passing on knowledge about a particular country but rather with teaching the content knowledge of subjects such as biology, geography, mathematics, physics, chemistry or history. The subjects are usually taught by Polish teachers who are not only content teachers but also have a good knowledge of the foreign language, that is, English, German or French.

In the Spanish model the language is inherently linked with the target culture. Apart from learning the language, the learners acquire knowledge concerning the history, geography and culture of Spain. Consequently, L2 is not only seen as a tool, but it is also treated as a source of knowledge about the culture of the country. In most cases, CLIL streams specialise in the humanities and hardly ever are any science subjects, such as biology, mathematics, physics or chemistry, taught in this language. What is more, the teachers are of Spanish origin, who do not speak Polish and therefore only one language (Spanish) is present during the lessons. In the Spanish model, a Polish teacher teaches Geography in Polish and a Spanish teacher in Spanish. What is very significant in this model is that Polish and Spanish are not used simultaneously during one lesson – the lesson is either in Polish or in Spanish. It should be mentioned that there are cases when a Polish teacher is required to teach the content subject in Spanish but he/she should always do it in the target language. It is underlined that Polish should not be used during the content lessons.

Curricular models – summary

As can be observed, teachers vary with respect to teaching resources, preferred interaction patterns, proportions between the use of L1 and L2, approaches to erroneous performance and the emphasis on content- or language-related elements. These differences undoubtedly result from teachers' qualifications and competence in integrating content and language elements. Only a small number of teachers have formal qualifications to teach both the content and the language subject, and the majority of content teachers have no education in second language methodology. It must be noted that, apart from one post-graduate course initiated at the University of Warsaw in 2010, there is no formal training available in CLIL methodology. Teachers interested in integrating language and content can attend short-term courses as a part of their in-service training only. Due to the lack of a coherent CLIL methodology (Coyle 2007; Iluk 2002; Wolff 2003) and insufficient pre- and in-service training, CLIL teachers develop their own teaching techniques and materials through trial and error. Because of the shortage of teaching materials or course books available on the market, teachers are forced to prepare their own materials based on diverse resources found in specialist literature or on the Internet. Alternatively, some choose to rely on content textbooks used in target language countries. It must be remembered, however, that neither the content nor the instructional objectives of teaching resources prepared in other countries comply with the curricular requirements in the Polish educational context (Papaja 2014). The quality of teaching greatly depends on the teachers' intuition, beliefs and ability to adjust their teaching to learners' needs. The differences observed in teaching techniques also stem from different levels of language competence among content teachers. In schools with French, Spanish and German as the media of instruction, some of the content subjects are taught by native speakers of a given language. In English streams, however, most of the teachers are of Polish origin, and only some of them have lived and worked in the target language countries. Teachers insecure about their language proficiency tend to opt for Model D, in which the use of English is limited and the teaching process is to a large extent based on resources. Moreover, such teachers focus on the content and are less likely to pay attention to the linguistic features of L2.

It is suggested that administrative decisions have a significant impact on the shape of CLIL education in Poland (Pawlak 2010; Wolff and Otwinowska-Kasztelanic 2010). The lack of a uniform curriculum for content subjects taught through the medium of a foreign language is yet another factor determining the existence of CLIL models in Poland. Regardless of whether the lesson is taught through the mother tongue or a foreign language, teachers need to realise all the curricular objectives stipulated in the core curriculum for the content subject. In some schools, no extra time is allotted to subjects taught through L2; therefore, teachers need to adjust the amount of L2 or to apply teaching techniques and materials that would allow them to discuss the entire content required by externally imposed curricular objectives. Due to the limited use of L2 in content subjects, Models C and D seem to prevail in such schools.

Conclusions

As has been observed, CLIL provision in Poland is characterised by a significant flexibility and embraces different approaches developed in diversified learning environments. Although the amount of L2 and the teaching techniques used in CLIL content classes vary from classroom to classroom, certain regularities can be observed. This has allowed for the formulation of curricular models whose existence and frequency of implementation depend to a large degree on the amount of L2 used during the CLIL lessons, the number of hours devoted to content versus language teaching as well teacher/learner centeredness. The diversification in CLIL provision in Poland is inevitable due to insufficient regulations that would facilitate and standardise this educational approach in schools across the country. The formulation and understanding of the curricular models is necessary to evaluate the approaches currently being applied and compare them with real educational needs. Such a systematic approach to researching CLIL provision in schools offering different languages of instruction might, in the long term, contribute to the adoption of the most successful models on a larger, national scale.

It might be argued that a large number of models help to adjust the integration of content and language to a particular teaching context, which is determined by the accessibility to learning resources and learners' individual needs. Such flexibility may also help to implement CLIL in schools in which both content teachers and learners possess different levels of L2 competence.

On the other hand, such flexibility may cause too far-fetched interpretations of the concept. The adaptation of CLIL by various educational systems must at all times be in line with the notion of integrating content and language learning. More judicious use of the mother tongue, a consistent approach to code-switching and clear guidelines on how the linguistic and content objectives should be obtained are needed. Moreover, clear aims and anticipated outcomes of this type of education should be stated.

The analysis of the Bilingual Education Research Project outcomes prove the existence of what Dalton-Puffer (2007, 4) calls a gap between 'local grassroots activities and the supra-national level,' that is, between the actions of individual teachers or schools and the transnational initiatives supported by European organisations. This problem could be solved by the national education authorities' willingness to develop national curricula for CLIL programmes, establish clear certification criteria, support the introduction of purpose-designed textbooks as well as subsidise teacher training and educational equipment in schools. Secondly, there is an urgent need for research in the field, the results of which may lead to the development of uniform aims and a methodological basis of CLIL. Although the improvement and expansion of CLIL requires considerable expenditure and a substantial workload for teachers, it should not be regarded as an obstacle. CLIL is not solely an interesting alternative to language learning. It has a broader educational dimension: it contributes to the development of multilingualism, promotes European integration and helps the learners to enhance the academic skills necessary for their educational and professional careers in the future.

Note

1. Act of 6 January 2005 on National and Ethnic Minorities and on the Regional Language and The School Education Act of 7 September 1991 (with further amendments)

References

Baetens-Beardsmore, H., ed. 1993. *Models of Bilingual Education*. Clevedon & Philadelphia, PA: Multilingual Matters.
Coyle, D. 2007. "Content and Language Integrated Learning: Towards a Connected Research Agenda for CLIL Pedagogies." *International Journal of Bilingual Education and Bilingualism* 10 (5): 543–562. http://www.tandfonline.com/doi/abs/10.2167/beb459.0
Coyle, D., P. Hood, and D. Marsh. 2010. *CLIL Content and Language Integrated Learning*. Cambridge: Cambridge University Press.
Czura, A., K. Papaja, and M. Urbaniak. 2009. "Bilingual Education and the Emergence of CLIL in Poland." In *CLIL Practice: Perspectives from the Field*, edited by D. Marsh, P. Mehisto, D. Wolff, R. Aliaga, T. Asikainen, M. J. Frigols-Martin, S. Hughes, and G. Lange, 172–178. Jyväskylä: CLIL Cascade Network, University of Jyväskylä.
de Bot, K. 2001. "The Need for Research on CLIL in Europe." In *Profiling European CLIL Classrooms – Languages Open Doors*, edited by D. Marsh, A. Maljers, and A.K. Hartiala (p. 12). Jyväskylä: University of Jyväskylä.
Dalton-Puffer, C. 2007. *Discourse in Content and Language Integrated Learning (CLIL) Classrooms*. Amsterdam: John Benjamins.
Dzięgielewska, Z. 2008. *Nauczanie dwujęzyczne w Polsce i Europie* [Bilingual education in Poland and Europe]. Warszawa: CODN.
European Council. 2002. *Barcelona European Council. Presidency Conclusions*. Press Release 100/1/02.
Eurydice. 2006. *Content and Language Integrated Learning (CLIL) at School in Europe*. Strasbourg: European Commission.
Eurydice. 2008. *Key Data on Teaching Languages at School in Europe*. Strasbourg: European Commission.

Gajo, L., C.S. Stern, and M. Zając. 2005. *Rapport d'évaluation des sections bilinguesfrancophones en Pologne* [A Report on Bilingual Education in French Sections in Poland]. Warsaw: CODN and French Embassy in Poland.

Iluk, J. 2002. "Problemy kształcenia dwujęzycznego w Polsce." Języki Obce w Szkole. Numer Specjalny [Problems of Bilingual Education in Poland. JOWS]. *Nauczanie dwujęzyczne [Bilingual Education]* 6: 27–36. http://www.bc.ore.edu.pl/dlibra/docmetadata?id=19&from=&dirids=1

Marsh, D., A. Maljers, and A. K. Hartiala. 2001. *Profiling European CLIL Classrooms – Languages Open Doors* [Profiling European CLIL Classrooms – Languages Open Doors]. Jyväskylä: University of Jyväskylä.

Marsh, D., M. Zając, H. Gołębiowska, A. Czura, A. Gapińska, K. Papaja, M. Roda, and M. Urbaniak. 2008. *Profile Report Bilingual Education (English) in Poland – Overview of Practice in Selected Schools.* Warszawa: CODN.

Mehisto, P., D. Marsh, and M. Frigols. 2008. *Uncovering CLIL: Content and Language Integrated Learning in Biligual and Multilingual Education.* Oxford: Macmillan Education.

Multańska, M. 2002. "Nauczanie dwujęzyczne w polskim systemie oswiaty." Języki Obce w Szkole. Numer Specjalny [Bilingual Education in Polish Schools. JOWS]. *Nauczanie dwujęzyczne [Bilingual Education]* 6: 77–79. http://www.bc.ore.edu.pl/dilibra/doccontent?id=265&dirids=1

Nikula, T. 1997. "Terminological Considerations in Teaching Content through a Foreign Language." In *Aspects of Implementing Plurilingual Education Seminar and Field Notes*, edited by D. Marsh, B. Marsland, and T. Nikula, 5–9. Jyväskylä: Continuing Education Centre, University of Jyväskylä.

Papaja, K. 2014. *Focus on CLIL. A Qualitative Evaluation of Content and Language Integrated Learning (CLIL) in Secondary Education.* UK: Cambridge Scholars Publishing.

Pawlak, M. 2010. "Zintegrowane kształcenie przedmiotowo-językowe: założenia, praktyka, perspektywy [Content and Language Integrated Learning: Assumptions, Practice and Perspectives]." *Języki Obce w Szkole Numer specjalny: CLIL w polskich szkołach* 6: 13–26. http://www.bc.ore.edu.pl/dlibra/docmetadata?id=265&from=&dirids=1

Roda, M. 2007. "Edukacja bilingwalna w Polsce na tle innych krajów Unii Europejskiej [Bilingual Education in Poland in Comparison to Other European Union Countries]." In *Nauczanie języków obcych. Polska a Europa* [Teaching Foreign Languages. Poland vs. Europe], edited by H. Komorowska, 57–81. Warszawa: Academica SWPS.

Tatoj, C., R. Majewska, M. Spychała, M. Zajac, and E. Piech. 2008. *Raport ewaluacyjny – sekcje dwujęzyczne z językiem hiszpańskim w Polsce* [Evaluation Report – Spanish Bilingual Sections in Poland]. Warszawa: CODN.

Wolff, D. 1997. "Content-Based Bilingual Education or Using Foreign Languages as Working Languages in the Classroom." In *Aspects of Implementing Plurilingual Education*, edited by D. Marsh, B. Marsland, and T. Nikula, 51–64. Jyväskylä: University of Jyväskylä.

Wolff, D. 2003. "Content and Language Integrated Learning: A Framework for the Development of Learner Autonomy." In *Learner Autonomy in Foreign Language Classrooms: Teacher, Learner, Curriculum and Assessment*, edited by D. Little, J. Ridley, and E. Ushioda, 211–222. Dublin: Authentik.

Wolff, D. 2007. "CLIL: Bridging the Gap between School and Working Life." In *Diverse Contexts – Converging Goals. CLIL in Europe*, edited by D. Marsh and D. Wolff, 15–26. Frankfurt am Main: Peter Lang.

Wolff, D., and A. Otwinowska-Kasztelanic. 2010. "CLIL – przełomowe podejscie w edukacji europejskiej [CLIL – A Crucial Approach in European Education]." *Języki Obce w Szkole. Numer specjalny: CLIL w polskich szkołach* (6): 7–13. http://www.bc.ore.edu.pl/dlibra/docmetadata?id=265&from=&dirids=1.

Wolski, P., B. Kurzawińska, A. Sochal, M. Torenc, E. Orłowska, and M. Zajac. 2010. Edukacja Dwujęzyczna w Polsce. Język niemiecki. Raport ewaluacyjny – Praktyka w wybranych szkołach [Bilingual Education in Poland. German. Evaluation Report – Practice in Selected Schools]. Warszawa: CODN.

Zielonka, B. 2007. "CLIL in Poland." In *Windows on CLIL – Content and Language Integrated Learning in the European Spotlight*, edited by A. Maljers, D. Marsh, and D. Wolff, 147–153. Netherlands: European Platform for Dutch Education.

Learning to become a CLIL teacher: teaching, reflection and professional development

Cristina Escobar Urmeneta

Department of Language Education, Universitat Autònoma de Barcelona, Barcelona, Spain

This case study is part of a larger project which aims to determine the usefulness and validity of a model of a pre-service content and language integrated learning (CLIL) teacher education programme inserted in a Master's degree, whose main pedagogical option is to achieve teacher empowerment through cycles of collaborative teaching and shared reflection. More specifically, the two-fold goal of the study is to describe the nature of the student–teacher's main accomplishments on her teaching practice, if any, as well as on the quality of her reflection on that teaching practice; and to identify and characterise key stages in her developmental process throughout. The analysis adopts an ethnographic perspective and explores fragments of videotaped CLIL science lessons in English/L3 and other multimodal data (student–teacher's journal, academic reports and instructor's field notes) collected in a master's degree for secondary teachers in Barcelona, where Catalan and Spanish are co-official. Through Multimodal Conversation Analysis and Ethnographic Content Analysis, the study reconstructs the developmental process undertaken by the informant throughout one academic year. The analysis traces the student–teacher's progress both in the practical handling of the specific challenges of the CLIL lessons and in her progressive understanding of key issues in the domain of Second Language Acquisition (SLA); it also shows how teaching practice and reflection shape and fuel each other. In addition, it illustrates how CLIL teachers may benefit from tools developed in the field of Applied Linguistics in order to improve their professional skills.

Introduction

The last 15 years have witnessed an outburst of content and language integrated learning (CLIL) programmes all over Spain (Lasagabaster and Ruiz de Zarobe 2010). The interest in the teaching of content-subjects through a foreign language (FL) – usually English – is also present in Catalonia, a region where already two languages – Catalan and Spanish – are legally regulated as a means of instruction in compulsory and post-compulsory education. Thus, when English enters Catalan schools as a working language, it becomes the third language of instruction (Escobar Urmeneta and Nussbaum 2010; Pérez-Vidal and Juan-Garau 2011). This outbreak coincided in time with the launching by the Spanish Ministry of Education of a 60-ECTS Master's degree, whose official guidelines, surprisingly, do not include any reference to CLIL.

It is in this context that the Bellaterra Teacher Education (TED) Master's Degree decided to adapt its offer so as to fulfil all the requirements set by the Ministry on the one hand, while simultaneously presenting all student–teachers with some basic information on CLIL, and offering them the option to relate to CLIL settings three of the mandatory course units or modules, namely (a) classroom-based research module, (b) internship and (c) Master's Dissertation (MD). The detailed procedure followed in the so-called *Bellaterra Model* which is presented in Escobar Urmeneta (2010). Table 1 shows the basic course structure, as well as the CLIL-related contents and the codes for the mandatory assignments relevant for the study.

Literature review
Dissociative vs. integrative TED models
TED models can be classified into two broad categories: dissociative and integrative programmes (Escobar Urmeneta 2010). In the first, teacher-training syllabi are based on lists of theoretical principles and teaching techniques are systematically presented in lectures. This type of Cartesian training usually reproduces in TED paradigms omnipresent at all levels in education, where:

> The teacher talks about **reality** as if it were **motionless, static, compartmentalized, and predictable**. (…) contents which are **detached from reality, disconnected** from the totality that engendered them and could **give them significance**. Words are **emptied of their concreteness** (…). The outstanding characteristic of this narrative education, then, is the **sonority of words, not their transforming power**. (Freire 1992, 57, emphasis added)

University lectures are then complemented with internship periods in practicum schools. Dissociative approaches are based on the assumption that the student–teachers, when in schools, will automatically be able to apply to their lessons the teaching techniques that derive from the theory taught at university. Unfortunately, classroom observation shows that once at work the contents presented in lectures are categorised by the novice practitioners as 'sonorous words' 'detached' from the here-and-now challenges that the lessons impose on them. As a result, the theoretical principles and teaching procedures taught at university come to lack all kind of 'transforming power'.

Table 1. Course structure.

Schedule	October–November	November	December–February	March–April	May–June
Period	7 weeks	2 weeks	8 weeks	6 weeks	10 weeks
Activities	Lectures	Internship 1	Lectures	Internship 2	Autonomous work
CLIL-related contents	Introduction to CLIL and classroom observation.	Video-recording lessons.	Introduction to teacher-led inquiry	Video-recording lessons.	Orientations for MD
Assignments (code)		Practice 1 (P1)	Reflection 1 (R1)	Practice 2 (P2)	Reflection 2 (R2); MD (R3)

Conversely, integrative approaches to TED attempt to bring theory and practice together and advocate that teacher-led enquiry is central to teacher's development. They include, among others *Action Research* (Carr and Kemmis 1986), *Reflective Teaching* (Richards and Lockhart 1996) or *Teacher Empowerment* (Short 1992). Other non-labelled models emphasise the importance of *classroom observation* (Lasagabaster and Sierra 2004) or *University–School Partnership* (Tsui, Edwards, and Fran 2009).[1]

In this vein, Schön (1987) theorised the *Reflection-in-action/Reflection-on-action* model for TED. According to Schön, *Reflection-on-action* allows the teacher to go back to particular teaching situations and explore how she acted and why she acted the way she did, as deep reflection requires time and distance. It is hypothesised that in doing so, teachers will gain deeper understanding on teaching situations and classroom life, which will result in the improvement of their professional skills and their capacity to reflect on them.

The *Bellaterra Model* departs from an integrative approach to TED deeply rooted in a sociocultural view of education (Lantolf 2000; Mercer 2000; Vygotsky 1930/1978) and an interactivist view on Second Language Acquisition (SLA) (Firth and Wagner 1997; Mondada and Pekarek Doehler 2004). This framework emphasises the interdependence of social and individual processes in learning, and attributes the quality of the conversations in which participants engage a central role in education. This rationale is instantiated in the alternation of cycles of action and reflection, triggered by a number of course assignments and sustained, aided and pushed forward by discussions held in tutorials, one-to-one conferences, lectures and informal exchanges. The literature is viewed as one more *conversationalist*, especially valuable once the student–teachers have some practical knowledge, that is, once the student–teachers have questions and data to bring into their readings.

Teacher-led interaction in CLIL classrooms

FL classrooms differ from L1 classrooms in many ways. One of them is the relevance attributed by teachers to the learners' participation in the co-construction of discourse. Walsh (2006) coined the term *classroom interactional competence* (CIC) to refer to the complexities of classroom discourse observed in FL classrooms in order to afford students interactional space:

> Classroom discourse varies in response to the unfolding task-structure and in accordance with stated pedagogic goals. A teacher's 'talk' may be high or low; it may involve the use of extended silence; it may be typified by extensive explanations; it may require form- or content- focused feedback; it may use display or referential questions. The variability of language used in response to the work-in-progress enables learners to play a more prominent part in the jointly constructed discourse. (130)

Although teachers are not the only participants responsible for it, CIC is very much determined by the choices they make during the unfolding of the lessons.

A set of recent studies using conversation analysis (CA) have described a number of qualitative differences in the way teacher–class interaction is enacted in CLIL settings (Escobar Urmeneta, in progress; Escobar Urmeneta and Evnitskaya, forthcoming a; Evnitskaya 2012; Escobar Urmeneta and Evnitskaya, forthcoming b; Evnitskaya and Morton 2011). These studies show that successful CLIL lessons present all the characteristics identified by Walsh (2006) as components of CIC in FL classrooms, which can be grouped into three main categories: (a) the use of learner-convergent language, including the abundant use of gesture; (b) the facilitation of interactional space so that learners are given the opportunity to contribute to the class conversation and (c) the 'shaping' of learner contributions by seeking clarification, modelling, paraphrasing, reiterating or repairing the learners' productions.

Since teacher-led interaction accounts for two-thirds of all the talk in CLIL classrooms with the total or quasi-total absence of extended teacher monologue (Dalton-Puffer 2007), it appears that offering student–teachers opportunities to develop efficient ways to manage academic conversations in a FL seems an unavoidable content in any TED course.

The case of Pilar

Context

This case study is part of the DALE-APECS project[2] on CLIL Science Classrooms. The data were collected at *El Firmament* School, located in an underprivileged working neighbourhood in metropolitan Barcelona, where the predominant academic profile among parents is that of basic compulsory education. As a result of a blend of sociocultural and educational factors, students at the age of 15 showed a competence level in English which roughly ranged between a Common European Framework of Reference for Languages (CEFR) A1 and a low A2. It is in these adverse conditions that a team of teachers chose to start up a CLIL programme, as they considered that schools need to become agents for social change, rather than the institutionalisation of inequality. The assumption behind this audacious resolution was that the running of a CLIL programme –together with other simultaneous actions– would not only better the students' exit levels in English but also contribute to the improvement of the students' self-esteem by allowing them access to English, a form of 'capital' (Bourdieu 1986) highly valued by the Catalan society.

In order to overcome the many possible obstacles ahead, it was decided that the English teachers, the Science teachers, with the assistance of student–teachers (English and Science) would work together in the ad hoc planning, co-teaching and evaluation of CLIL Science Teaching Units to be piloted in selected groupings. The outcomes of this school-led action-research process would be used to design a comprehensive CLIL Science curriculum available to all the students in the school (see Escobar Urmeneta [2011] for a detailed presentation of the experience).

Method

Pilar's case was selected for close examination because she happened to be a good informant, as she was not intimidated of sharing her (un)certainties with peers, mentors or tutor. The study is an interpretive reconstruction of the key stages in the process of action, reflection and change undergone by Pilar throughout one academic year. The resulting narrative aims to trace cause–effect relationships between practice and reflection, if any, and assess the validity of the formative proposal in terms of progress made by the student–teacher along the course and the programme's potential for professional lifelong development.

The conversational data selected for this study were collected in slots corresponding to Science lessons covering mandatory curriculum contents (*Trophic chains* and *Pressure*), which were taught wholly in English under the supervision and the assistance of the Science mentor and the collaboration of the English mentor. All data are approached in an emic way, respecting the significance attributed by the participants to the different events.

Five mandatory assignments have been used to portray Pilar's development at particular points in the process and to capture empirical evidences of change: (a) a video-recorded lesson taught in Internship 1 (coded 'P1'); (b) a self-reflective report on P1 (coded 'R1'); (c) a video-recorded lesson taught in Internship 2 (P2);[3] (d) a self-reflective report on her progress from P1 to P2 (R2) and (e) MD, (coded 'R3'). The former assignments provide two main types of data: conversational, extracted from the videotaped lessons, and textual, derived from the reports and MD. Field notes have been referred to provide supplementary contextual information when convenient.

The interactions in P1 and P2 were transcribed using Transana software, employing conventions based on those proposed by Jefferson (2004) (Appendix 1). Non-verbal actions are described using line-to-line narratives (Evnitskaya 2012). Additional contextual information is provided with video screenshots, whereas English translation of the Catalan or Spanish utterances is offered in parallel to the original text. By means of Multimodal CA, which approaches classroom talk as conversation (Kupetz 2011; Markee 2005; Seedhouse 2005), the study sets out to discover how 'messages and the meanings derived from them are co-constructed by partners-at-talk as the interaction unfolds' (Dalton-Puffer 2007, 37), which will allow identifying the student–teacher's development from P1 to P2 in the way she conducts teacher-led explanations.[4]

Written documents are approached using Ethnographic Content Analysis (Altheide 1987), that is, recurrent issues, words or themes are tracked over R1, R2 and R3 in order to identify patterns and processes. Finally, the findings derived from the analysis of the scripts and those of the reports are related to one another in order to reconstruct the developmental process undertaken by the informant throughout the academic year and how teaching and reflecting may have influenced one another.

Narrative

October

The story began in October, when the student–teachers had been presented with a number of videotaped lessons to observe. They were informed that they would be required to record several lessons and select three short excerpts to present and discuss them once they would be back at university. Pilar had expressed then her distrust of being recorded, but finally accepted it as one more of the many demands imposed by the institution.

November

Pilar started her internship period in November. Her experience with CLIL began with a Teaching Unit on *Trophic Chains* to be taught to a class of 30 14-year-old students. Excerpt 1[5] corresponds to a transitional moment when the student–teacher aims to present an activity intended to revise facts related to nutrition, where the use of a teacher-made chart and a set of cards are meant to help low-proficiency learners to contribute to the co-construction of the academic explanation. One student at a turn is supposed to read-out the card, add some relevant information about the content in the card and stick it onto its corresponding place in the chart. The screenshot in Figure 1 corresponds to Line 10 in the transcript.

The lesson begins with Pilar's long monologue (Lines 1–46) in front of an attentive class. In Line 1 (L.1), Pilar announces a new activity and immediately self-translates the announcement into Catalan. The announcement is followed by focusing the students' attention on the chart using a number or multimodal resources: pointing (L.4), comprehension check (L.6) and teacher's movement towards it and two pauses (L.4 and L.7). In L.9, a new bit of information is introduced (it is empty), followed by a pause and self-translation used as a means to speed up the explanation (L.10). From L.12 to L.15, Pilar continues adding bits of information using different resources to aid understanding such as intonation, pauses, repetition, contrast, definition or gesture. The rest of the transcript evidences Pilar's ability to get and hold the students' attention and win and sustain a cooperative audience who complies with the student–teacher and tries hard to satisfy her demands all throughout the excerpt.

However, the more than abundant use of gesture, the pauses she introduces in her speech (L.1, 10, 14,19), the comprehension checks (L.12, 17, 26), the pervasive resort to code switching used by the student–teacher (L.3, 10, 19, 22, 28, 34, 70, 72) and other resources do *not* result in a successful learner-oriented conversation. The students' abundant verbal and non-verbal contributions (L.27, 47, 48, 49, 50, 51, 53, 56, 59, 61, 62) evidence that, even if they are trying hard, they are unable to decipher the role that the different components of the complex teaching apparatus displayed by the student–teacher (explanation, chart and cards) play in the lesson. The result is that the students seem to drift rather than navigate the lesson.

Figure 1. 'It is empty'.

CONTENT AND LANGUAGE INTEGRATED LEARNING

Excerpt 1. Food web.

1.	Pilar	so↓ (.) now↑ (.) we are going to make another activity↓ (0.2)
2.		**una altra activitat↓** (0.9) we've got here a food web
3.		*another activity*
4.		(2.4) ((points at the chart on the whiteboard opposite the blackboard
5.		and students turn round to look at where she is pointing at))
6.	Pilar	okay?
7.		(4.7) ((Pilar approaches the chart while pointing at it, and students
8.		follow her with their gaze))
9.	Pilar	bu::t↑ (.) ((turns to students, looks at them))
10.		it is empty↓ (0.4) **està buida↓** (1.2)
11.		*it is empty*
12.		okay? this is a <u>food web</u>↓ ((points at the words 'food web' on the
13.		whiteboard)) (0.5) not a <u>food chain</u>↓ ((shakes finger while looking at
14.		students)) (0.7) food web↓ (0.5) it means a lot of arrows↓ (0.3)
15.		((follows some arrows with her finger))
16.	Blanca	((yawns))
17.	Pilar	can you see? ((gazes on Blanca))
18.	Blanca	((nods))
19.	Pilar	**moltes fletxes↓** (0.4) ((turns body to her right to address
20.		*many arrows*
21.		the other side of the classroom))
22.		**molts camins↓** ((traces some arrows with her finger))
23.		*many paths*
24.	Carme	xx? ((private turn))
25.		(1.1)
26.	Pilar	okay?
27.	SS	xxxx ((murmur))
28.	Pilar	so↓ (0.5) what we are go:ing to do↑ (0.3) **el què**
29.		*what*
30.		**anem a fer↑**(0.7) **és omplir↓** (0.4) to stick here↑
31.		*we are going to do is to fill*
32.		((presses the palm of her hand against the whiteboard making
33.		the gesture of sticking something)) (0.3)
34.		**enganxar↑**(0.6) ((looks at students))
35.		*Stick*
36.		which animals and plants↑ (1.3) ((continues pressing her palm
37.		against the whiteboard))
38.		[are going to be there↓ (1.1) okay?
39.	Blanca	[((fidgets with one corner of the chart))
40.		(2.0) ((Pilar starts moving back to the blackboard))
41.	Pilar	so:↓
42.		(5.7) ((Pilar returns to the blackboard, students follow her
43.		with their gaze))
44.	Roger	(what about (.) this one?)
45.		(0.6)
46.	Pilar	[who wants (.) to start?]
47.	Roger	[((points at a certain item on the chart)) xxxx]
48.	Antoni	it's the same↓
49.	FS(?)	which one?
50.	Nerea	start↓
51.	Irene	[**el sol**↓ ((laughs))
52.		*the sun*
53.	Antoni	[**arriba↓** (.) **arriba del todo↓**
54.		*at the top at the very top*
55.	Jeni	[((points at a certain item on the chart))
56.	Fani	[((looks at the teacher and raises her hand))

110

Excerpt 1. *Continued*

57.	MS(?)	[a la derecha↓
58.		*to the right*
59.	Irene	allí↓ ((points at a certain item on the chart))
60.		*There*
61.	Mireia	[((points at a certain item of the chart and then raises her hand))
62.	Helena	[sun↓
63.	Pilar	Fani↓
64.	Antoni	[ah↓ (.) no↓
65.	Blanca	[((points at a certain item on the chart))
66.	MS(?)	jo! (.) jo!
67.		*me me*
68.	Pilar	°you will-° ((hands Fani a card)) (0.4) so↓ (0.4)
69.		you have to come here↑ ((accompanies Fani to the front of the chart)) (.)
70.		**has de venir aquí**↑((gazes at Fani)) (.)
71.		*you have to come here*
72.		and tell us↓ (1.0) **i dir-los-hi**↓ ((gazes at the class)) (.)
73.		*and tell them*
74.		this is the sun↓ (.) okay? (1.0)

December

On-campus lessons restarted at the end of November with lectures and small-group tutorials, some of them dedicated to discuss the videotaped lessons selected by the student–teachers to this purpose. Using a previously prepared report card as a prompt, Pilar presented the lesson corresponding to the excerpt analysed above. Her card read 'I worked hard preparing the activity and the materials but I don't know why I am not sure about the results'. Pilar's brief introduction was followed by the viewing of the episode by the group. The viewing was followed by a lively small-group discussion where problems were discussed and ideas for improvement suggested (Source: instructor's field notes).

January

At the beginning of January, Pilar handed in her first self-reflective report (R1), where she analysed the lesson corresponding to Excerpt 1. A number of fragments which are representative from different sections in that paper will be briefly dealt with following the order established by the student–teacher.

First, Pilar uses the Introduction mainly to define the two objectives of her report (Passage 1, emphasis added).

Passage 1. Objectives

> There are two objectives in doing this observation: the first one is to be aware of the *real amount of the students' exposure to FL* in this class (…); and the second one is to use this study *to improve this aspect in my future classes* by using strategies which increase the *amount and the quality of learners' exposure to FL* and thus, also improve the learners'' chances of making good progress.

Three ideas stand out from this statement of intent: (a) the amount of exposure to English was limited in the lesson observed; (b) both quantity and quality of exposure

> 1　T: So, now, we are going to make another activity. Una altra activitat. We've got here a food web, OK? But... it is empty. Està buida. OK? This is a food web, not a food chain. Food web. It means a lot of arrows, can you see? Moltes fletxes, molts camins. OK? So, what we are going to do, el què anem a fer és omplir, to stick here, enganxar, which animals and plants are going to be there. OK? So... who wants to start?

Figure 2. Transcript.

to the FL play an important role in Foreign Language Acquisition (FLA) and (c) *the study* will allow the student–teacher to improve these two aspects.

The *transcript's* (Section 2, p. 1) early position in the report also suggests that the conversational data have played a prominent role in Pilar's reflective work. It contains exclusively verbal data in the form of standard text (Figure 2). On the other hand, the students' non-verbal and verbal attempts to contribute to the lesson go unnoticed.

Her *Analysis* (Section 3) begins with a question formulated in the first person which accepts the fact that the student–teacher used too much L1[6]. She answers her question using her fresh memories of the event: the pressure of time made her forget that the true goal was learning (Passage 2).

Passage 2. The real objective

> "Why do I use so much L1? (...) (the reason) that may explain why I used to translate so much was the pressure due to the *lack of time*. (...) I thought I had to finish all the activities I had prepared (...). *This led me to forget that the real objective of the classes was to make students learn, independently of the number of activities* (...)" (My emphasis)

From then on, Pilar sets to do some bibliographical research on how to improve her communication skills in teaching contexts. The theoretical constructs she prioritises include Comprehensible Input and Affective filter (Krashen 1982) and Negotiation of meaning (Long 1983). Consistent with them Pilar produces a list of strategies – in the form of teaching tips for action (Passage 3) – to improve the quantity and quality of the input she provides students with. One of those tips reveals Pilar's discovery of the importance of *wait time*.

Passage 3. Some of the tips listed by Pilar

> Teacher's talk:
> - Use simpler vocabulary and syntax
> - Repetitions
> - Periphrasis and hyperonyms
> - Voice (tones)
> - Adapting the level of complexity of the speech
> - Reduce the speed of the messages, if necessary
> - Introduce more pauses
> - A generous amount of waiting time should be allowed (minimum: 8 seconds)
> - Visual support:
> - Gestures and facial expressions
> - Give the oral instructions also in written
> - Drawings, images ...
> (...)

In spite of the importance Pilar attributes to input, she has also been able to find support for the use of the L1. Accordingly, she devotes one whole section to the 'Justified use of L1', which concludes with a list of contexts where the use of the L1 is 'correct'. Finally, the student–teacher manages to self-assess her performance against the criteria on the list (Passage 4).

Passage 4. 'Correct uses of the L1'

| maintain motivation |
| provide context |
| promote full understanding when it is essential |
| allow them to use L1 in interaction, although the teacher uses the FL. |
| establish limits between different sequences of the discourse |

| check students' comprehension (…) |

| In the video, some *correct use* of L1 can be seen in turns 17, 36 and 38[7] because I use L1 not to translate something that I have already said in English, but to demand students to translate these words into English(…) |

March

January and February were spent in lectures, tutorials and visits to the Professional Development Schools (PDS). The second period of internship began in March. Excerpt 2 belongs to the second lesson on a unit on *Pressure* taught to a class of 30 15-year-old students. For them, this unit is their first experience with CLIL. Figure 3 corresponds to L.23 in the transcript.

Pilar begins the lesson trying to connect the contents discussed the previous day with the new contents, and is determined to do so by engaging students in a teacher-led conversation. In order to achieve her two-fold goal, she uses a variety of conversational resources, including the pervasive use of questions instead of direct

Figure 3.   Claudia's bid.

CONTENT AND LANGUAGE INTEGRATED LEARNING

Excerpt 2. Pressure.

1.	Pilar	do you (.) <u>remember</u> yesterday we talk about the <u>pressure</u>?
2.		(7.3) ((Pilar writes 'pressure' on the blackboard))
3.	Pilar	and↓ ((looks at students))
4.		(1.1)
5.	Pilar	we did some <u>exercises</u>↓ ((points at dossier)) (.) you know?
6.		(0.6)
7.	Pilar	to (.) <u>know</u>↑ (.) the definition of pressure↓ ((points at the word
8.		'pressure' on the blackboard))
9.		(1.0)
10.	Pilar	does anybody remember? (.) what we said yesterday?
11.		(0.7)
12.	Pilar	about pressure?
13.		(1.2)
14.	Pilar	do you remember?
15.		(1.5)
16.	Pilar	anyone?
17.		(1.5)
18.	Pilar	in English:? (.) Catala:n? (.) don't worry↓
19.		(1.7)
20.	Pilar	do you remember (0.4)
21.		the definition of pressure? ((points at the word 'pressure' on the blackboard))
22.		(1.1)
23.	Claudia	((raises her hand))
24.		(0.7)
25.	Pilar	Claudia↓
26.	Claudia	**la pressió (.) és la relació que hi ha entre la superficie (0.6) i:: la força↓**
27.		*pressure is the relationship between surface and force*
28.	Pilar	((nods)) very good↓
29.		(0.8)
30.	Pilar	in this definition that Claudia has said↓ ((points at Claudia while looking at
31.		students)) (0.5) does anybody know any word in <u>English</u>?
32.		(1.1)
33.	Pilar	Sandra↓
34.		(4.6) ((Sandra checks her notes))
35.	Sandra	((reads out)) pressure (0.3) is the (0.3) m: rela- (0.6)
36.		relationship between (0.4) e:::hrm (0.3) force +'forθe+↑
37.		(0.4)
38.	Pilar	force +fɔrs+↓
39.		(0.6)
40.	Sandra	((finishes reading)) <u>force</u> +fɔrs+ (.) and surface↓
41.		(0.6)
42.	Pilar	very good↓
43.		(0.6)
44.	Pilar	a:nd do you remember some <u>example</u>? (.)
45.		(0.7)
46.	Pilar	that we did yesterday?
47.		(1.1)
48.	S(?)	m:?
49.	Pilar	do you remember the <u>flat</u> shoes? (.) and the <u>high heeled</u> shoes?
50.		(3.0) ((Pilar writes 'flat shoes' and 'high heel shoes' on the blackboard))

commands to set her demands, exact repetitions, reformulations, dissociating and regrouping demands, emphasis, writing on the blackboard, gaze and a generous amount of wait time after each time she defines or redefines her demand. The students' reluctance to take the floor in spite of the many opportunities offered does not seem to discourage the teacher, who eventually tries out one more strategy by reminding the students that the use of the L1 is acceptable. The first time she does so it has the function of eliciting the target definition (L.18), where the main problem lies in its conceptual *density* (Gajo 2007), and once she obtains it in the L1, she challenges the students to encode the definition into the L2. By doing so, temporarily, she manages to dissociate the conceptual challenge from the communicative challenge, and deal with each of them in isolation. The second time she encourages the use of the L1 has the purpose of *remediating*, the *opacity* (Gajo 2007) of everyday terms in the FL (*flat shoes*) by eliciting a translation from the students. It is interesting to highlight that she manages to accept the use of the L1 while she is able to stick to the target language all through the excerpt. All the conversational strategies deployed by the teacher allow the class to evolve from being an attentive but silent community at the very beginning of the lesson to a participatory one, where it has been clearly established that English is the default language. Likewise, in this plurilingual environment, the L1 is also welcome.

The lecture continues through triadic dialogue achieving a fluid interaction, thanks to the students' contribution the jointly constructed discourse (Walsh 2006; Wells 1999).

Recap 1: developments in CIC from November to March

Task design in P1 shows that Pilar was able to predict some of the specific challenges that CLIL was posing on her students, such as the difficulties they would face to contribute verbally to the development of the lesson given their limited command of English: the information the students obtained from the cards, had been predicted, should act as a support for their contributions to an interactive teacher-led explanation.

On the other hand, her excessive concern to comply with the schedule in her lesson plan seems to have led her towards an overuse of L1 and the construction of a monological explanation, when the purpose of the activity was to construct an interactive dialogical one (Wells 1999).

In P2, Pilar introduces a number of improvements in the way she conducts the lesson including the use of learner-convergent language; a variety of scaffolding procedures displayed, such as dissociating the content/language challenges or grading her demands up and down; the efficient management of wait time and turn allocating procedures; the way she deals with affective factors by acknowledging credit to individual students or removing emotional pressure from the students and the minimal but highly efficient use of L1 to sort out linguistic problems and ensure conceptual accuracy.

The way the student–teacher articulates all these strategies result into two major accomplishments. (a) Her capacity to lead the lesson almost entirely in the target language. The coincidence between the resources now incorporated and those listed in R1 (Passage 3) leads to conclude that becoming aware of the many possibilities available for the efficient use of the L2 and the L1 has had an impact on the way the student–teacher addresses learners.

(b) The student–teacher's newly gained ability to configure the necessary conditions to make it possible for the students to contribute to the completion of the initiation-response-feedback (IRF) sequences in spite of their extremely limited command of the language shows a general improvement in the way she articulates conversational and multimodal resources to provide students with interactional space.

May

Pilar's second self-reflective paper (R2) comprises four main sections: an introduction, data – which included analysis – discussion and conclusions, plus annexes and bibliography.

In the *introduction*, she presents the paper as part of an action-research process and states the focus of the paper and the questions that guide her inquire (Passage 5).

Passage 5. R2's questions

> "Finally the last step of this *action-research process* is to do this *second self-observation* task to check if all this has helped me *to improve as a teacher*. More specifically I have tried to answer these questions: a) Have I *increased the amount of input* in my classes?; b) Have I *increased the quality of this input*?; and c) *Which strategies* did I use to do this?" (Emphasis added).

As for her handling of *data*, Figure 4 shows a fragment of the transcript produced corresponding to a stage in the lesson soon after that transcribed in Excerpt 2.

Some of the conversational features incorporated in R2 which were absent in R1 are: short, long and very long pauses; vowel elongation; intonation patterns; pronunciation; teacher's non-verbal behaviour and code switching. The double signalling of L1 utterances (italics and highlights) reveals the degree of concern that this issue provokes in the student–teacher.

To organise her analysis, she uses the list of strategies produced in R1 to assess her own performance against them locating evidences in the transcript to support her claims and to identify areas which need 'to be improved'.

Figure 5[8] shows how aware the student–teacher is of the way she has bettered the way she modifies her speech using 'simpler vocabulary and syntax', 'repetition', 'periphrases and hyperonyms', 'pauses', 'wait time' and other multimodal resources not cited here for lack of space. As for her use of the L1, Passage 6 shows an instance of the analysis she performs in relation to this issue.

23	T: *Pes*, Tania, *molt bé* (..) The weight is the force here (3 seconds) So (..) this weight (.) this force (.) is concentrated in a very (.) little (.) surface (..) So, there is a lot of pressure, OK? (..) And which is the difference/? (.) If this woman is wearing (..) a flat shoe/? (..) Who can tell me/? Laia (.) Cristina.	- I point at the vocabulary written on the blackboard. - I write "= force" on the blackboard. - I underline the heel of the shoe. - I draw a flat shoe in the other foot of the woman.
24	S5: Que::: xxx xxx (..) Que es reparteix (? en molts punts).	- I nod my head.
25	T: Very good (.) Do you remember/ (.) *es concentra* (.) in English/?	
26	Students: Concentrate	

Figure 4. R2's transcript.

	VIDEO	REST OF SESSIONS
Teacher's talk		
Use simpler vocabulary and syntax	Turn 1 (*know the definition* instead of *define*)	
Repetitions	Turn 1 (*do you remember* is said four times)	
Periphrasis and hyperonyms	Turn 23 (*weight is a type of force*.)	
Voice (intonation)	--This has to be improved.--	
Adapting the level of complexity of the speech	--This has to be improved.--	
Reduce the speed of the messages, if necessary	--This has to be improved.--	
Introduce more pauses	Turn 23	
A generous amount of waiting time should be allowed (minimum: 8 seconds)	Turn 11 (I wait 3 seconds for the students' answers)	
Visual support		

Figure 5. Teacher talk.

Passage 6. Justified use of the L1

> In turn 25, I use Catalan not to translate something that I have already said in English (like I used to do in the first practicum), but to ask students to translate these words into English. I think this is a justified use of L1. (See transcript in Figure 4).

June. MD (R3)

By the end of June, Pilar handed in her MD (R3), a 44-page-long report which revisits the data in R1 and R2 approaching them from a broader perspective. For example, she incorporates a concern for the students' role in the collective process of teaching and learning, as well as for the attainment of the content-related goals (Passage 6, emphasis added). The use of the third person to refer to herself is also a noticeable variation which denotes effort to detach from the data.

Passage 6. R3's questions

> 3. Has the student–teacher increased the number of strategies the teacher uses to *achieve an effective interaction*?
>
> 4. Do these strategies promote possibilities for students' acquisition of knowledge, not only *language* but also *content* (…)?

In keeping with the former goals, the revised version of the transcripts incorporates the description of relevant actions performed by the students which may sign, for example, the difficulties they are experiencing at exact points in the lesson and/or the strategies they are using to overcome them (see 'ACTIONS' 8 and 9 in Figure 6).

Her analysis (Section 6) follows a sequential organisation. There, as well as in the Discussion (Section 7) and Conclusions (Section 8), Pilar adds to the ones used before a number of constructs absent in previous reports which help her attain deeper levels of conceptualisation and understanding of the intricacies of classroom interaction in CLIL settings; among them: *Scaffolding* (Wood, Bruner, and Ross 1976), *Zone of Proximal Development* (Vygotsky 1930/1978), *Situated Learning* (Mondada and Doheler 2004), *Focus on content* vs. *Focus on language* (Long 1991; Mohan 1986) or *Turn taking* and *Repair* (Seedhouse 2005). She is also capable of relating some of the most abstract concepts to the practical problems she has been able to identify in her lessons, and write a complementary, more elaborated ready-to-use list of do's and don'ts (Passage 7).

Passage 7. Opportunities to seize

> Moreover, provided that interaction also contributes to create the context, the teacher should also accept the changes occurring during the development of the task and look at them as an opportunity to learn and teach, and not as an error on the students' performance or (a problem) in the planning of the unit.

Her understanding of the CLIL classroom as a plurilingual environment and how the L1 may contribute to deal with the density of the content are also enhanced. This last accomplishment is illustrated in Passage 8, where turn 2 (Figure 6) is being analysed.

Passage 8

> Claudia answers (...) in Catalan (...). In this turn, we have evidence of the student's cognitive activity in the lengthening of the sounds and the pauses. (...) if any language different from English would have been forbidden, it would have been more difficult to achieve the students' participation because *they would have had to add the difficulty of the language to the difficulty of the content of the answer demanded by the teacher. (Emphasis added)*

Recap 2: development in Pilar's reflection from R1 to R3

In R1 (January), Pilar was able to identify a problem in *her* performance, formulate it in an operational way, find relevant literature on the matter and produce a set of conclusions in the form of teaching tips that would help her to overcome the problem identified. In R2 (May), she checked her new data against the formulated tips. In R3 (June), she approaches the same conversational data overcoming her exclusive concern for her *own* performance and manages to put the learners' contributions in focus as well.

A combination of several factors may provide an explanation for this huge step forward. First, the prominence given to 'wait time' in R1 hints that the evolution started there at a very practical level even if she was not able to theorise about it. Second, deep reflection demands time and concentration, which Pilar seems to have found in the last weeks of the course, when lectures were over. Third, learning to teach and learning to reflect on teaching in academic ways seem like two daunting demands; it appears that the student–teacher could not progress in both of them at the same rate and needed to prioritise one thing at a time. Fourth, reflection also demands distance; the fact that Pilar was not involved in any more teaching and that

CONTENT AND LANGUAGE INTEGRATED LEARNING

TURN	NAME	UTTERANCES	ACTIONS
2	CLA	la pressió: (.) és (.) la relació: que hi ha (.) entre la superfície (.) i: la força\ |6|	|6| The teacher nods her head.
3	PIL	very good\ (..) in this definition |7| that Claudia has said/ (.) does anybody know any word in English/ (..) Sandra\	|7| The teacher points at the student who has just talked.
4	SAN	the pressure is the rila- +rilationsip+\ |8|	|8| The student is reading the answer in the dossier.
5	PIL	yes	
6	SAN	between (.) eh::: +forse+ |9|	|9| The student does not read.
7	PIL	force\	
8	SAN	force\ (.) and the surface\	

Figure 6. R3's transcript.

she went over the data for a second time surely contributed to the detachment she shows in R3. Last but not least, the academic demands set by the MD itself may have played a relevant role in how Pilar placed herself in front of the assignment, how she approached it and the outcomes that derived from it.

Conclusion

In P1, Pilar plans an activity aimed at favouring the students' participation. Unfortunately, the way the activity is enacted – including inefficient use of L1, insufficient wait time or inability to make sense of the students' reactions – shows that Pilar is not able to grasp the difficulties experienced by the students and interactively adapt her explanation accordingly (Escobar Urmeneta and Evnitskaya, forthcoming b). Recording, selecting, transcribing and analysing her own practice allowed the student–teacher to modify her own classroom practice as a CLIL teacher. Thus, in P2, Pilar makes good progress in her use of learner-convergent language and in the way she monitors the class and paces her agenda introducing an array of conversational strategies, thus enabling learners to play a more prominent part in the jointly constructed discourse (Walsh 2006).

One of those strategies which deserve special attention is code choice. The role that the L1 plays in the learning of a FL is a very much debated one (Cook 2001; Levine 2011; Macaro 2001, among others). This issue becomes a particularly hot one in content-driven CLIL classrooms where the learning of the content-matter is at stake (Moore, Nussbaum, and Borràs 2012; Nussbaum and Cots 2011). In this respect, the analysis shows that the way the L1 was used in P1 (the student–teacher's mechanical self-translation in order to speed up the lesson) was counterproductive as it favoured neither comprehension nor fruitful participation. Conversely, P2 shows that by allowing learners to express their content understandings in L1, the students were able to overcome the block they were facing due partly to their poor command of the language, partly to the density of the content.[9] This case in point illustrates that it would be incorrect to attribute Pilar's improvement in CIC to the simple use of a set of teaching strategies which will automatically offer predictable results (i.e. use vs.

avoidance of the L1). On the contrary, the differences observed between P1 and P2 show that it is *how* conversational and multimodal resources are articulated in a locally situated manner to respond to the particular needs made relevant by participants in the course of the activity which made Pilar succeed in accomplishing the interactively constructed explanation so hardly sought for (Escobar Urmeneta, in progress).

We can attribute this developed sensitivity to the interplay of the transforming power of the repeated cycles of teaching practice and reflection and the distinct demands created by the CLIL context, which, combined, lead the student–teacher to experiment alternative ways of doing in order to overcome the acutely perceived difficulties caused by the FL (Escobar Urmeneta 2009).

It was not the object of the paper to find out whether Excerpt 2 is an exemplary piece of teaching; however, noteworthy, the progress made by Pilar in these few weeks is, the road ahead is long and the challenges as a teacher, many. But the maturity the student–teacher reaches at the end of the course in the way she deals with data and literature suggests that she has gained sufficient autonomy to be able to take the lead of her own education. For all this, it can be concluded that the course makes a potentially valuable lifelong training programme.

The analysis also shows how CLIL teachers may benefit from procedures, tools and constructs developed in the field of Applied Linguistics in order to improve their professional skills in multilingual environments. The ones identified in this study are basic transcription of selected extracts, familiarity with central concepts related to SLA when perceived as relevant by the student–teachers and tools from CA.

To finish with, one extremely relevant pedagogical issue which has been marginally referred to in the paper is that of the advisability of offering content-driven CLIL courses to low-proficiency students (see Denman, Tanner, and de Graaff 2013), who often tend to be students coming from less favoured sociocultural milieus. Although this study cannot be conclusive on this issue, the conversational data examined here suggests that when there is a will, there is a way. It also unmistakably shows that the challenges teachers and learners face in these contexts are extremely high. Undoubtedly, focused research on this issue is needed.

Notes
1. Inquiry-based professional development in CLIL has also been vindicated by Coyle, Hood, and Marsh (2010).
2. Academic Discourse in a Foreign Language: Learning and Assessment of Science Content in the Multilingual CLIL Classroom, funded by the Spanish Ministry of Science and Innovation (Reference: EDU2010–15783).
3. Although the Units designed by Pilar under the supervision of her mentors made abundant use of peer and group work, lab work and information and communication technologies (ICT), the excepts she selected for discussion correspond to teacher-led sequences, as tends to be the case among novice teachers.
4. For detailed line-by-line CA of the excerpts, see Escobar Urmeneta (in progress).
5. Conversational data were gathered and transcribed by Escobar Urmeneta, Evnitskaya, Fuentes and Jiménez.
6. The term 'L1' is used by the student–teacher to refer to Catalan. However, for some of the students in the two groups observed Catalan may not have been the/a family language.
7. The turns cited in passage 4 correspond to a later stage in the lesson not transcribed here. The turn numbers in all passages taken from the student–teacher's reports are the original ones assigned by her. In order to avoid confusion, I am using 'lines' instead of 'turns' to

8. locate conversational phenomena in the researchers' more elaborated transcripts (Excerpts 1 and 2).
8. Turn numbers as assigned by the student–teacher. Turn 1 corresponds to lines 1–25 as transcribed in Excerpt 2. Turn 11 to a later stage in the lesson not transcribed here. Turn 23 appears in the student–teacher's transcript in Figure 4.
9. The presence of the camera may have also contributed to the initial reserve shown by the students.

References

Altheide, D. L. 1987. "Reflections: Ethnographic Content Analysis." *Qualitative Sociology* 10 (1): 65–77. doi:10.1007/BF00988269.

Bourdieu, P. 1986. "The Forms of Capital." In *Handbook of Theory and Research for the Sociology of Education*, edited by J. G. Richardson, 46–58. New York: Greenwood Press.

Carr, W., and S. Kemmis. 1986. *Becoming Critical: Education Knowledge and Action Research*. London: Falmer Press.

Cook, V. 2001. "Using the First Language in the Classroom." *Canadian Modern Language Review* [*La Revue canadienne des langues vivantes*] 57: 402–423. doi:10.3138/cmlr.57.3.402.

Coyle, D., P. Hood, and D. Marsh. 2010. *CLIL: Content and Language Integrated Learning*. Cambridge: Cambridge University Press.

Dalton-Puffer, C. 2007. *Discourse in Content and Language Integrated Learning*. Amsterdam: John Benjamins.

Denman, J., R. Tanner, and R. de Graaff. 2013. "CLIL in Junior Vocational Secondary Education: Challenges and Opportunities for Teaching and Learning." *International Journal of Bilingual Education and Bilingualism* 16 (3): 285–300.

Escobar Urmeneta, C. 2009. "Cuando la lengua de la escuela es diferente de la lengua familiar [When the Language of the School is not the Family Language]." *Cuadernos de Pedagogía* 395: 46–51. http://www.cuadernosdepedagogia.com/

Escobar Urmeneta, C. 2010. "Pre-service CLIL Teacher-Education in Catalonia: Expert and Novice Practitioners Teaching and Reflecting together." In *CLIL in Spain: Implementation, Results and Teacher Training*, edited by D. Lasagabaster and Y. Ruiz de Zarobe, 189–218. Newcastle: Cambridge Scholars Publishing.

Escobar Urmeneta, C. 2011. "Colaboración interdisciplinar, Partenariado y Centros de Formación Docente: Tres ejes para sustentar la formación del profesorado AICLE [Collaboration Across Disciplines, Partnership and Professional Development Schools: Three Pillars to Lay the Foundations of Teacher Education for CLIL]." In *Learning Through Another Language*, edited by C. Escobar Urmeneta and L. Nussbaum, 203–230. Cerdanyola: Servei de Publicacions de la Universitat Autònoma de Barcelona.

Escobar Urmeneta, C. Submitted. "Do Good Ingredients Make a Good Stew? The Complex Articulation of Interactional Resources in Successful Teacher-Led Explanations in a CLIL Science Classroom."

Escobar Urmeneta, C., and N. Evnitskaya. 2014. "Do You Know Actimel? The Adaptive Nature of Science Explanations in a CLIL Classroom." *Language Learning Journal*: 42 (2): 165–180. DOI:10.1080/09571736.2014.889507.

Escobar Urmeneta, C., and L. Nussbaum. 2010. "Politiques, pratiques et perspectives de l'éducation linguistique en Espagne [Politics, Practices and Perspectives on Language Education in Spain]." *Sociolinguistica* 24: 120–133. http://www.degruyter.com/view/j/SOCI.2010.24.issue-1/9783110223323.120/9783110223323.120.xml

Escobar Urmeneta, C., and N. Evnitskaya. 2013. "Affording Students Opportunities for the Integrated Learning of Content and Language. A Contrastive Study on Classroom Interactional Strategies Deployed by Two CLIL Teachers." In *Teaching Languages in a Multilingual Context: the Catalan Case*, edited by J. Arnau. Clevedon: Multilingual Matters and Institut d'Estudis Catalans:158-182.

Evnitskaya, N. 2012. "Talking Science in a Second Language: The Interactive Co-Construction of Dialogic Explanations in the CLIL Science Classroom." PhD diss., Universitat Autònoma de Barcelona.

Evnitskaya, N., and T. Morton. 2011. "Knowledge Construction, Meaning-Making and Interaction in CLIL Science Classroom Communities of Practice." *Language and Education* 25 (2): 109–127. doi:10.1080/09500782.2010.547199.

Firth, A., and J. Wagner. 1997. "On Discourse, Communication, and Some Fundamental Concepts in SLA Research." *The Modern Language Journal* 81: 285–300. doi:10.1111/j.1540-4781.1997.tb05480.x.

Freire, P. 1992. *Pedagogy of the Oppressed*. New York, NY: Continuum Publishing Co.

Gajo, L. 2007. "Linguistic Knowledge and Subject Knowledge: How Does Bilingualism Contribute to Subject Development?" *The International Journal of Bilingual Education and Bilingualism* 10: 563–581. http://www.tandfonline.com/doi/abs/10.2167/beb460.0

Jefferson, G. 2004. "Glossary of Transcript Symbols with an Introduction." In *Conversation Analysis: Studies from the First Generation*, edited by G. H. Lerner, 13–23. Philadelphia: John Benjamins.

Krashen, S. 1982. *Principles and Practice in Second Language Acquisition*. Oxford: Pergamon.

Kupetz, M. 2011. "Multimodal Resources in Students' Explanations in CLIL Interaction." *Novitas-ROYAL (Research on Youth and Language)* 5 (1): 121–142. http://www.novitasroyal.org/archives/vol-5-issue-1

Lantolf, J. P. 2000. *Sociocultural Theory and Second Language Learning*. Oxford: Oxford University Press.

Lasagabaster, D., and J. M. Sierra, eds., 2004. *La observación como instrumento para la mejora de la enseñanza-aprendizaje de lenguas* [Classroom Observation as a Tool for the Improvement of Language Teaching and Learning]. Barcelona: Horsori.

Lasagabaster, D., and Y. Ruiz de Zarobe, eds., 2010. *CLIL in Spain: Implementation, Results and Teacher Training*. Newcastle: Cambridge Scholars Publishing.

Levine, G. S. 2011. *Code Choice in the Language Classroom*. Bristol: Multilingual Matters.

Long, M. H. 1983. "Native Speaker/Non-native Speaker Conversation and the Negotiation of Comprehensible Input1." *Applied Linguistics* 4 (2): 126–141.

Long, M. H. 1991. "Focus on Form: A Design Feature in Language Teaching Methodology." In *Foreign Language Research in Cross-Cultural Perspective*, edited by K. De Bot, R. Ginsberg, and C. Kramsch, 39–52. Amsterdam: John Benjamins.

Macaro, E. 2001. "Analysing Student Teachers? Codeswitching in Foreign Language Classrooms: Theories and Decision Making." *The Modern Language Journal* 85: 531–548. doi:10.1111/0026-7902.00124.

Markee, N. 2005. "Conversation Analysis for Second Language Acquisition." In *Handbook of Research in Second Language Teaching and Learning*, edited by E. Hinkel, 355–374. Mahwah, NJ: Erlbaum.

Mercer, N. 2000. *Words and Minds: How We Use Language to Think Together*. London: Routledge.

Mohan, B. A. 1986. *Language and Content*. Reading, MA: Addison Wesley.

Mondada, L., and S. Pekarek Doehler. 2004. "Second Language Acquisition as Situated Practice: Task Accomplishment in the French Second Language Classroom." *The Modern Language Journal* 88: 501–518. doi:10.1111/j.0026-7902.2004.t01-15-.x.

Moore, E., L. Nussbaum, and E. Borràs. 2012. "Plurilingual Teaching and Learning Practices in 'Internationalised' University Lectures." *International Journal of Bilingual Education and Bilingualism* 1–23. doi:10.1080/13670050.2012.702724.

Nussbaum, L., and J. M. Cots. 2011. "Doing Learning Languages in a Multilingual Context: Pragmatic Aspects of Classroom Discourse in Catalonia." In *The Pragmatics of Catalan*, edited by L. Payrató and J. M Cots, 331–359. London: De Gruyter.

Pérez-Vidal, C., and M. Juan-Garau. 2011. "Trilingual Primary Education in Catalonia." In *Trilingual Primary Education in Europe*, edited by I. Bangma, C. van der Meer, and A. Riemersma, 68–92. Leeuwarden: Mercator European Research Centre on Multilingualism and Language Learning.

Richards, J. C., and C. Lockhart. 1996. *Reflective Teaching in Second Language Classrooms*. Cambridge: Cambridge University Press.

Schön, D. A. 1987. *Educating the Reflective Practitioner: Toward a New Design for Teaching and Learning in the Professions*. San Francisco, CA: Jossey-Bass.

Seedhouse, P. 2005. "Conversation Analysis and Language Learning." *Language Teaching* 38 (04): 165–187. doi:10.1017/S0261444805003010.

Short, P. M. 1992. "Dimensions of Teacher Empowerment." Pennsylvania State University, Program in Educational Administration. (ERIC Record No. ED368701).
Tsui, Amy B. M., G. Edwards, and L. R. Fran. 2009. *Learning in School-University Partnership. Sociocultural Perspectives.* NY: Routledge.
Vygotsky, L. S. 1930/1978. *Mind in Society.* Cambridge, MA: Harvard University Press.
Walsh, S. 2006. *Investigating Classroom Discourse.* London: Routledge.
Wells, G. 1999. *Dialogic Inquiry: Towards a Sociocultural Practice and Theory of Education.* Cambridge: Cambridge University Press.
Wood, D., J. S. Bruner, and G. Ross. 1976. "The Role of Tutoring in Problem Solving." *Journal of Child Psychology and Psychiatry* 17 (2): 89–100. doi:10.1111/j.1469-7610.1976.tb00381.x.

Appendix 1: Transcript conventions

(.)	Unmeasured (micro-)pause of less than two-tenths of a second.
(1.5)	Measured pauses in seconds.
=	'Latching' (no gap) between utterances produced by the same speaker or different speakers.
over[lap 　[overlap	Start of concurrent speech.
word	Underlining indicates speaker's emphasis.
°word°	Talk which is softer than that surrounding it.
↓	Falling intonation.
↑	Low-rising intonation, suggesting continuation.
?	Rising intonation, not necessarily a question.
cu-	Sharp cut-off.
:	Stretching of the preceding sound, more colons more stretching.
Xxx	Unintelligible fragment with one 'x' equal to one syllable.
word	Utterances produced in any other language that is not English.
((laughs))	Description of speaker's non-verbal actions.
`courier new`	Translation into English of original L1 utterances.

How CLIL can provide a pragmatic means to renovate science education – even in a sub-optimally bilingual context

Maria Grandinetti[a], Margherita Langellotti[b] and Y.L. Teresa Ting[c]

[a]*English Department, 'IPSSS L. Da Vinci', Cosenza, Italy;* [b]*Science Department, Liceo Scientifico 'Galileo Galilei', Calabria, Paola, Italy;* [c]*The Department of Chemistry and Chemical Engineering, The University of Calabria, Cosenza, Calabria, Italy*

This study responds to the Italian Ministry of Education mandate that, starting the 2013–2014 academic year, CLIL be implemented in the *final* year of high school, during content time, by content teachers with C1-level competence in English. This decision raises numerous concerns, at least in Calabria: most content teachers have, at best, B1-level English competence and consider CLIL the final straw in an overburdened scholastic curriculum. Secondly, EFL teachers without sufficient content competence are reluctant to contribute to CLIL initiatives, seeing themselves reduced into 'walking (technical) dictionaries.' Content-driven task-based activities were therefore developed to enable both the EFL teacher (Grandinetti) to work within her comfort zone on an advanced-level science topic and an experienced science teacher (Langellotti), with 'only' B1-level English-competence, to fulfil the L1-science curriculum. Such 'professional limitations' prompted the development of CLIL activities which necessarily scaffold between *comprehensible language* and *accessible content*, transforming teacher-centred lecturing into learner-centred learning. The materials used and the theories guiding their development are presented, alongside analyses of classroom discourse. Positive learning outcomes were obtained and more importantly, maintained, especially from normally disaffected students. Since the sub-optimally bilingual reality of Calabria may reflect many international contexts, delineating how content and language teachers 'can CLIL' within their comfort zones will ensure that CLIL contributes successfully to international mainstream bilingual education.

1. Introduction

Upon debuting as an acronym in the 1990s, Italian foreign language (FL) educators readily joined their European colleagues in welcoming CLIL as a 'European solution to [the] European challenge' (Marsh 2002) of ensuring that citizens master not one but two FLs. This enthusiasm was further justified by the hopes that embedding content subjects within an FL would provide more authentic contexts for FL-*use* and thus FL-*learning*. However, since Italy began 'forcing' CLIL into *content* classrooms (e.g. Gazetta 24/12/2011[1]) it is receiving a rather arid reception from content teachers, and their FL colleagues are increasingly more disenchanted: this Decree mandates that, by the 2013–2014 academic year, lyceums and technical institutions must implement CLIL in the final year of study, in one non-lingual discipline, during the content lesson by a content teacher with C1-Level *English* competence. A science teacher must, for example, during her already limited 2h/week of science lessons, use CLIL and her C1-level English to move the science curriculum forward. This raises several concerns for professionals in both content education and EFL instruction.

Firstly, it calls upon a nationwide abundance of teachers who are not only content competent, but also fluent in English. This emphasis on language competence has led to the misunderstanding that CLIL is simply 'doing it in English', thus overlooking the problem that *learning* probably cannot happen when teachers use C1-level FL tongues to explain to learners' A2-level FL ears. Education is about *learning*, not teaching: if lectures on geometry, physics or geography are already challenging in our mother tongue, straining our A2-level competence to comprehend a C1-level FL lecture about these topics would not only not spark interest in these subjects, it would probably abate any inkling of love for the FL. Especially if you are 16 and have not chosen to study 'this stuff.' In fact, articles in a special issue of *Science*, report how, when ex-Anglophone colonies in Africa used English, an 'elitist FL', to teach science, the outcome was dismal: 'teachers do most of the talking while learners understand little and remain silent and passive' Webb (2010, 449).

In non-immersion contexts such as Italy, CLIL must not reinvent this dysfunctional 'just do it in English' process (Lasagabaster and Sierra 2010). Italy is, in fact, one of the least multilingual nations in Europe (Eurobarometer 2006). In addition, Italy classified poorly in the 2006 PISA-OECD (2006) survey, especially in the area of science and maths literacy. There is therefore a national urgency to renovate science education: CLIL, applied to science education must move the science curriculum forward, and do so well. Attempts to either simplify content for the sake of FL instruction or focus on 'microlanguage' beg the question: 'better a monolingual surgeon who knows her anatomy well or a multilingual one who doesn't?' While learning content terminology has its place, reducing the final year of compulsory science education into 'microlanguage' does little to prepare students for university entrance exams. Besides, EFL professionals cannot be reduced to walking dictionaries.

Interestingly, these far-from-ideal conditions have prompted CLIL practitioners in Italy to develop CLIL-learning processes which not only move the content curriculum forward but do so within both the FL comfort zone of the content teachers as well as the content comfort zone of their EFL colleagues. This chapter discusses such a process and presents data from two CLIL science lessons undertaken at an Italian Scientific Lyceum, representing a truly grassroots effort to meet a national mandate on bilingual education: aware that she would soon need to implement CLIL in her classrooms, Langellotti, an experienced science teacher (25 years of teaching), along with Grandinetti, an EFL colleague, sought out Ting, a CLIL researcher in the nearby university for suggestions. The concerns were that Langellotti had limited EFL competence, mastering 'only' B1-level English and Grandinetti had limited content competence, knowing too little upper secondary science to do more than simply 'OK-ing the general English' of scientific texts taken from different sources. Despite such 'limitations' both teachers recognised their joint expertise could nonetheless be (and had to be) better optimised and potentiated through 'this imposition called CLIL'.

This established a three-way collaboration which, at the time of this writing, is into its second successful year.[2] Our collaboration sought to answer the question 'how can CLIL help Content teachers who are sub-fluent in the FL move advanced-level content forward?' Here, we discuss how, because of this 'sub-optimal' context, CLIL prompted the design of learning materials on human heart anatomy which, when implemented, naturally led to learner-centred classroom dynamics. It should be noted that, as classroom practitioners seeking pragmatic solutions, our research methodology is post-positivistic and qualitative in nature (Denzin and Lincoln 1994): rather than testing hypotheses which have been established a priori, we sought to understand whether and how our approach to CLIL supports (or not) learning in the natural setting of the CLIL classroom. As such, our method *is* the process: we do not have, therefore, a 'Methods & Materials' section since the method of materials development was the actual process of producing the materials. Therefore, in Section 2, we discuss how traditional learning materials were transformed into CLIL-learning materials, presenting not only the full set of materials, but also the theoretical framework guiding our materials development. We also provide a detailed analysis of how the tasks systematically scaffolded between familiar language and unfamiliar content, or vice versa. Section 3 presents data collected on classroom dynamics and discourse during the implementation of these CLIL-learning materials (Section 3.1). Likewise, samples of successful and sustained learning are presented to illustrate that CLIL can indeed support both content learning and language acquisition. Finally, this research reflects classroom-situated teacher training at its best: while the CLIL researcher (Ting) implemented the two CLIL lessons, Maria and Margherita assumed the role of participant observers, scrutinising learning processes from their respective perspectives of EFL instruction and science education. These experienced teachers delineated how the use of ad hoc CLIL-learning materials facilitated learning (Section 3.2), concluding that CLIL can be much more than the sum of its parts. Since teacher-led classroom investigations using qualitative research methods provide a prime source of insight into (in)effective classroom practices (Eisner 1991; Hargreaves 1996), it will be teachers' narratives (Goodson and Sikes 2001; Ting 2005) such as that presented here, which may convince sceptical colleagues that CLIL, done well, can indeed offer a pragmatic means for obtaining rather positive learning outcomes despite rather 'far-from-ideal' conditions.

2. The process: from traditional to CLIL

Without the fluency to 'just do it' in English, CLIL obliged Margherita, despite 25 years of classroom experience, to reconsider her role as science teacher: what could she, sub-fluent in English, actually do to help her learners, also sub-fluent in English, to nonetheless master the science curriculum. One solution is the use of content-driven English-based learning *tasks*, much like those used in language education (e.g. see Robinson 2011). The transformation of curricular content into tasks prompts the first change in classroom practice. Rather than considering how to *teach* the topic 'heart', it becomes necessary to delineate a sequence of micro-content-objectives which cumulate towards the content-learning objectives established by the L1-science curriculum. Table 1 lists the microlearning objectives which Teresa had previously used to develop a set of CLIL-learning materials on the 'human heart' (Ting et al. 2006): since these materials fulfilled the curricular objectives for Margherita's students, they were used in this study.

However, to sensitise both Maria and Margherita to the issue of 'comprehensible science input' (Snow 2010), they were invited to analyse the lexical density of the

Table 1. Micro-learning-objectives of the L1-Science curriculum.

Micro-leaning-objectives	
1	Distribution and relative size of atria and ventricles; symmetry
2	Convention relating imagery and anatomy
3	Blood circulation: afferent and efferent vessels; one-way valves
4	Separate and coordinated function of the heart and lungs as 'the circulatory system'
5	Anatomy of contractions: nodes (SA–AV); Bundle of His; Purkinje fibers
6	Electrophysiology of contractions: nerve transmission; rhythm

Italian textbook (Boccardi 2011) which would have provided the prime input for traditional science lessons: a similar text from Wikipedia is presented in Excerpt 1, Supplementary Materials. This 'language analysis' sensitised both teachers, but especially the science teacher, to the fact that the language by which science makes itself science often 'transforms our L1 into a foreign language' (Halliday and Martin 1993). That being the case, feeding students a scientific text in an FL would undoubtedly discourage learning: it was therefore necessary to develop and use ad hoc CLIL-learning materials.

2.1. Defining a CLIL modus operandi

A *modus operandi* (Figure 1) was developed to help both teachers visualise the process guiding CLIL materials development (Ting 2011). The *modus operandi* interprets the CLIL acronym 'mathematically' to obtain a [50:50]/[Content: Language] ratio which solicits the question: 'whose language does the [50/Language] refer to?' Since the answer is obviously the language of the *learner*, not the teacher, this Core-CLIL-Construct asks *if*, *how* and *how well* the *learner* is acquiring, using and mastering the FL. This initiates a shift towards a learner-centred learning environment. This Core-CLIL Concept establishes three concrete *ways of proceeding*, three CLIL-Operands. First of all, as learners must acquire content knowledge through an FL, for which they have limited linguistic resources, the CLIL-teacher must automatically ask 'is the input-language comprehensible? Do learners even understand the *language* that I, the book, or learning material, is using?' This is CLIL-Operand-1. Secondly, why would an Italian subject teacher bother to use English if not so her learners can *also* communicate effectively about content in English? This prompts CLIL teachers to automatically cultivate not only learners' receptive skills of reading and listening but also their productive skills of speaking and writing: CLIL-Operand-2 thus asks 'Can learners *use* language effectively to *obtain information, negotiate meaning, discuss hypotheses, construct knowledge* and *communicate understanding*?' This CLIL-Operand automatically inserts *academic discourse and literacy* into the learning agenda. Interestingly, these two Operands regarding *language*-instruction catalyse an important change in *content* education: When a teacher becomes aware that input *language* must be comprehensible, she naturally considers whether the input *content* is comprehensible. CLIL-Operand-3 thus asks 'Is the content presented in chewable and digestible aliquots?' Figure 1 illustrates how the Core-CLIL-Construct coordinates the three CLIL-Operands.

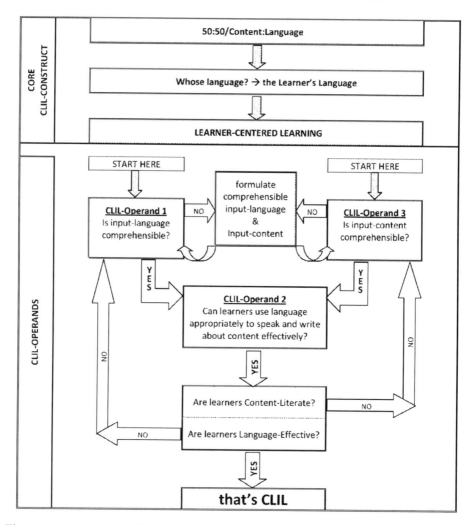

Figure 1. A mathematically derived CLIL *modus operandi* (from Ting, 2011).

2.2. Operationalising the modus operandi: from theory to practice

Operating in a context where both teachers and students are sub-fluent in the target FL prompts two major considerations and thus changes in classroom dynamics. The first is that, since the teacher cannot provide prolonged teacher-fronted instruction, s/he is obliged to seek alternative ways of instructing. Likewise, given the passive nature students usually approach science education, even in L1 (probably in reaction to traditional teacher-fronted instruction), we would not expect learners to engage in extensive discussions on unfamiliar new content in a less-than-familiar FL. We therefore designed CLIL-learning materials which sought to engage learners in tasks which, once completed, provided them with all necessary *new content* knowledge: since the teacher was sub-fluent in the FL, the tasks were designed so that it was not necessary for learners to seek explanations on content from the teacher. The full set of CLIL-learning activities used in this study are presented in the Supplementary Materials. Due to space limitations, we analyse only the CLIL-activities developed to fulfill the first four learning objectives defined in Table 1. To fully appreciate the CLIL-learning process through which our learners attained new content knowledge, the reader is strongly advised to assume the role of *'participant researcher'* (Denzin and Lincoln 1994) by first engaging with these materials as a 'learner' before proceeding to the following analysis of how the theories of CLIL-good practice presented in the Operandi were operationalised for actual learning.

To complete Exercises 1 and 2, learners rely on familiar elementary level English to form grammatically correct questions and answers. Learners thus obtained, in comprehensible language, information regarding the first micro-objective regarding how the four chambers of the heart are organised. However, since language comprehension is no guarantee of content understanding, Exercise 3 asks learners to choose the correct schematic representation for summarising the information. To do this, learners must revisit Exercises 1 and 2 to extract content from what was a mere language puzzle. Exercise 4 then asks students to redraw the correct representation: in constructing 'their own heart diagram', learners gain ownership of this new knowledge (Bransford, Brown, and Cocking 1999). Exercise 5 uses a seemingly straightforward exercise on English definite and indefinite articles to inform students of the standard academic convention regarding how to read left–right laterality of textbook images of the heart (micro-objective 2). However, when students must then 'simply' label the left and right sides of their heart diagram, they must, once again, reprocess the language exercise for content.

These activities exemplify how, using an FL for content-instruction establishes natural scaffolding processes, whereby unfamiliar content can be scaffolded upon familiar language. When the content is unknown, the content-cognitive demand (CCD) is high (Figure 2). We must therefore ensure that the *language* in which this new content is embedded is easy: language-cognitive demand (LCD) must be low. Effective CLIL instruction must thus equilibrate between the CCD and the LCD. Low LCD does not mean, however, oversimplified language. In fact, the 'familiar language' upon which unknown content is scaffolded in Exercise 1 actually focuses on areas of English which are challenging for Italians: e.g. confusion between *much* and *many*; *named* and *called* correspond to only *chiamato* in Italian; *by* and *from* to only *da* in Italian, making it more efficient to learn *different from* as a chunk, as visualised in the exercise; and Question 5 highlights how, unlike Italian, subject drop is not possible English. Finally, since the English definite article is one of the biggest challenges for Italian EFL learners, Exercise 5 reviews the English definitive article as gateway into content information.

Since CLIL attends to both content and language learning, these language-reviewing moments are a natural scaffold into totally unknown content. Although,

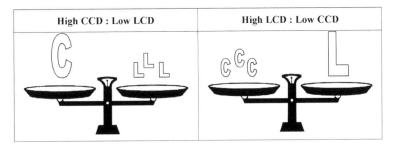

Figure 2. Ideal CLIL-materials must maintain equilibrium between Content-Cognitive-Demand (CCD) and Language-Cognitive-Demand (LCD).

EFL learners whose L1 is not Italian would require different language-focusing reviews, EFL expertise is nonetheless essential for delineating where language-focusing moments can be inserted to provide effective scaffolds into new content. In fact, since it is essential to ensure that unknown content is never embedded within unfamiliar language, EFL expertise is necessary to distinguish between the process of *reviewing* familiar language from that of *learning* new language. Scaffolding which equilibrates between the CCD and LCD is in line with what we know about *working memory* (e.g. Bransford 1979; Bransford, Brown, and Cocking 1999; Kandel 2006), a form of short-term memory whereby the complex myriad of sensory input is processed to identify which is worth attending to and code into 'a temporary piece of information'. If there is *understanding* or *strong emotional pertinence*, this information is recoded and stored in long-term memory (e.g. Kandel 2006). The important point for education is that these 'pieces of information' have a size limit: if we must remember the plumber's number only long enough to dial it, we can easily do so if the number does not exceed seven digits.

While no empirical research indicates how much 'CLIL information' would fill this 'seven digit unit' of working memory, common sense would suggest that, since learners must access new content through an FL, it is essential that CLIL materials equilibrate between content and language cognitive-demands: scaffolding from known-content-to-unknown-language or known-language-to-unknown-content considers the 'content and language familiarity and novelty continuum [whereby] language remains accessible as new concepts are introduced' Coyle, Hood, and Marsh (2010, 95).

In addition, language-review tasks allow us to adroitly move between implicit and explicit cognitive processes. This is exemplified in Exercises 1, 2 and 5: while learners actively work through relatively simple language tasks they are actually exposed to new content information, but *implicitly*. This covertly exposes learners to content information so that Exercises 3 and 4, which requires the *explicit* demonstration of content comprehension, become easy to complete. In fact, although no instructions are given for localising the interatrial and interventricular septi, if learners have mastered content information by this point in the game, they can easily localise these structures within their heart diagrams. Effective scaffolding between language and content can thus be used to harness implicit learning capabilities.

Seamlessly moving through the first set of tasks builds the learners' confidence and prepares them for the next set of activities, cultivating academic discourse literacy, which increases the language-cognitive load. Although there is also unknown content, Exercise 8 scaffolds this new content within linguistic cohesion devices (conjunctions, deictic referents and lexical links etc.) which provides learners the *linguistic logic* for completing Exercise 8, logically. Exercise 9 then explicitly draws learners' attention to how such linguistic devices are used to develop more effective discourse. Exercise 9 also provides the answers to Exercise 8, minimising the need for teacher intervention while maximising peer–peer collaborative learning time. Finally, since learning is happening through an FL, we must constantly evaluate whether learners have learnt what we intended. Exercise 10 evaluates content comprehension through a very simple output exercise which, again, obliges learners to revisit the previous two exercises for content information.

Exercise 11 employs the standard missing information gap-fill format. However, since the content is now embedded in academic discourse, a higher level of information processing is needed. Experience has shown that, when using this task to deal with academic information, having students orally ask for missing information leads to their simply reading the sentences aloud, pausing at the gaps for their partners to do an 'oral-gap-fill'. This does little for learning content and effective communication. Exercise 11 thus obliges learners to generate their inquiries in writing. This heightens cognitive engagement with both content and language, since learners must first identify the exact piece of information missing so to formulate an effective question. Then, being obliged to write out their questions calls upon prolonged focused attention on unfamiliar content lexis during the voluntary action of writing (Mangen and Velay 2010). In fact, despite eight years of English, Italian university students still produce *whit* rather than *with*, and this is surely not for want of input since *with* is the sixteenth most frequent English word[3].

Learners then concretise this new knowledge fulfilling micro-objective 3 by completing the left side of their heart diagrams. Since the motivation to complete a half-finished heart diagram is high, Exercise 12 is a combined reading–listening exercise which provides students information for completing the right side of their heart diagrams. Exercise 13 reviews content knowledge acquired thus far. To ensure that deep-level understanding of content was attained, students were asked a set of higher order thinking (HOT) questions (Wellington and Osborn 2001; see Supplementary Materials) requiring knowledge transfer (Bransford, Brown, and Cocking 1999): to answer these questions correctly, students must have *learnt* not only where the relevant anatomical structures are, but also have *understood* the function of the circulatory system.

3. Results and discussion

3.1. Classroom dynamics and learning outcomes

The CLIL science activities shown in the Supplementary Materials were used to present two 90-min lessons on human heart anatomy to 19 16-year-old students during regular science lessons on two consecutive weeks (the regular Science hour was combined with part of the subsequent English hour in these two occasions). A total of 148 min of CLIL learning time was video-recorded and transcribed. Using the videos and transcripts, each of the three authors worked individually to code classroom events such as who was talking (e.g. teacher-talk or student-talk) the direction of the utterance (e.g. teacher-to-student talk, student-to-student-talk, student-to-teacher-talk) and the *purpose* of each utterance (see below): the few instances whereby utterances were coded differently were discussed so to reach an agreed categorisation. Since the CLIL activities aimed for task-based learning, it is not surprising that teacher talk did not dominate the learning time (Table 2): the videos of the CLIL science lessons were, in fact, characterised by collaborative talk between learners while completing the CLIL activities.

3.1.1. Teacher-led instructional talk

While teacher talk accounted for ca 46% of the learning time in the first lesson, in the second lesson where a video-clip was used, instructional talk was reduced to 29% of the learning time. Table 3 delineates the *purpose* of instructional talk during 125 utterances over a 20-min segment, when the teacher was correcting Exercises 1–5.

Table 2. Classroom interaction dynamics.

Lesson	Learning time (video-recording)	Teacher-led instruction talk (% learning time)	Non-teacher-led talk (% learning time)
Lesson 1: objectives 1–3	72 minutes[a]	33 minutes (45.8%)	38 minutes (52.8%)
Lesson 2: objectives 4–6	76 minutes[a,b]	22 minutes (28.9%)	41 minutes (53.9%)

[a]Difference between the duration of the lesson and video-recording is accounted for by breaks.
[b]A video of 13 minute was used in lesson 2, accounting for 17.1% of the learning time.

Table 3. Purpose of teacher-talk in a 20 minute segment of Lesson 1.

Purpose of teacher-talk	Number of utterances
Classroom management	41
Soliciting student reflection and response	18
Cultivating learning attitudes	6
Content comprehension check and FL-L1 terminology codes	40
Explanation	20

Of the 41 utterances related to classroom management, 33 were shorter than 10 words, with the purpose of moving the correction process forward, e.g. 'does everyone agree?', 'number 5 please', 'check with each other to see if you have the same answer'. In the longest utterance of this type, the teacher actually first solicited student reflection in Italian and then code-switched to model the English question form, *'perché avete scelto questa come risposta...Why? Why is that the right answer? Discutete perché questa è la risposta giusta*, OK?' The last phrase invites students to reflect on why the correct choice was indeed correct. These results corroborate CLIL-classroom observations reported by Dalton-Puffer (2007, 32) who reports that 'teacher monologue is hard to find...In fact, there is no extended teacher monologue at all in the data corpus(!)'

Instructional talk advising students of their learning attitudes ranged from simply encouraging more extended utterances 'say the whole sentence' to suggestions for successful learning (referring to Ex. 2):

> T: Allora...scusate...stop! Guardate lì c'è spazio per scrivere, giusto? Sulla destra se scrivete a, b, c, imparate l'inglese? *[excuse me...look there, there's space to write in, right? On the right, if you write a, b, c, do you learn English?]*
>
> S(chorus): no
>
> T: noooo...sapete già scrivere a, b, c, giusto? Quindi, riscrivete tutta la frase...[...you already know how to write a, b, c, right? SO, re-write the whole sentence...]

Although the number of utterances differs between the last two typologies of teacher talk, they actually illustrate how attention was balanced between content and language. The 40 utterances used to check content comprehension took place over two minutes and accounted for the longest series of turns. Here, the initiation-response-feedback (IRF) cycle was used to implement gameplay using a 'how do you say *Italian-term*' structure to check that students had learnt content terminology:

T: OK, now, let's see...symmetry, symmetry, what does that mean, symmetry?

S(chorus): *simmetria*

T: uh-hu (confirmatory tone)...how do you say *camera superiore*?

S(chorus): upper chambers

T: OK, how do you say...*sangue*

S(chorus): blUd

T: blood (models correct pronunciation)

S(chorus): blood

//

T: how do you say simmetria destra-sinistra

S (chorus): left-right symmetry

T: symmetry...symmetry (models correct pronunciation)...how do you say...*diverso da*

S (chorus): different from.

In addition to seamlessly moving between the terminology codes of both languages, the students always maintained the English adjective–noun order, syntactically contrary to their L1. They had also successfully assimilated the chunk '*different from*' focused on in Exercise 1. This gameplay took only two minutes but was worthwhile as it enabled the teacher to also identify unlearnt language:

T: how do you say fino a

S(some voices): at rest

T: no...fino a...fino a

S(chorus): up to

T: bravi! Fino a trenta litri...how do you say fino a trenta litri...

S(chorus): up to 30 litres

Therefore, in addition to ensuring that discipline terminology has been acquired, we should also focus on sub-technical language such as *up to* or *at rest* (Wellington and Osborne 2001; Benjamin 2005), especially since such language has transdisciplinary applications.

In fact, two of the longest instructional-talk classified under 'explanation' related to Exercise 5 whereby 39 utterances were used to revise the English definite article, particularly difficult for Italian EFL-learners. The teacher dedicated more than a minute to this language-instruction, but used L1 to ensure that the students could understand her examples, which would have been an incomprehensible stream of English.

3.1.2. Non-teacher-led talk

Given that even the small amount of instructional talk did not provide extensive content explanations, the question is, therefore, when did content learning take place? Figure 3 shows that 87% of the non-teacher-talk time of both lessons was devoted to peer-to-peer interactions during which students collaborated to complete the CLIL activities (Supplementary Materials). Considering that non-teacher-talk time accounts for an average of 39 min per lesson, collaborative task completion thus accounted for almost 32 min (43%) of each of the 74-min lessons. Collaborative learning was supported by the occasional elicitation of responses; however, this represented only 13% of non-teacher-talk time of both lessons and thus only 7 min of each lesson: Collaborative work was indeed an active student-determined process.

While task completion provided the main source of learning, this was supported through instructional-talk and occasional elicitation of responses. The following segment of instructional talk shows the real-time evolution of learning through student–teacher interactions which used both Italian and *English*. At [time-0], students were concluding Exercises 8–9 and readying themselves for teacher-led task correction:

> S1(inter-group dialogue): la relazione tra...lungs and body...io ho messo qui because it summarise (sic)...perchè spiega la relationship...[the relationship between – I put this here – because it explains the -]
>
> S2(to teacher): non so come spiegare che la D è buona per concludere... *[I don't know how to explain why D is good for concluding]*
>
> T1: it's about *language* (emphasis)
>
> S2(to teacher): è giusta la D? *[is D correct?]*

Rather than answering the student, the teacher drew the class together for a 2-min instructional talk, in Italian, on the importance of using language precisely, 'especially for science...since you must always express thoughts coherently...you cannot just

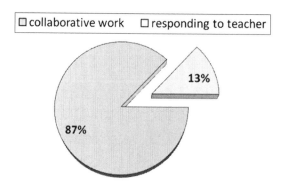

Figure 3. Distribution of non-teacher-talk time.

shoot off terminology and nor can you shoot off a sentence anywhere. This applies to both science and all other communications, right?' The teacher also invited students to notice how good writing is characterised by linguistic devices, which are necessary regardless of language. In checking Exercise 9, the teacher again used the IRF cycle to *review* how the sentences cohered into a well-written paragraph. While Exercise 8 provided implicit learning of cohesive devices, Exercise 9 very naturally prompted students into peer-peer instructional-discussions which explicitly analyzed and addressed discourse cohesion. By the time task correction was at question 7 [time-13.24], when the teacher asked 'so what is the word?' student S2 of the above transcript who, 13 minutes prior, did not know how to explain why D was an effective concluding sentence, answered, in English, 'this'. To evaluate whether students had indeed realised how word choices determine communication, the teacher continued:

S2: **this** relationship

T: This...questa...Allora se noi dovessimo scrivere un altro paragrafo, come potremmo modificare D in modo che possa essere utilizzato per *iniziare* il discorso? [*this...so, if we were to write another paragraph, how would we modify D so that it could be used to **start** the entire paragraph?*]

S(chorus): **The** relationship

Students' understanding that the *function* of a sentence can be changed by replacing an attended anaphoric *this* with the definite article is a good step towards academic literacy, regardless of language or content.

3.1.3. Sustained learning outcome

Increased awareness of academic discourse was evident two months following the lessons, when students were asked to write an ungraded essay showing what they recalled about heart anatomy. Interestingly, the high quality of learning can be exemplified through what weaker students wrote. Briefly, in Calabria where unemployment has hovered at 30% for several decades, teachers are reluctant to fail students since, if classes become too small, students are redistributed, reducing the number of classes and thus teaching posts the following year (Ting and Watts, 2008). Students may thus proceed through school regardless of their performance. Student, SV, is one such student, totally disaffected, uninvolved and unabashedly returning blank exam papers to the teachers. What is noteworthy of SV's essay two months following the lessons was that it was not blank (Figure 4). In fact, SV had first written '*Il cuore è costituito da 4 camere muscolari: atrio destro e atrio sinistro, ventricolo destro e ventricolo sinistro*' before deciding to also include a topic sentence, '*il sistema circolatorio è il trasporto di sangue ed è costituito dal*' which, as indicated with the curved line on the left, should come before *cuore*. However, as any good writer knows, changing one part of a text requires a revision of the existent: SV thus also added '*che a sua volta*' between '*cuore*' and '*è costituito....*' The final self-edited sentence with the [new additions] read, '[The circulatory system is the transport of blood (sic) and is comprised of] the heart [which in turn] is comprised of four muscular chambers: right atrium and left atrium, right ventricle and left ventricle.' Granted the logic in 'the circulatory system is the transport of blood' is imprecise, as also 'all those substances' (tutti quei materiali) which the circulatory system transports to and from cells (concept 2) and the fact that the *aorta* is not a vein

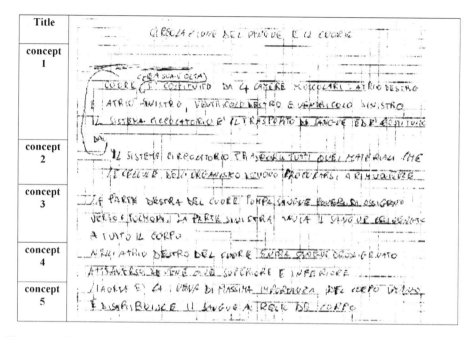

Figure 4. Essay written by a disaffected learner two months following the lessons.

but an artery (concept 4). However, SV chose 'substances' rather than 'stuff' (*cose*). Most importantly, although expressing himself in L1, SV had not only attained and retained learning-objectives 1–4 (see Table 1), he was showing signs of academic literacy.

A concern regarding CLIL is whether students fully comprehend concepts learnt through an FL and if they can verbalise this understanding, also in L1 (Dalton-Puffer 2007). And, can students do so within the limited learning time available? It may be essays from weak students such as SV which illustrate the potential of CLIL. In fact, the essay written by an average student (Figure 5) started by parroting so perfectly the sentences of the CLIL activities (Part 1) that the teachers wondered whether student had copied from a handout (see note at bottom of sample). Spelling mistakes of general purpose words with L1-cognates such as *sistema* (Part 1) and drop of the third person 's' (Part 5) actually assured us that the student was not copying. Analysis of the text showed that, while this student has notable mnemonic capabilities (Parts 1 and 3), she was, where necessary, able to manipulate both content information and language. For example, Part 2 shows a correct self-generated summary of micro-objective 1. Part 4 shows how the student readily adapted the original sentences from Exercise 12a regarding anatomy of the left side of the heart to correctly discuss the anatomical structures and processes occurring on the right side of the heart: content information had been successfully learnt. In addition, even in the simple listing of additional thoughts (Part 5), the student adjusted the sentences from Exercise 6 by removing the subordinating *which* so to suit her current communicative needs. Interestingly, this student is very shy, so much so that the teacher did not know she could use English so well.

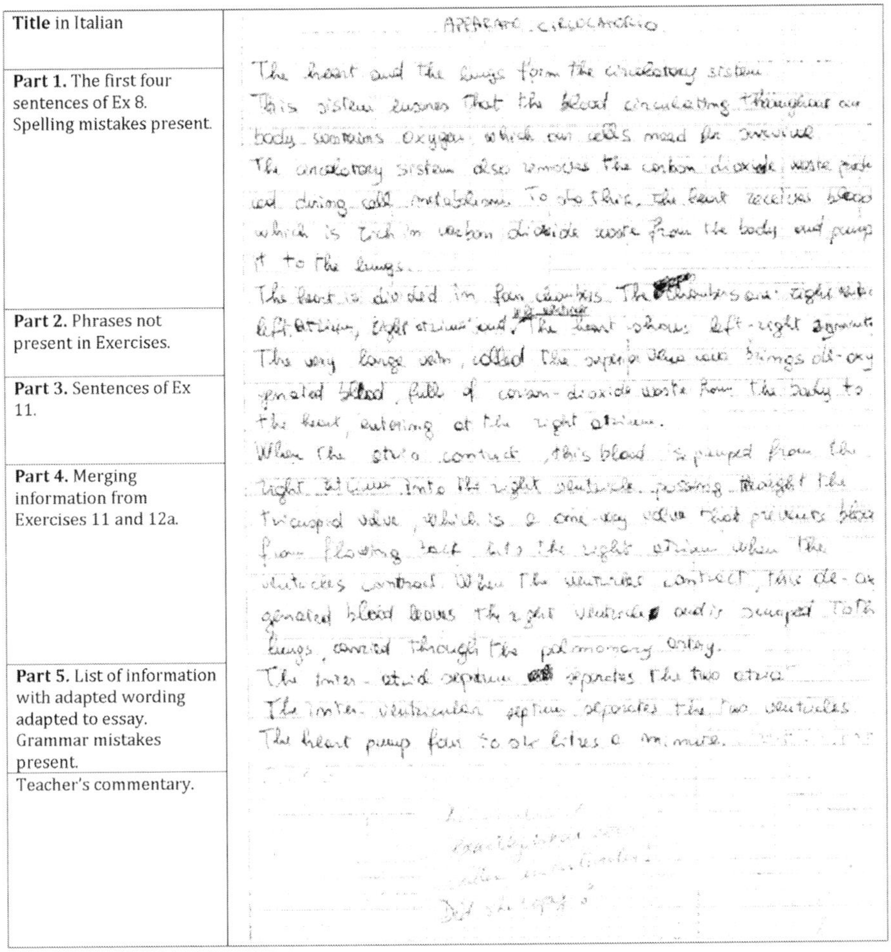

Title in Italian	APPARATO CIRCOLATORIO
Part 1. The first four sentences of Ex 8. Spelling mistakes present.	The heart and the lungs form the circulatory sistem. This sistem ensures that the blood circulating throughout our body contains oxygen which our cells need for survival. The circulatory sistem also removes the carbon dioxide waste produced during cell metabolism. To do this, the heart receives blood which is rich in carbon dioxide waste from the body and pumps it to the lungs.
Part 2. Phrases not present in Exercises.	The heart is divided in four chambers. The chambers are: right [illegible] left atrium, right atrium and [illegible]. The heart shows left-right asymmetry.
Part 3. Sentences of Ex 11.	The very large vein, called the superior vena cava brings de-oxygenated blood, full of carbon-dioxide waste from the body to the heart, entering at the right atrium.
Part 4. Merging information from Exercises 11 and 12a.	When the atria contract, this blood is pumped from the right atrium into the right ventricle passing through the tricuspid valve, which is a one-way valve that prevents blood from flowing back into the right atrium when the ventricles contract. When the ventricles contract, the de-oxygenated blood leaves the right ventricle and is pumped to the lungs, carried through the pulmonary artery.
Part 5. List of information with adapted wording adapted to essay. Grammar mistakes present.	The inter-atrial septum separates the two atria. The inter-ventricular septum separates the two ventricles. The heart pump four to six litres a minute.
Teacher's commentary.	[illegible]

Figure 5. Essay written by an average learner two months following the lessons.

3.2. Teachers' reflections

Our collective reflections on the lessons identified how CLIL prompted at least five changes in classroom dynamics which probably contributed to drawing even the weaker and shier students into the learning circle.

3.2.1. CLIL classroom dynamics which support learning

The first change involves attention to comprehensible instruction language: CLIL-Operand-1. Although there are no direct empirical studies based on academic texts, there is ample neurobiological research to indicate that academic texts are probably not highly 'brain compatible.' Using surface electrodes to record evoked response potentials (ERP), sentences such as 'he spread his toast with butter and socks' elicit a neuroelectrophysiological response (N400) following the semantically incongruent input, 'socks' (Kutas and Hillyard 1980). Likewise, sentences such as 'the horse raced by the barn fell' elicit neuroelectrophysiological responses (P-600) which reflect the reprocessing of *syntactically opaque* input (Hinojosa, MartIn-Loeches, and Rubia 2001).

Imagine how difficult it is for a learner to read and understand Excerpt 1 in Supplementary Materials which addresses the same learning objectives as the CLIL activities. If we remove unknown discipline-specific terminology, common words used in uncommon ways and unfamiliar ways of languaging we would remove 31% of the words and obtain:

> The human heart is a muscular= that ==== through the == and is one of the most == organs in the human body. The heart is divided into four main ==: the two == are called the left and right = and two ==== are called the right and left =.The two == are the == and the two == are the ==.

These remaining 52 words are void of content and offers little for language learning. While science education has recognised that science discourse is often off-putting, rendering science downright alienating (Halliday and Martin 1993), this way of languaging scientific understandings is the staple of science education, requiring several rereadings so to learn (or is it memorise?) enough for the exam (e.g., Bransford, Brown, and Cocking 1999). Lexically dense spoken scientific discourse, in no matter what language, does not make for enthralling input. Obliging teachers to be more language aware is probably the most significant way CLIL changes classroom dynamics.

Secondly, language aware teachers naturally become more content aware, questioning whether content information has been re-dimensioned into chewable aliquots, CLIL-Operand-3. This awareness is the second way CLIL changed classroom dynamics since content awareness prompted us to first decompose the topic of 'human heart' into a list of microlearning objectives. In delineating smaller learning-objectives (Figure 6), it was possible to then design learning tasks which moved students seamlessly towards a deeper level understanding of the topic at hand: the teachers chose an 'increasingly more powerful' arrow to reflect their observations of how students became increasingly more confident learners as the learning community seemed to grow.

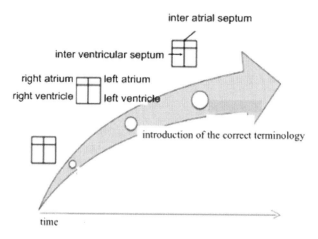

Figure 6. Seamless transition through smaller learning objectives builds students' confidence as learners.

Task-based learning probably accounts for the third reason even disaffected students joined in. Although weaker learners immediately assumed their bored observer stance, they soon became curious to see why their classmates were so engaged in seemingly purposeful discussions and conversations. And, since both language and content were comprehensible, weaker learners soon found themselves *successfully collaborating* to solve the language puzzles and complete their heart diagrams. Thus the fourth way CLIL made it possible for all learners to join in and stay in: since the tasks used an FL, the learning process was slowed down, enabling even the weaker to 'stay aboard.' In addition, since learning was regularly evaluated, both teachers and students themselves could identify and correct misconceptions in real time: nobody lagged behind.

These observations on task-based learning made the teachers realise that, in the past, while lecturing, they could not observe learning. Being able to observe the learning habits of each student enabled the teachers to provide, in real time, individualised suggestions on learning strategies. In addition, traditionally, slowing down meant entering a vicious cycle governed by weakness whereby information is constantly rehashed to prevent the weak and disaffected from actually sleeping. This sacrifices the enthusiasm and potential of stronger students. Using the CLIL activities, since knowledge-construction came through task completion, it was possible for the good learners to set the pace of learning within each group. However, since the micro-objectives came in digestible chunks, it was also possible for the good learners who finished first but were only themselves learning, to discuss new knowledge with the weaker learners of their group, providing explanations rather than simply the correct answer. The good thus pulled the weak along and slowing down did not mean diluting or rehashing the content.

Finally, the fifth way CLIL facilitated learning permeates beyond the CLIL classroom and returns to the issue of language and is related to how CLIL contributes to cultivating literacy. Granted academic language is rather difficult for students to comprehend and thus *learn from*, it is nonetheless necessary for our learners to become extremely comfortable with it. Indeed, why would an Italian teacher bother using an FL to teach her subject if not so her learners can also generate well-written texts in that FL? This is CLIL-Operand-2: can the learners use the target FL effectively to *obtain information, negotiate meaning, discuss hypotheses, construct knowledge,* and *convey understanding*? While being able to comprehend academic text/talk is a step in the right direction, full literacy is when an individual is also able to *write* and *speak* academically, should the need arise. Widespread anecdotal evidence lamenting the inability of students to write well (e.g., Pearson, Moje, and Greenleaf 2010) indicates that, years of *reading* coherently written textbooks does not guarantee the ability for *writing* coherently written texts (Benjamin 2005; Schleicher 2010). Full academic literacy, up to *production*, must therefore be cultivated, actively and systematically, even in L1 (Osborne 2010). In addition, the process of putting knowledge into written language moves the learner from hands-on learning into minds-on understanding (Wellington and Osborne 2001).

3.2.2. Benefits beyond the CLIL classroom?

A prime learning objective of the CLIL activities presented here was therefore to move learners from BICS (Basic Interpersonal Communication Skills) towards CALP (Cognitive Academic Language Proficiency). Referring to immigrant learners,

Cummins (1981) found that while BICS can be achieved after 2–3 years of immersion, CALP can take twice as long, but attainment determines these young people's future academic success: CALP must, therefore, be an objective in CLIL instruction (CLIL-Operand-2). Cummins' *Framework for Developing FL-Proficiency* (1984), which considers how cognitively demanding an FL-learning task is as a function of how familiar a communicative context is, has been used to guide CLIL materials development Coyle, Hood, and Marsh (2010) and can be further adapted for CLIL science education by considering the concept-cognitive load of the science concept at hand (Figure 7). Such a science-proficiency framework evaluates the *efficacy* of learning-tasks by intersecting how accessible the language of instruction is for the learner (CLIL-Operand-1) with how familiar and tangible the science concept can be rendered (van den Broek 2010: CLIL-Operand-3). Topics which are familiar, such as 'the heart', would allocate into Zones A and A.' Others such as *gluons* and *bosons*, much appreciated by subnuclear particle physicists but difficult to grasp for those outside their community, are examples of concepts allocating into Zones B and B.' While there are concepts in Zone B which we must study in school (e.g. atoms, electrons, metabolism), most scholastic-level science can be made accessible through language-aware learning processes which present concepts in chewable chunks. Adding on academic literacy, moves from Zone A towards minds-on learning in zone A.' Literacy development ensures more deep-level transferable understanding of concepts which learners will then need to grasp concepts in Zone B.

An unexpected result we would like to share echoes the aforementioned reports on how academic literacy determines academic success. We found that, although limited, learning through CLIL may have nonetheless improved students' general academic performance. This emerged when all the teachers of this CLIL class noted a significant increase in the end-of-year grade point average, especially of the weaker students (Table 4). In fact, of the four students who had failed the year prior, only one did worse by 0.1 points while the other three increased their grade points by an averaged advancement of 0.7 points. Improved academic performance was, not

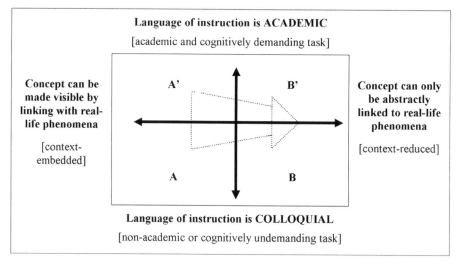

Figure 7. A science/academic-proficiency framework for evaluating the efficacy of science-learning tasks: adapted Cummins (1984: square brackets show original axial correlates).

Table 4. End-of-year average grades of the 19 learners.

Student	Overall final grade average: year prior to CLIL experience	Overall final grade average: year of CLIL experience	Difference
1	5.3	5.2	−0.1
2	5.4	5.8	0.4
3	5.4	6.4	1.0
4	5.6	6.3	0.7
5	6.8	7.1	0,3
6	6.8	7.4	0.6
7	7.0	7.7	0.7
8	7.0	7.5	0.5
9	7.1	7.1	0
10	7.1	7.6	0.5
11	7.4	7.2	−0.2
12	7.4	7.7	0.3
13	7.4	7.3	−0.1
14	7.5	7.4	−0.1
15	8.0	8.2	0.2
16	8.2	9.0	0.8
17	8.2	8.2	0
18	8.4	9.0	0.6
19	8.6	9.2	0.6
	Class average 7.08	Class average 7.44	

Notes: 6 = pass; up to 6 *Sufficiente* (in need amendment); 6–7 *Discreta*; 7–8 *Buona*; 9 *Ottima*.

surprisingly, also seen with the stronger students, with only three losing slightly on their already good grades, two maintaining their high grades but 10 improving their grades by an average of 0.51 points.

Whether only two CLIL lessons account for such improvements would require additional studies to verify, with the question being if even small amounts of training on academic literacy does indeed support overall academic performance (Cummins 1981, 1984; Pearson, Moje, and Greenleaf 2010; Webb 2010). However, it should be noted that, as discussed in Section 3.1.2, one of the rare moments of extended teacher talk concentrated learners' attention to the 'power of language' (Knorr-Cetina 1981; Fairclough 1991; David and Lemke 2000). Therefore, albeit very limited, attention to academic discourse was both intense and extremely overt. If we consider that *literacy* is rarely addressed anywhere else in the curriculum, even a brief encounter may have sufficed to give students that extra piece of 'insight' they needed to navigate academically languageD input and subsequently produce more effectively written essays, as did student SV.

4. Conclusions

Albeit an experienced science teacher, having 'only' B1-level EFL obliged Margherita to reconsider traditional teacher-centred lecturing: CLIL could not be 'just do it in English'. This 'linguistic limitation' of the content teacher is actually a blessing since it sensitises content experts to the fact that, even in L1, discipline-specific discourse often seems like an FL for those outside the discourse community (Wenger 1998; Halliday and Martin 1993). And, since learners must acquire discipline knowledge through an FL, CLIL teachers must consider whether their students understand the language of instructional input. Becoming more language aware naturally leads a

CLIL teacher to evaluate if content is also being presented in comprehensible aliquots. Therefore, in calling for *language aware instruction*, CLIL automatically also moves towards *content-aware education*. Since new content knowledge is being acquired through an FL, it is also necessary to constantly evaluate whether learners are learning what we intended: whether input has become intake. Any process that constantly evaluates both the comprehensibility of both language and content plus how well learning is taking place, focuses on *the process of learning* rather than *the act of teaching*. This alone makes for better education.

The results demonstrate that, through appropriately designed CLIL learning materials, the use of an FL for science education actually facilitated science learning. Being aware of learners' limited linguistic competence in the FL, CLIL teacher-talk is limited, leaving much more room for student-led interactions. Our findings corroborated those of Dalton-Puffer (2007, 32) who observed that CLIL classrooms are characterised by a predominance of 'class interaction [which accounts] for at least two thirds of all the talk'. In fact, since extensive teacher talk is rare, students cannot just wile away the time listening (or daydreaming) passively: they must do something. In this study, this something was CLIL learning tasks designed to optimise the quantity and quality of peer-to-peer interactions through which learners successfully attained micro-concepts which together, achieved the national curriculum. Although classroom exchanges rarely involved teacher-fronted explanations of content, students' essays collected two months following the CLIL lessons clearly confirm that content-learning was successful. More importantly, content knowledge was well consolidated, even in weaker learners. Interestingly, although the use of CLIL tasks greatly reduced teacher talk and seemed to slow down the learning process, neither content understanding nor language competence was diluted. In fact, when tasks are properly scaffolded between the content and language cognitive loads, learners can actively collaborate and construct not only new understandings regarding content but also cultivate academic language competence. Since this academic literacy is transferable between languages and across disciplines, the ability to confidently navigate academic discourse can contribute significantly to students' academic success.

CLIL has evolved from simply a way to increase FL exposure, *ergo* FL learning, into a pragmatic and effective approach for renovating education (Ting 2011). Interestingly, it is the more experienced teachers who immediately appreciate how and why CLIL can significantly potentiate their classroom practice: with years of less-than-satisfying classroom experience behind them, seeing CLIL work for the good, the bad and the disaffected, drawing all learners into the learning circle, provides an immense boost of professional energy. Planned well, a gradual nation-wide implementation of CLIL will be able to harness this energy successfully (e.g., Dalton-Puffer 2007; Lasagabaster and Ruiz de Zarobe 2010). In fact, into our second year of collaboration, Margherita is on her own: equipped with her unlimited content competence and empowered by the CLIL materials, plus some audio recordings for honing learners' pronunciation, Margherita is witnessing active knowledge construction at work, again, despite her 'limited English'. Since most of the world does not abound with Oxbridge graduates in science, history, maths, etc., delineating how teachers such as Margherita can comfortably use an FL to successfully move their content curriculum forward will contribute to successful bilingual education in non-immersion realities.

Notes

1. GAZZETTA UFFICIALE DELLA REPUBBLICA ITALIANA 24-12-2011, *Serie generale* – n. 299 http://www.uil.it/uilscuola/sites/default/files/dm-clill_gu_299_del_24_12_2011.pdf
2. Since this chapter represents the product of enthusiastic three-way collaboration between complementary professional roles and expertise, the authors are listed in alphabetical order. However, for the sake of academic merit, Grandinetti and Langellotti should be credited with the laborious transcription of the videos, obviously the teacher reflections (Section 3.2) and the organisation of the quantitative CLIL classroom data; Ting with the design of the CLIL-materials used, data analysis and research design and the writing of the chapter.
3. http://www.world-english.org/english500.htm

References

Benjamin, A. 2005. *Writing in the Content Areas*. Larchmont, NY: Eye on Education.
Bloome, D., and J. Lemke, eds. 2000. "The Disempowerment Game" *Linguistics and Education* 10: 391–458. http://www.sciencedirect.com/science/journal/08985898/10.
Boccardi, V. 2011. *Moduli di Biologia*. Brescia: La Scuola.
Bransford, J. D. 1979. *Human Cognition: Learning, Understanding, and Remembering*. Belmont: Wadsworth.
Bransford, J. D., A. L. Brown, and R. R. Cocking. 1999. *How People Learn: Brain, Mind, Experience and School*. New York: The National Academy of Sciences.
Coyle, D., P. Hood, and D. Marsh. 2010. *CLIL*. Cambridge: Cambridge University Press.
Cummins, J. 1981. "Age on Arrival and Immigrant Second Language Learning in Canada: A Reassessment1." *Applied Linguistics* II (2): 132–149. doi:10.1093/applin/II.2.132.
Cummins, J. 1984. *Bilingualism and Special Education: Issues in Assessment and Pedagogy*. Clevedon: Multilingual Matters.
Dalton-Puffer, C. 2007. *Discourse in Content and Language Integrated learning (CLIL) Classrooms*. Amsterdam: John Benjamins.
Denzin, N. K., and Y. Lincoln. 1994. *Handbook of Qualitative Research*. London: Sage.
Eisner, E. W. 1991. *The Enlightened Eye: Qualitative Inquiry and the Enhancement of Educational Practice*. New York: Macmillan.
Eurobarometer. 2006. *Europeans and Their Languages. Special Eurobarometer 243*. Brussels: European Commission.
Fairclough, N. 1991. *Discourse and Social Change*. Cambridge: Polity Press.
Goodson, I., and P. Sikes. 2001. *Life History Research in Educational Settings: Learning from Lives*. Buckingham: Open University Press.
Halliday, M. A. K., and J. R. Martin. 1993. *Writing Science*. London: Falmer Press.
Hargreaves, D. 1996. *Teaching as a Research-based Profession: Possibilities and Prospects*. London: Teacher Training Agency (Annual Lecture).
Hinojosa, J. A., M. MartIn-Loeches, and F. J. Rubia. 2001. "Event-Related Potentials and Semantics: An Overview and an Integrative Proposal." *Brain and Language* 78 (1): 128–139. doi:10.1006/brln.2001.2455.
Kandel, E. 2006. *In Search of Memory: The Emergence of a New Science of Mind*. New York: W.W. Norton.
Knorr-Cetina, K. D. 1981. *The Manufacture of Knowledge*. Oxford: Pergamon.
Kutas, M., and S. A. Hillyard. 1980. "Reading Senseless Sentences: Brain Potentials Reflect Semantic Incongruity." *Science* 207 (4427): 203–205. doi:10.1126/science.7350657.
Lasagabaster, D., and Y. Ruiz de Zarobe. 2010. *CLIL in Spain: Implementation, Results and Teacher*. Newcastle upon Tyne: Cambridge Scholars.
Lasagabaster, D., and J. M. Sierra. 2010. "Immersion and CLIL in English: More Differences Than Similarities." *ELT Journal* 64 (4): 367–375. doi:10.1093/elt/ccp082.
Mangen, A., and J. L. Velay. 2010. "Digitizing Literacy: Reflections on the Haptics of Writing." In *Advances in Haptics*, edited by M. H. Zadeh, 385–401. Rijeka, Croatia: InTech.

Marsh, D. 2002. *The Relevance and Potential of Content and Language Integrated Learning (CLIL) for Achieving MT+2 in Europe*. European Language Council Report. http://web.fu-berlin.de/elc/bulletin/9/en/marsh.html

Osborne, J. 2010. "Arguing to Learn in Science: The Role of Collaborative, Critical Discourse." *Science* 328 (5977): 463–466. doi:10.1126/science.1183944.

Pearson, P. D., E. Moje, and C. Greenleaf. 2010. "Literacy and Science: Each in the Service of the Other." *Science* 328 (5977): 459–463. doi:10.1126/science.1182595.

Robinson, P. 2011. "Task-based Language Learning: A Review of Issues." *Language Learning* 61: 1–36. doi:10.1111/j.1467-9922.2011.00641.x.

Schleicher, A. 2010. "Assessing Literacy across a Changing World." *Science* 328 (5977): 433–434. doi:10.1126/science.1183092.

Snow, C. E. 2010. "Academic Language and the Challenge of Reading for Learning about Science." *Science* 328 (5977): 450–452. doi:10.1126/science.1182597.

The Programme for International Student Assessment-Organization for Economic Co-operation and Development (PISA-OECD). 2006. http://www.oecd.org/dataoecd/15/13/39725224.pdf

Ting, Y. L. T. 2005. *The Value of Narrative Inquiry in Professional Development*. Rende: The University of Calabria Press.

Ting, Y. L. T. 2011. "CLIL...Not Only Not Immersion But Also Much More than the Sum of Its Parts." *ELT Journal* 65 (3): 314–317. doi:10.1093/elt/ccr026.

Ting Y. L. T., Miceli, C., Newell, J., and Parise, F. G. 2006. "Voices from the CLIL Classroom: What Do Subject Teachers, Language Teachers and Students Have to Say about What Makes for Successful CLIL." TESOL-Italy 31st National Conference, Napoli, November 3–4.

Ting, Y. L. T., and M. F. Watts. 2008. "Narrative Inquiry: Defogging Expatriate Expectations." In *Immigrant Academics and Cultural Challenges in a Global Environment*, edited by J. Femi and Kolapo, 73–106. Amherst: Cambria.

van den Broek, P. 2010. "Using Texts in Science Education: Cognitive Processes and Knowledge Representation." *Science* 328 (5977): 453–456. doi:10.1126/science.1182594.

Webb, P. 2010. "Science Education and Literacy: Imperatives for the Developed and Developing World." *Science* 328 (5977): 448–450. doi:10.1126/science.1182596.

Wellington, J., and J. Osborne. 2001. *Language and Literacy in Science Education*. New York: Open University Press.

Wenger, E. 1998. *Communities of Practice: Learning, Meaning, and Identity*. Cambridge: Cambridge University Press.

Supplementary material for this chapter can be found on page 165 of this volume

Genre-based curricula: multilingual academic literacy in content and language integrated learning

Francisco Lorenzo

School of Humanities, Pablo de Olavide University, Seville, Spain

> This study addresses academic literacy in content and language integrated learning (CLIL) secondary education. More precisely, this chapter focuses on attempts to meet modern standards for language competences set in areas like Europe, where the notion involves multilingual academic competence. The study centres on new proposals for language organisation in CLIL education based on genres resulting in a *multilingual genre map across the curriculum*. The feasibility of this model was proven in the author's national context in an attempt to improve language competence levels. The study provides a revision of the language theory in CLIL classroom practice that sits ill with traditional structural formalism and is better served through multilingual genre-based, functional semiotic models. Textual examples and genres will come from the area of History.

Introduction

A major factor in the quality of bilingual teaching is the proper matching of language and content, a process known with different names: sheltering, scaffolding or integration. However, despite the existence of various investigation strands around an issue which constitutes the core of content and language integrated learning (CLIL) – the *I* in the acronym for integration – further attention is needed in an area too often taken for granted.

To put this study into perspective, a revision of the research on the interface of language and content was made. The main issues on this front have been to date are as follows:

(1) The linguistic adaptation and grading of disciplinary content so that it becomes understandable for students with limited competence in the vehicular language, a process known as *rediscursification* (Musumeci 1996; Adger, Snow, and Christian 2003; Crossley et al. 2007; Lorenzo 2008).
(2) The layer of the language system wherein content and language should be integrated, i.e. whether the focus of integration should involve the lexico-grammar only – identifying the lexical and morphosyntactic items which correspond to the presentation of a maths lesson on *integers* or a music lesson on *medieval polyphony* – or whether, alternatively, there could be integration

at higher linguistic levels such as involving text types, macro-functions or genres (Mohan 1986; Mohan and Beckett 2003; Mohan and Slater 2005; Lorenzo and Moore 2010).

(3) The description of language behaviour in the CLIL classroom, and of the learning processes involved (Coonan 2007; Dalton-Puffer and Smit 2007; Dalton-Puffer, Nikula, and Smit 2010; Lorenzo 2007; Moore 2011).

(4) The specificities of the language of the disciplines and the particular difficulties that L2 students have to deal with in each: maths (Jäppinen 2005; Lemke 2002), science (Macken-Horarik 2002; Zwiers 2006) or history (Achugar 2009; Llinares and Morton 2010; Scheleppegrell and Colombi 2002).

Against the backdrop of this research on the interface between language and content, this chapter sets out to study integration at a textual level both in the L1 and L2. With this, we intend to respond to a request made by educational administrations which, in adding new vehicular languages in their former monolingual schools, have seen the need to provide new curriculum arrangements where integration of areas and languages are accounted for. The chapter will consider genre-based programmes as an adequate frame for subject and language integration in CLIL settings; genres as they appear not only in language courses but also more importantly in courses in which the focus is generally not on language per se, as is the case with history, science or technology. This will finally result in the proposal of a multilingual *genre map across the curriculum*, a selection of genres that form an articulated language curriculum and which will involve all the languages of schooling and all the disciplines. For reasons of space, the discussion here will focus mainly on the subject of history. The feasibility of this model was proven in the author's national context in an attempt to improve communicative language competence by embracing multilingual, genre-based, functional semiotic models.

Genre-based teaching and CLIL

Practice of sentential grammar units is said to contribute to real language competence only if they are seen within the larger frame of textual and/or cultural units – see Kress (2007) on the transition from breath units to textual units in communication and Mohan and Slater (2005) on social practice as a unit of culture that involves cultural knowledge and cultural action. On these bases, European language policies have attempted to consolidate and upgrade advanced literacy with programmes that highlight semantic units –macro-functions or genres – in all school disciplines, arrangements known under labels such as *integrated language curriculum* or *languages across the curriculum* (Bruce 2008; Vollmer 2006).

One such approach is the genre-based syllabus, which also aims at delineating a framework for overall language competence in different sociolinguistic environments: the workplace, the academy or the school. Various definitions in the literature underline its being indebted to classical rhetorical tradition; genres are defined as 'rhetorical actions that we draw on to respond to perceived repeated situations' (Hyland 2002, 116) or 'the rhetorical structures fundamental to various forms of communication in a culture' (Hyland 2004, 29). Furthermore, genres are seen as the textual result of social interaction and given the power granted to those who excel at their composition, the case is made that they should be the central language units in curricula to warrant equality in education (Feez 2001; Kress 2007).

As an approach to language education, genre programmes were originally related to the study and practice of communicative functions and notions, which motivated the former label *New Rhetoric* (Johns 2002). Alternative approaches have been the Languages for Specific Purposes strand, more focused on the genres produced by particular, usually professional, discourse communities (Bhatia 1993). However, genres have only become a major approach in education through the proposal of the Sydney School which, drawing on systemic functional linguistics, has substantiated the semantic components of the language as the focus of classroom discourse (Martin and Rose 2003; Hüttner 2007).

Notwithstanding major aspects like sequencing and implementation, genre-based programmes ultimately consist of an arrangement of texts set for reading and a sequence of genres that need to be produced in formal learning settings. Various terms have been used for these arrangements, and all of them revolve around the principle of cognitive processing during the reception and production of texts of increasing complexity: *genre chain* (Swales 1990, 2004), *mixed genres portfolio* (Hyland 2002) or *genre systems* (Hyland 2004). As such, it has become a very popular approach to language education and it is likely to draw more attention, if only because it represents the linguistic rationale that organisation for economic co-operation and development (OECD) international benchmarking systems such as programme for international student assessment (PISA) and progress in international reading literacy study embrace (OECD 2010).

Despite their popularity, genre-based programmes have been mostly used for monolingual education. Their occasional use for second language development includes the education of linguistic minorities of vernacular languages (see Thomson and Hari [2006] in South Africa), language immigrant education (see Azevedo [2010] for outstanding results in language competence of young immigrants in a reduced span of time in Sweden) or for the planning of foreign languages in official programmes (see the case of Spanish as a second language at Instituto Cervantes [2006]).

These instances aside, genre-based programmes have rarely – if ever – been adopted for full-fledged school programmes comprising all disciplines and vehicular languages as in multilingual CLIL schools. There are reasons to believe, however, that genre-based education sits well with the goal of academic, multilingual, advanced literacy and that genres could prove useful in CLIL implementation (Lorenzo, Casal, and Moore 2009; Lorenzo, Moore, and Casal 2011; Ruiz de Zarobe 2009). Various reasons uphold this belief.

Genre-based education language teaching is integrated with content

Genre level integration of content and language demands attention to the textual properties of the discourse of the disciplines: the discourse of science, the discourse of history, etc. Integration requires an understanding of the discourse features that communities of practice – historians, mathematicians or technologists – use to arrange their textual products since, when it comes down to it 'the macrostructure of a text is based on knowledge of the organization of events and situations in the real world' (Van Dijk and Kintsch 1983, 59).

The cognitive nature of the interface between language and content in the areas is well known. The transition from content to language is virtually demiurgic in the sense that content cognitive clusters of data structures are not visible but language is, content knowledge as mental schemata arranged in brain structures is not linear and language is. That being the case, a CLIL methodology would need to clarify how knowledge structures in the disciplines (causality in history or multiplicity in maths) match textual structures. This would imply the study of the function/form mappings in the discourse of the school disciplines and insights from the structure of area texts, the so-called *rhetorical moves* (Swales 1990, 2004). This approach would lead to the ultimate goal of this study: a genre map of area-related textual products that help develop multilingual academic literacy in CLIL.

Genre learning is based on discourse semantic units

Corpus analysis of CLIL classroom discourse shows that content and grammar relations are not fixed and consequently the integration of content and language cannot be expressed through one-to-one correspondences between sentential grammar units and content units (Lorenzo and Moore 2010). The CLIL teaching profession often believes that students need to know individual below sentence-level grammar items for content learning: compound progressive verb tenses to understand World War II in history, reciprocal pronouns for symbiotic relations in science and spatial prepositions to learn about the pulley system in technology in L2. However, students are more in need of semantic notions which link content and language, notions which for the said content topics could be contrasting past actions, duality and movement in space. Therefore, a genre-based approach to CLIL education would rely more on formulaic sequences and fixed sentence fragments related to content units than sequences of grammar rules. Needless to say, this calls for a linguistic approach above the level of the sentence which incorporates discourse and pragmatic factors into its grammatical framework. Grammar theories of this kind include systemic functional grammar (Halliday and Hasan 2006) and other recent contributions like construction grammar (Salmon 2010).

Genre learning needs attention to formal semiotic components

Genre theorists repeatedly hold that functional aspects of language and genres cannot be acquired through occasional unstructured language contact or semiotic osmosis (Eggins and Martin 2003). A systematic awareness-raising and practice of the components of texts is necessary for genre acquisition. Genre methodology can inform CLIL on how to avoid language being taken for granted, a common malpractice of content teachers in bilingual settings which results in *sink or swim* situations. Moreover, content teachers are eminently qualified to undertake this kind of multilingual integrated language education for one major reason: they are knowledgeable of their area content genres and will feel their teaching is legitimate. Content teachers in bilingual settings, for many of whom grammar teaching is an alien field and supposedly beyond their area responsibilities, report uneasiness when they become involved in explicit language instruction. However, when it comes to drawing students' attention to the formal linguistic properties of their area genres – a commercial memo for business teachers, a fieldwork observation sheet in science or an arithmetic problem in maths – their involvement in the task is seen as wholly appropriate.

Genre-based multilingual curriculum: a case from monolingual Southern Europe

The Eurydice (2006) report on CLIL in Europe shows the wide application of educational bilingualism in many latitudes of the continent. In Andalusia, an educationally autonomous region in wider Spain, several CLIL aspects have received attention. Despite the high approval rate amongst stakeholders and the sustained L2 competence gains of the CLIL network, an assessment and evaluation of the bilingual sections programme (Lorenzo, Casal, and Moore 2009) revealed shortcomings in some areas. Chief among them was teachers' difficulties with the process of content and language integration, the coordination of disciplinary and language teachers, the development of specifically designed CLIL material and, in close relation to the ends of this chapter, the lack of a comprehensive language programme which would set goals and tasks for all languages and areas in the curriculum.

As a result, the local administration took action with a number of projects worth quoting in case it might provide for other CLIL networks: the production of an open-access bilingual textbook library surpassing 4000 pages of ready-to-use CLIL lessons, the publication of self-teaching programmes for CLIL teachers' in-service training and the publication of genre-based materials for bilingual schools, including implementation guidelines and sample units (Junta de Andalucía 2008, 2010, 2011).

Among other collaborations with the administration, this author – as part of a team of researchers and secondary schoolteachers – was involved in the production of a multilingual academic programme across the curriculum, which in essence consists of a *genre map* covering a full educational level (a 2-year course in post-compulsory education). The genre map involved content areas (maths, science or history) and language areas which contributed to an overall genre repository with genres: (1) in the school's first language, (2) in the second languages used to teach content in CLIL courses, (3) in a second language in FL teaching and (4) in classical languages (Latin and Greek were adds-on in the curriculum). This new approach was designed as a guideline for language programming in CLIL educational curricula. Following the structure of the European language portfolio, students were asked to compile all the discursive products created and hence produce a genre archive. The implementation of this approach in schools has received attention from the local High Inspectorate and has provided promising results in the advance of academic literacy as measured by PISA standards (Goméz and Arcos 2007). Later, the initiative has been further pursued by the Spanish Ministry of Education, and an appointed committee is currently working on a full multilingual genre proposal that is to be implemented statewide under the label *Proyecto Lingüístico de Centro (School Language Programme*; Organismo Autónomo de Programas Europeos 2011).

Table 1 shows a section of such a genre map. In it, the science area encourages students to engage with genres such as the scientific chronicle and fieldwork notes. For history, a course that will be further studied below, the task was to produce a timeline and read annals. In the course of philosophy where the issue was the 'Logical structure of thought and physical reality', the textual demands centred on watching an online philosophy lecture from a virtual repertoire of academic talks and producing a verse in the Japanese tradition (haiku) whereby the theme of the lesson is

Table 1. A genre map section of a CLIL program.

Contemporary science (English)	Spanish language and linguistics (Spanish)	Philosophy and citizenship (Spanish)	English as a foreign language (English)	Mathematics (Spanish)	Contemporary History (English)
Innovation and technological developments Input: the research article Output: patent registration form	The technological challenges to humanism Input: the scientific research protocol Output: the abstract	Argumentation and fallacy Input: the philosophical essay Output: the philosophical digression	Getting a position in the hi-tech job market Input: the news item Output: the work interview	Polynomial equations Input: the maths power point presentation Output: the theorem	The Cold War. Input: The parliamentary speech Output: the timeline
The human species Input: the scientific chronicle Output: fieldwork notes	Creative writing and poetic experience Input: computer-generated short stories Output: the haiku	The logical structure of thought. Input: the virtual academic talk Output: the outline	The symbolic species Input: diaries Output: observation sheets	Probability and infinite dimensional analysis Input: The scientific essay Output: the oral presentation	The European Construction Input: Constitution excerpts Output: the historical essay

Note: All the lesson titles have been translated into English to keep language consistency throughout the chapter. Originally, the textual products demanded from students were either in English or Spanish as it was a bilingual programme, and these were the vehicular languages of the courses. The actual language used in each particular course appears in brackets.
The words 'input' and 'output' in the boxes mean, respectively, the genres that students received and the genres students produced.

encapsulated as an axiom. Language courses include academic genres that students need to develop as part of their overall literacy competence and other types of text related to their future professional careers. In the English course, in line with a typical English as a Foreign Language approach, student's role play a job interview and browse a job offer section in a financial newspaper when they do the lesson, *Getting a position in the hi-tech job market*. Even courses on so-called non-communicative languages like Latin involve students in discursive practice – translating adapted texts and in an oral genre of Latin tradition: the *controversia*. Other textual types included writing Pompeian style graffiti or funeral inscriptions in Latin. In short, what the table intend is to convey at a glance that all subjects, without exception, must make textual contributions and this takes the shape of a genre map.

The project has been instrumental in providing guidelines for content and language integration and may be inspirational for other CLIL settings. The following section looks at different routes which might be taken to further refine the proposal.

Key variables for genre selection

However inspirational, the model proposed might have been – and CLIL schools in Andalusia certainly used it to comply with the administrative requirement to formulate the integrated curriculum – its programming of genres for textual reception and production was somewhat random. The model was inclusive of all languages and areas and had genres as a cornerstone for textual production and reception but it lacked a clear path for genre selection based on cognitive and textual criteria. In view of this limitation, this section sets forth principles for the elaboration of a graded sequence of texts of increasing textual complexity that could gear the growth of academic language in the various tongues used at CLIL schools in secondary education. The section will discuss four macro-variables which help draw a comprehensive genre map including all areas and languages, and their respective teachers, in a coordinated way. For the sake of precision, examples will come from the discipline of history only, although the discussion claims full validity for other subjects.

It must be added at this point that the study of the linguistic dimension of school subjects is high on the agenda of European language policies, with on-going programmes to make content teachers mindful of the language properties of their areas (see Beacco [2010] for an inspirational frame of reference for the development of *historical literacy*).

Subject area genres

Historians often refer to their area as discursive construction, a linguistic reconstruction of the past by an omniscient teller. It follows from this that the linguistic rendition of History as a discipline must have some bearing on its learning and understanding. From the point of view of content, the learning of history demands an internal construction of the past world. In its barest forms, history is a sequence of content schemata, data strings upon which students learn and form historical constructs such as conflict, liberation, secession, union, warfare or more gestalt categories like cause and consequence. As a result, students transfer these new knowledge structures into their world knowledge and develop a worldview and a transmitted ideology (Coffin 2006; Christie and Maton 2011). Of interest, here is that

Table 2. A genre-based syllabus for a CLIL history course.

	L1	L2
Input genres		
Argumentative	Sermon Parliamentary speech Libel Panegyric Poster	Historical argument case Historical argument and practice
Expository	Edict Proclamation decree Estate concession Capitulation act Treaty Bill of rights	Historical paper Historical dissertation Historical research report
Descriptive	Chorology Chorography	Chorology Chorography
Narrative	Chronicle News pamphlets Cosmogony Sagas Annals Biographies	Chronicle News pamphlets Cosmogony Sagas Annals Biographies
Instructive	Historical timeline Social pyramid	Historical timeline Social pyramid
Output genres		
Argumentative	Historical argument case Historical argument and practice	
Expository	Historical paper Historical dissertation Historical timeline Historical research report	
Descriptive	Historical summary Historical essay review	Historical summary Historical essay review
Narrative	Historical case study report	Historical case study report
Instructive	Historical Q&A exercise History quiz In-class historic essay	Historical Q&A exercise History quiz In-class historic essay

the construction of historical knowledge rests upon a number of genres which involve all possible macro-structures and text typologies: argumentative, expository, descriptive, narrative and instructive. Beyond this basic textual typology, there is a very wide range of history genres with diverse componential organisation (the above-mentioned rhetorical moves). History genres include primary sources (bills of rights, speeches, placards); secondary sources, i.e. the telling of history (chronicles, biographies, annals) and academic genres for the learning of history only (historic timeline, historical essay review). The selection of the appropriate items of the historic genre set into an articulated whole with the rest of the areas is the contribution of history to language education. Table 2 features a whole selection of historic genres that could be used in CLIL upper secondary education with students with an advanced level of L1 and an intermediate level of L2 which permits their partial learning of content through a language other than their L1. More details on the rationale of the table follow below.

Language status

Traditionally, learning history through a second language has been thought to add a bonus to the education of students as they are empowered when given access to alternative reconstructions of the past incorporating alternative voices, alternative languages. That was the reason, in post-war Europe with the rebirth of bilingual programmes, why Germany and neighbouring France agreed to teach history courses in their reciprocal languages. The rationale was that students were thought to gain in intellectual sophistication and be empowered with the linguistic means to interpret the past beyond the narrow-mindedness of monolingualism if history was learnt in the language of the other (Vázquez 2007). Other similar cases have been unsuccessful. A case in point is the teaching of History in the Middle East, which attempted a new multilingual focus with the publication of *Learning each other's historical narrative: Palestinians and Israelis*. This history handbook for ninth and tenth graders which used both Hebrew and Arabic was considered inappropriate by both sides, who thought historical conditions were not ripe to concede the other's accounts of their common history (Adwan and Bar-on 2003).

However, the teaching of history through a second language can also undermine learning, as research into the teaching of history courses through a majority language to immigrant students has shown. The discourse of history involves functions – recording, explaining and/or arguing about the past – for which advanced linguistic resources are necessary (Coffin 2006; Scheleppegrell and Colombi 2002; Achugar 2009). For L2 users, understanding and producing historical narratives are not aided by latent meanings, convoluted syntax, cline to abstraction and the often biased cause and effect links. The methods employed to integrate language and content are various: deconstructing historical discourse, studying bias through the lens of historical thinking and enhancing and labelling discourse chunks with their semantic functions (Zwiers 2006).

In the end, a full genre map needs to account for the fact that genre selection must be streamlined according to the levels of students in the given language and that historical discourse cannot exceed students' language competence. The genre components of Table 2 provide for this.

Text typology

The line drawn between texts and genres is not clear and conceptual overlapping is not uncommon in textual classifications. Some formulations conceive of genres as abstract ideas because 'what we see are texts, not genres' (Hyland 2004, 13). Schools like systemic functional linguistics simply do not distinguish between the concepts – texts and genres – preferring more general categories of rhetorical basic structures called macro-genres.

Terminological considerations aside, most genre-based programmes, have tried to provide full coverage of the best known text typologies: argumentative, expository, descriptive, narrative and instructive texts. Historical genres can be listed for all these text types, as in Table 2. As one of the most basic and familiar text types, personal recounts follow the structure of oral narratives well known to children prior even to the development of literacy. More elaborated rhetorical text types are used for advanced historical discourse functions: the rendition of facts in time (biographies, historical recounts) or the development of cause and agency (accounts and explanations). The highest degree of discourse complexity appears with the rendition of multiple causes and effects, a level in which writers can show critical attitudes and generate new discourses (expositions and discussions). As is mentioned in critical studies writings (Martin and Rose 2003; Martin, Maton, and Matruglio 2010), the discourse of history has two major turning points: the comprehension and production of causation and, at a later point in language growth, the comprehension and production of multiple factorial causality. With this classification in mind, Table 2 provides a parameter that could benchmark conceptual and linguistic historical content complexity in a second language.

One step further in the analysis of the texture of history is the study of its rhetorical structure. By way of example, the account of the handover of La Florida from Spanish to American sovereignty through the Adams-Onis real estate sale document lends itself to both historical and linguistic analyses, simultaneously. Compound analysis would look not only at the historical conditions around the event but also at the genre structure of the document. Students would learn that such a genre involves a number of textual moves: the presentation of the particulars, the description of the assets and the list of terms and conditions that frame the agreement. Needless to say, the content of the area is part of that structure and students learn the linguistic categories alongside the history content.

This integrated scheme has one further advantage: content teachers have an implicit knowledge of the textual organisation of their particular genres. Unlike the ordinary reader or even the professional linguist, CLIL history practitioners have an implicit knowledge on the rhetorics of historical genres such as cosmogony, chronicle or treaty. This being so, the organisation of an integrated curriculum along genres truly involves content teachers, who can teach the idiomaticity of the historical expressions used, present language functions students may lack, and scaffold language difficulties.

In close relation to the varying textual demands of different genre types, the classification in Table 2 is based upon the consideration that at intermediate levels of language competence – like those found in CLIL settings – the capacity to produce genres of an argumentative or expository kind is very limited, given the linguistic demands of these textual types. It must be noted that among the discursive functions found in genre types involving factorial explanations, the following can be found: expressing the internal organisation of factors, the intervention of generic participants or the expression of judgement. The proper rendering of these functions in a second language implies the use of multiple embeddednes, long textual units and structures like complex nominals, to mention only some of the major indices of syntactic complexity (Lu 2010).

Input and output genres

Finally, the proposal here incorporates a clear division between the texts students receive and the texts that they produce. The reason for this balance is not only that there is a tendency for bilingual classroom discourse to focus on receptive skills but also that without careful planning of students' textual interventions and the context in which they will be produced, their production will be lacking in accuracy and appropriateness. Llinares and Morton (2010) have traced CLIL secondary school students' discourse in the history class. Their findings do not only recognise students' incorrect interpretations of historical processes: 'in lower secondary grades, students may see history in terms of biographical narratives in which historical events are explained by the actions of people rather than by more abstract historical processes' (2010, 49), they also observe that students' interventions change across classroom situations in such a way that more numerous, richer and more varied historical explanations are produced in interviews than in classroom discussions. It seems to be that historical content is best presented when the student can rest upon other peers to scaffold their messages and produce complete answers with more historical content; an arrangement which allows for some attention relief when peers in the conversation fill the gaps that students leave, especially in a second language.

If output deserved attention, that is also the case with input in historical discourse. Oteiza (2009) has scrutinised historical content in secondary school textbooks to find that at times linguistic resources are used to systematically hide agentivity when reporting controversial historical events like *coups d'etat*. For that reason, input also needs to be considered so students can have a proper understanding of historical categories and facts. CLIL History teachers need to find a balance between primary sources in their original form without any further linguistic adjustments and other textual sources which mediate the narration of history with discursive devices that make content understandable (Lorenzo 2008). In the end, the input/output axis in our genre map refers to the concept of *sayability* and *hearability*, the potential for communicative participation that students can achieve both in classrooms and outside.

In the genre map in Table 2, primary source genres are not considered input genres in an L2 in the argumentative and expository categories. As mentioned above, arguments in a sermon or an edict use language resources which far exceed CLIL students' interlanguage. Language grading in the form of adjustments is needed and once this process is done, the input text is not a primary source anymore since a historian or a teller has intervened and mingled with the original text. This is a well-known fact in historiography, hence the rendering of history as a discursive creation.

Another factor for the classification of genres in the table is that some input genres in an L2 can be output genres in an L1, i.e. ideally students will reach a level of historic expertise and L1 language command to give their own rendering of the past.

Conclusion

As regards language-related aims in CLIL settings, content teachers do not only contribute to second language competence, they are also responsible for the development of multilingual academic literacy. Our main thrust here is that to this end, content and language teacher collaboration should first involve the drafting of a road map for classroom discourse. Based on this cooperative scheme, students would be exposed to and would produce a number of genres involving many areas and languages. This we have called a multilingual genre map across the curriculum.

Although the study reports real CLIL implementation, some crucial areas remain to be addressed. Future research is needed on the interface between area content genres and their actual rhetorical texture, a research strand with implications not only for second language learning but also for language education in general. Also, future multilingual genre map exploration will cast some light on the core concept of integration, which leaves teachers feeling lost, in their own words, like making 'stabs in the dark' (Cammarata and Tedick 2012, 257). Advanced multilingual literacy, like all complex issues, will demand complex remedies, and one-sided individual moves of teachers or areas may be insufficient for the challenge. The scheme report shows that whole-school coordinated plans, for all their complexity, are worth being given a chance.

Acknowledgements

This chapter was done under the auspices of the ConCLIL project funded by the Academy of Finland. We want to express our gratitude to Prof. Tarja Nikula at the Center of Applied Language Studies (University of Jyväskylä) for her leadership in this project. We also want to thank the two anonymous reviewers for their insightful comments and Yolanda Ruiz de Zarobe for her assistance and advice as the guest editor of this volume.

References

Achugar, M. 2009. "Designing Environments for Teaching and Learning History in Multilingual Contexts." *Critical Inquiry in Language Studies* 6 (1): 39–62. doi:10.1080/15427580802679377.
Adger, C. T., C. Snow, and D. Christian. 2003. *What Teachers Need to Know about Language.* Washington, DC: Center for Applied Linguistics.
Adwan, S., and D. Bar-on. 2003. *Learning Each Other's Historical Narrative: Palestinians and Israelis.* Beit Jallah: Prime Publication. http://vispo.com/PRIME/leohn1.pdf
Azevedo, C. 2010. *Will the Implementation of Reading to Learn in Stockholm Schools Accelerate Literacy Learning for Disadvantage Students and Close the Achievement Gap?* Multilingual Research Institute: A report on school-based Action Research. http://www.readingtolearn.com.au/images/pdf/October/stockholm%20r2l%20report.pdf
Beacco, J. C. 2010. *Items for a Description of Linguistic Competence in the Language of Schooling Necessary for Learning/Teaching History. An Approach with Reference Points.* Brussels: Language Policy Division, Council of Europe. http://www.coe.int/t/dg4/linguistic/Source/Source2010_ForumGeneva/1_LIS-History2010_en.pdf
Bhatia, V. K. 1993. *Analysing Genre: Language Use in Professional Settings.* London: Longman.
Bruce, I. 2008. *Academic Writing and Genre.* London: Continuum.
Cammarata, L., and D. J. Tedick. 2012. "Balancing Content and Language in Instruction: The Experience of Immersion Teachers." *The Modern Language Journal* 96: 251–269. doi:10.1111/j.1540-4781.2012.01330.x.
Christie, F., and K. Maton. 2011. *Disciplinarity: Functional Linguistic and Sociological Perspectives.* London: Continuum.
Coffin, C. 2006. "Reconstructing Personal Time as Collective Time: Learning the Discourse of History." In *Language and Literacy: Functional Approaches*, edited by R. Whittaker, M. O'Donnell, and A. McCabe, 15–45. London: Continuum.
Coonan, C. M. 2007. "Insider Views of the CLIL Class Through Teacher Self Observation-Introspection." *International Journal of Bilingual Education and Bilingualism* 10: 625–646. doi:10.2167/beb463.0.
Crossley, S. A., P. McCarthy, M. Louwerse, and D. McNamara. 2007. "A Linguistic Analysis of Simplified and Authentic Texts." *The Modern Language Journal* 91 (1): 15–30. doi:10.1111/j.1540-4781.2007.00507.x.
Dalton-Puffer, C., and U. Smit, eds. 2007. *Empirical Perspectives on CLIL Classroom Discourse.* Frankfurt: Peter Lang.
Dalton-Puffer, C., T. Nikula, and U. Smit, eds. 2010. *Language Use and Language Learning in CLIL Classrooms.* Amsterdam: John Benjamins.
Eggin, S., and J. Martin. 2003. "El contexto como género: una perspectiva lingüística funcional [Context as Genre: A Functional Linguistic Perspective]." *Signos* 36 (1): 85–105. doi:10.4067/S0718-09342003005400005.
Eurydice. 2006. *Content and Language Integrated Learning (CLIL) at School in Europe.* Brussels: European Commission. http://www.coe.int/t/dg4/linguistic/Source/Source2010_ForumGeneva/1_LIS-History2010_en.pdf
Feez, S. 2001. *Text-Based Syllabus Design.* Sydney: Macquaire University.

Goméz, A., and D. Arcos. 2007. "Plan de mejora de la competencia lingüística: Elaboración del proyecto lingüístico de centro [Improving Language Competence: School Genre Maps]." *Avances en Supervisión Educativa. Revista de la Asociación de Inspectores de Educación de España* 7, 13–27. http://www.adide.org/revista/index.php?option=com_content&task=view&id=224&Itemid=49

Halliday, M., and R. Hasan. 2006. "Retrospective on SFL and Literacy." In *Language and Literacy: Functional Approaches*, edited by R. Whittaker, M. O'Donnell, and A. McCabe, 15–45. London: Continuum.

Hüttner, J. I. 2007. *Academic Writing in a Foreign Language:* An Extended Genre Analysis of Student Texts. Frankfurt am Main: Peter Lang.

Hyland, K. 2002. "Genre: Language, Context and Literacy." *Annual Review of Applied Linguistics* 22 (1): 113–135. http://dx.doi.org/10.1017/S0267190502000065

Hyland, K. 2004. *Genre and Second Language Writing.* Ann Arbor, MI: University of Michigan Press.

Instituto Cervantes. 2006. *Plan curricular del Instituto Cervantes* [Instituto Cervantes Official Curriculum]. Madrid: Biblioteca Nueva.

Jäppinen, A.-K. 2005. "Thinking and Content Learning of Mathematics and Science as Cognitional Development in Content and Language Integrated Learning (CLIL): Teaching Through a Foreign Language in Finland." *Language and Education* 19 (2): 147–168. doi:10.1080/09500780508668671.

Johns, A., ed., 2002. *Genre in the Classroom: Multiple Perspectives.* Mawhaw: Lawrence Erlbaum.

Junta de Andalucía. 2008. *El Curriculum integrado de las lenguas* [A Language Integrated Curriculum]. Sevilla: Consejería de Educación. http://www.juntadeandalucia.es/averroes/impe/web/contenido?pag=/contenidos/B/InnovacionEInvestigacion/ProyectosInnovadores/Plurilinguismo/Seccion/CVIntegrado/cil

Junta de Analucía. 2010. *Proyecto lingüistico de centro* [A School Genre Map]. Sevilla: Consejería de Educación. http://www.juntadeandalucia.es/educacion/webportal/web/proyecto-linguistico-centro

Junta de Andalucía. 2011. *Biblioteca de materiales AICLE* [The CLIL Lesson Archives]. Sevilla. Consejería de Educación. http://www.juntadeandalucia.es/educacion/nav/contenido.jsp?pag=/Contenidos/OEE/programasinternacionales/AICLE/materiales

Kress, G. 2007. "Meaning, Learning and Representation in a Social Semiotic Approach to Multimodal Communication." In *Language and Literacy: Functional Approaches*, edited by R. Whittaker, M. O'Donnell, and A. McCabe, 16–37. London: Continuum.

Lemke, J. L. 2002. "Multimedia Genres for Scientific Education and Science Literacy." In *Developing Advanced Literacy in First and Second Languages*, edited by M. J. Scheleppegrell and C. Colombi, 21–44. Mawhaw: Erlbaum.

Llinares, A., and T. Morton. 2010. "Historical Explanations as Situated Practice in Content and Language Integrated Learning." *Classroom Discourse* 1 (1): 46–65. doi:10.1080/19463011003750681.

Lorenzo, F. 2007. "An Analytical Framework of Language Integration in L2-Content Based Courses." *Language and Education* 22: 502–515. doi:10.2167/le708.0.

Lorenzo, F. 2008. "Instructional Discourse in Bilingual Settings: An Empirical Study of Linguistic Adjustments in Content and Language Integrated Learning." *Language Learning Journal* 36 (1): 21–33. doi:10.1080/09571730801988470.

Lorenzo, F., and P. Moore. 2010. "On the Natural Emergence of Language Structures in CLIL. Towards a Theory of European Educational Bilingualism." In *Language Use and Language Learning in CLIL Classrooms*, edited by C- Dalton-Puffer, T. Nikula, and U. Smit, 23–38. Amsterdam: John Benjamins.

Lorenzo, F., S. Casal, and P. Moore. 2009. "The Effects of Content and Language Integrated Learning in European Education: Key Findings from the Andalusian Bilingual Sections Evaluation Project." *Applied Linguistics* 31: 418–442. doi:10.1093/applin/amp041.

Lorenzo, F., P. Moore, and S. Casal. 2011. "On Complexity in Bilingual Research: The Causes, Effects, and Breadth of Content and Language Integrated Learning: A reply to Bruton." *Applied Linguistics* 32: 450–455. doi:10.1093/applin/amr025.

Lu, X. 2010. "Automatic Analysis of Syntactic Complexity in Second Language Writing." *International Journal of Corpus Linguistics* 15: 474–496. doi:10.1075/ijcl.15.4.02lu.

Macken-Horarik, M. 2002. "Something to Shoot for: A Systemic Functional Approach to Teaching Genre in Secondary School Science." In *Genre in the Classroom: Multiple Perspectives*, edited by A. John, 64–79. Mawhaw: Lawrence Erlbaum.

Martin, J. R., and D. Rose. 2003. *Working with Discourse: Meaning Beyond the Clause*. London: Continuum.

Martin, J. R., K. Maton, and E. Matruglio. 2010. "Historical Cosmologies: Epistemology and Axiology in Australian Secondary School History Discourse." *Signos* 43: 433–463. doi:10.4067/S0718-09342010000500003.

Mohan, B. 1986. *Language and Content*. Reading MA: Addison-Wesley.

Mohan, B., and G. H. Beckett. 2003. "A Functional Approach to Research on Content-Based Language Learning: Recasts in Causal Explanations." *The Modern Language Journal* 87: 421–432. doi:10.1111/1540-4781.00199.

Mohan, B., and T. Slater. 2005. "A Functional Perspective on the Critical 'theory/Practice' Relation in Teaching Language and Science." *Linguistics and Education* 16 (2): 151–172. doi:10.1016/j.linged.2006.01.008.

Moore, P. 2011. "Collaborative Interaction in Turn-Taking: A Comparative Study of European Bilingual (CLIL) and Mainstream (MS) Foreign Language Learners in Early Secondary Education." *International Journal of Bilingual Education and Bilingualism* 14: 531–549. doi:10.1080/13670050.2010.537741.

Musumeci, D. 1996. "Teacher-Learner Negotiation in Content-Based Instruction: Communication at Cross-Purposes." *Applied Linguistics* 17: 286–325. doi:10.1093/applin/17.3.286

OECD. 2010. *PISA 2009 Results: What Students Know and Can Do – Student Performance in Reading, Mathematics and Science (Volume I)*. http://browse.oecdbookshop.org/oecd/pdfs/browseit/9810071E.PDF.

Organismo Autónomo de Programas Europeos. 2011. *Proyecto Lingüístico de Centro* [School Language Genre Map]. Madrid: Ministerio de Educación. http://proyectolinguisticodecentro.es/

Oteíza, T. 2009. "Solidaridad ideológica en el discurso de la historia: Tensión entre orientaciones monoglósicas y heteroglósicas [Ideological Solidarity in the Historical Discourse: Tension Between Monoglossic and Heteroglossic Orientations]." *Revista Signos* 42: 219–244.

Ruiz de Zarobe, Y. 2009. *Content and Language Integrated Learning: Evidence from Research in Europe*. Clevedon: Multilingual Matters.

Salmon, W. N. 2010. "Formal Idioms and Action: Toward a Grammar of Genres." *Language and Communication* 30: 211–224. doi:10.1016/j.langcom.2010.01.002.

Scheleppegrell, M. J., and M. C. Colombi. 2002. *Developing Advanced Literacy in First and Second Languages*. Mawhaw: Lawrence Erlbaum.

Swales, J. M. 1990. *Genre Analysis*. Cambridge: Cambridge University Press.

Swales, J. M. 2004. *Research Genres: Explorations and Applications*. Cambridge: Cambridge University Press.

Thomson, C., and M. Hari. 2006. "Implementing the Genre Approach in a South African School." In *Language and Literacy: Functional Approaches*, edited by R. Whittaker, M. O'Donnell, and A. McCabe 56–72. London: Continuum.

Van Dijk, T., and W. Kintsch. 1983. *Strategies of Discourse Comprehension*. New York: Academic Press.

Vázquez, G. 2007. "Models of CLIL: An Evaluation of its Status Drawing on the German Experience." *A Critical Report on the Limits*, Revista Española de Lingüística Aplicada, Número Monográfico, 95–112.

Vollmer, H. J. 2006. *Language Across the Curriculum*. Brussels: Language Policy Division, Council of Europe. http://www.coe.int/t/dg4/linguistic/Source/Prague07_LangCom_VollmerEd_EN.doc.

Zwiers, J. 2006. "Integrating Academic Language, Thinking, and Content: Learning Scaffolds for Non-Native Speakers in the Middle Grades." *Journal of English for Academic Purposes* 5: 317–332. doi:10.1016/j.jeap.2006.08.005.

Discussion: towards an educational perspective in CLIL language policy and pedagogical practice

Jasone Cenoz

Department of Research Methods in Education, University of the Basque Country, UPV/EHU, Gipuzkoa, Spain

This volume includes eight studies on different aspects of language policy pedagogical practices, and teacher training in school contexts where a foreign language is used to teach curricular content (CLIL). This is a very welcome contribution because it provides additional perspectives to former studies that had focused on the linguistic outcomes of CLIL as compared to non-CLIL students. Successful language learning as well as successful content learning is necessarily linked to good pedagogical practices by well-trained teachers who use appropriate materials. This volume also provides the opportunity to hear the voices of the stakeholders involved in CLIL.

Even though one of the main features of CLIL is the balance between language and content and *advocates a 50:50/Content:Language CLIL-equilibrium* (Ting 2010, 3), this volume approaches CLIL from a language rather than from a content perspective. The main idea is to teach foreign languages efficiently and less attention is paid to the way content is learned. This attention to language rather than content reflects the general trend in Europe where CLIL has attracted mainly scholars in Applied Linguistics, English language teacher educators and practitioners. This does not have to be seen as a problem because research is needed from different perspectives and the language learning perspective is very relevant in an increasing multilingual and multicultural world. However, as we will see later there are potential risks when CLIL is considered just an English/foreign language teaching approach.

This volume brings together CLIL studies in nine European Union states (Austria, Finland, Germany, Italy, the Netherlands, Poland, Spain, Sweden, and UK) and with the exception of the UK, all the other situations involve English as the target language. French, Spanish, and German are also discussed in the chapter by Czura and Papaja (this volume) on CLIL education in Poland and minority languages (Gaelic, Kashubian, and Catalan) are mentioned but not discussed in other chapters. Immigrant languages, which are not usually part of the school curriculum, are not addressed in this volume either. There is an interesting point when comparing the UK to the rest of the countries which clearly reflects the strength of English. While the need to learn English is taken for granted and reinforced by language policies in most countries in Continental Europe, in the UK the issue is to study or not to study a foreign language. As Coyle (this volume) reports, foreign language learning is in decline in England and Scotland. Other differences that can be seen in the CLIL contexts in this volume are the level of exposure to English in different countries (Sylvén, this volume) and the level of language competence achieved by students in different European Union countries (European Commission 2012). English is more a second than a foreign language in countries like Sweden or the Netherlands as compared to countries such as Spain or Italy where exposure to English is more limited and the level of English proficiency is lower.

All the chapters in this volume are on CLIL in Europe. However, it can be seen that CLIL refers to a wide diversity of situations. Coyle (this volume) refers to CLIL when *thematic or subject content and foreign languages are integrated* and this includes *thematic study in language classes*, which is quite different from the context of the other chapters using a foreign language as the language of instruction for teaching one or more content subjects.

The diversity of CLIL situations can be most clearly seen in the chapter by Czura and Papaja who identify four curricular models in CLIL and several types within each model in a single country, Poland. These models and types are arranged according to the amount of L2 used in the classroom, the focus on language or content, and classroom didactics. The diversity of situations can also be seen in the chapter by Sylvén who discusses the poor results of CLIL in Sweden by comparing the CLIL situations to that of three other countries: Finland, Germany, and Spain. She analyses the differences regarding the amount of research carried out, teacher education, age of onset, and exposure to English outside school. The comparison is somehow problematic because the information about the countries is very superficial and does not reflect the diversity of situations within each of the countries but it does show that CLIL can refer to quite different teaching and learning contexts.

Some of the chapters in this volume (Coyle; Escobar Urmeneta; Grandinetti, Langellotti, and Ting) focus on good pedagogical practices so as to identify teaching and learning practices that are considered effective. The findings of these studies can be very useful for CLIL teachers in different contexts and this is certainly an area that needs further development. These good practices are necessarily linked to specific pre- and in-service training for teachers and the development of appropriate materials (see Lorenzo, this volume). An interesting point is to see to what extent the good CLIL practices identified in this volume are necessarily linked to CLIL or just good practices for language teaching independently of the approach used. For example, Grandinetti, Langellotti, and Ting explain the need to insert language-focusing moments to provide effective scaffolds into new content. This teaching strategy is not new and has a long tradition in non-CLIL second language classes (Doughty and Williams 1998).

Challenges and future directions

After highlighting some of the trends that can be found in this volume the next step is to look at some challenges of CLIL and directions for future research from a broader perspective. CLIL is usually linked to educational contexts although Mehisto, Marsh, and Frigols (2008, chapter 1) consider that CLIL also includes CLIL camps, student exchanges, local projects, international projects, family stays, modules or work–study abroad. In this volume, CLIL is part of regular education. Within this context, a clear distinction can be made between conceptualizing CLIL as a language teaching approach or as an educational approach.

CONTENT AND LANGUAGE INTEGRATED LEARNING

CLIL as a language teaching approach

As it has already been said CLIL has attracted language teaching scholars, teacher educators, and practitioners, particularly those in the field of English as a second/foreign language. Traditionally, curricular content has not been taught in English language classes. However, this does not mean that content has not been included in foreign language classes. In fact, it is almost unavoidable to do so because the readings, audiovisual materials and discussions that are used as teaching resources in non-CLIL language classes can also be considered content and can be related to other subjects in the curriculum. A unit with readings and audiovisual material on hunger in Africa in an English language textbook in a non-CLIL class can provide as much content as a unit on the solar system in a CLIL program based on thematic study in the English language class. The possibility to integrate language and content and to develop efficient teaching and learning strategies and good practices is available in both cases. The main difference, which is quite important from a curricular perspective, is that if the solar system is part of the syllabus of the Science class it is more likely that there is coordination between the teaching of the two subjects than in the case of the non-CLIL EFL class. In non-CLIL classes, content is just a resource to teach and learn language, while content is expected to be an integral part of the learning process in CLIL classes.

Most CLIL experiences reported in this volume go beyond teaching subject content in the EFL class into teaching non-language subjects in a foreign language. This situation is quite different from the traditional EFL class and is often considered an innovative approach (Eurydice 2006). However, using a second/foreign language as the language of instruction for non-language subjects is not only the main characteristic of Canadian immersion programs but also has a long tradition in European bilingual programs (Baetens-Beardsmore 1993). For example, the bilingual/partial immersion program aimed at Spanish L1 students in the Basque Autonomous Community in Spain (model B) has several subjects of the school curriculum taught through the medium of Basque, the L2. This program has existed for over 30 years and has been systematically evaluated for outcomes in the L1, L2, and content subjects (see Cenoz 2009). Basque is not a foreign language in the Basque Country but its minority status implies that many students in this program have almost no exposure to Basque outside school. It is likely that students in CLIL programs in some of the countries reported in this volume have more contact with English outside school than Spanish L1 students with Basque outside school. Similar programs exist in other regions with minority languages in different European countries but they are not always considered as examples of CLIL. As Cenoz, Genesee, and Gorter (2014) point out it is still difficult to distinguish CLIL learning environments from non-CLIL learning environments because of its diversity and its close relationship to other content and language-integrated programs such as immersion. It is therefore urgent to develop a clear definition of CLIL and to devise a taxonomy of its major forms. Some attempts are made in this volume (Sylvén; Czura and Papaja) and they need further development.

Even though most of the chapters in this volume report studies on the teaching and learning of English, there are also references to work with other European languages. Identifying language policies and good practices can work across languages. CLIL programs and research need to exchange their experience and their findings with long established bilingual/immersion programs so that they learn from each other and they identify their strong and weak points.

This volume provides examples of classroom-based research, on strategies to integrate language and content and on specific teaching training to integrate language and content. This research line is crucial because any language teaching program, CLIL or not, needs effective pedagogies to be successful. At the same time, there is a need for theoretical and empirical development so as to contribute to better language and content teaching for different second and foreign languages in Europe and elsewhere (Ruiz de Zarobe and Cenoz, 2015).

CLIL as an educational approach

As Coyle (this volume) points out great care has to be exercised when making claims *about the effectiveness of CLIL.* The ambiguity of the scope of CLIL and the diversity of CLIL contexts makes it difficult to identify the effect of CLIL on language and subject content learning. There is some evidence suggesting that CLIL learners obtain better results in English as a foreign language than non-CLIL learners but they often have more hours of instruction and students are also sometimes selected to take part in CLIL programs (Bruton 2011). The chapters by Hüttner, Smit, and Dalton-Puffer and by Denman, Tanner, and Graaff are examples of CLIL programs implemented in contexts where students were not selected to take part in CLIL programs but they do not focus on the outcomes as compared to students in non-CLIL programs.

If we just focus on CLIL as a foreign language teaching approach and we control for the time of instruction allocated to the target language, there is no reason to believe that learning content matter through the foreign language produces better results than having the same amount of instruction in foreign language classes. Why should students learn more English in a history or biology class than in an English language class? Marsh (2008) explains that through drawing content from academic subjects, CLIL can develop higher order language skills but there is no reason to believe that these skills cannot be developed in language classes as well. In fact, a non-CLIL language teacher can use a wider variety of resources to develop higher order language skills. Good language learning practices can certainly take place in CLIL but they can also take place in foreign language classes.

The strength of CLIL emerges when we consider it as an educational program that takes into account the whole curriculum and not only the learning of a foreign language. By integrating language and content, CLIL provides the opportunity of having additional exposure to the foreign language without extending the school timetable. This exposure can be limited to the use of the target language as the language of instruction and result in incidental learning of the target language (see for example in this volume, Hüttner, Smit, and Dalton-Puffer and some types in Czura and Papaja. When teaching a subject through the medium of a foreign language there are also CLIL contexts in which specific instruction to integrate language and content takes place (see for example Grandinetti, Langellotti, and Ting, this volume).

There is robust evidence from bilingual/immersion programs in Canada and Europe showing that students achieve a higher level of proficiency in the second language when they use the second language as the language of instruction (see for example Genesee 2004; Cenoz 2009). This is to be expected, with or without systematic teaching strategies to integrate language and content, because of the amount of exposure. The crucial findings of research on bilingual/immersion programs is that this improvement in second language proficiency is done at no cost for the development of the first language and the knowledge of content subjects. This does not mean that students would not have achieved even a higher level of proficiency in the target language if they had taken second/foreign language classes for the same amount of time. However, schools cannot usually afford having a large amount of language classes instead of subject classes and using a second/foreign language as the language of instruction can be an effective way to combine language and content. If we want to assess the effect of CLIL, it is necessary to adopt an educational perspective in the study of CLIL. This means considering CLIL as an approach that is related to the whole curriculum and not just limited to foreign language teaching. From a theoretical and empirical point, this perspective implies bringing together research traditions in bi/multilingualism and second language acquisition (Cenoz and Gorter 2011; Ortega 2014). Research on good practices in CLIL and on stakeholders' voices such as the studies reported in this volume is also useful because it can contribute to identify effective strategies in language and content integrated teaching. It is important to assess how effective some of these strategies are by conducting comparisons within CLIL contexts that share the same characteristics. It is also necessary to carry out studies to assess the impact of CLIL on content and all the languages in the curriculum taking into account the need to be very cautious about the cause–effect relationships.

Another point that deserves consideration in future research when we move away from the narrow perspective of CLIL as a foreign language teaching approach is the need to expand it to all the languages being learned and/or used by learners. CLIL learners are multilingual or in the process of becoming multilingual and have the potential to use their linguistic resources as a scaffold when learning and using languages. As Bialystok (2010) explains, bilingualism can have some general cognitive advantages related to metalinguistic awareness. If this is the case, it is desirable that these advantages are enhanced in CLIL classes. At the same time, it is important to look at the way multilinguals navigate between languages and are able to negotiate the multiple varieties of codes, modes, genres, registers, and discourses (Cenoz and Gorter 2011, 2015; Kramsch 2012). An educational perspective that goes beyond the foreign language teaching approach will give the opportunity for CLIL to integrate not only language and content but also all the languages in the students' multilingual repertoires.

Acknowledgements

I would like to acknowledge the funding by the Spanish Ministry of Economy and Competitiveness EDU2012-32191 and the Basque Department of Education, Research and Universities IT-362-10 (UFI 11/54).

References

Baetens-Beardsmore, H., ed. 1993. *European Models of Bilingual Education*. Clevedon, England: Multilingual Matters.
Bialystok, E. 2010. "Global-local and Trail-making Tasks by Monolingual and Bilingual Children: Beyond Inhibition." *Developmental Psychology* 46 (1): 93–105. doi:10.1037/a0015466.

Bruton, A. 2011. "Is CLIL so Beneficial, or Just Selective? Re-evaluating Some of the Research." *System* 39 (4): 523–532. doi:10.1016/j.system.2011.08.002.

Cenoz, J. 2009. *Towards Multilingual Education*. Bristol: Multilingual Matters

Cenoz, J., and D. Gorter. 2011. "Focus on Multilingualism: A Study of Trilingual Writing." *The Modern Language Journal* 95 (3): 356–369. doi:10.1111/j.1540-4781.2011.01206.x.

Cenoz, J., & Gorter, D. eds. 2015. *Multilingual education: between language learning and translanguaging*. Cambridge: Cambridge University Press

Cenoz, J., F. Genesee, and D. Gorter. 2014. "Critical Analysis of CLIL: Taking Stock and Looking Forward" Applied Linguistics 35:243-262.doi: 10.1093/applin/amt011

Doughty, C. and J. Williams, eds. 1998. *Focus on Form in Classroom Second Language Acquisition*. Cambridge: Cambridge University Press.

European Commission. 2012. *First European Survey on Language Competences*. http://ec.europa.eu/languages/eslc/docs/en/final-report-escl_en.pdf

Eurydice. 2006. *Content and Language Integrated Learning (CLIL) at School in Europe*. Brussels: Eurydice.

Genesee, F. 2004. "What Do We Know About Bilingual Education for Majority Language Students." In *Handbook of Bilingualism and Multiculturalism*, edited by T. K. Bhatia and W. Ritchie, 547–576. London: Blackwell.

Kramsch, C. 2012. "Authenticity and Legitimacy in Multilingual SLA." *Critical Multilingualism Studies* 1: 107–128. http://cms.arizona.edu/index.php/multilingual/article/view/9.

Marsh, C. 2008. "Language Awareness and CLIL." In *Encyclopedia of Language and Education. Vol 6. Knowledge about Language*, edited by J. Cenoz and N. Hornberger, 233–246. Berlin: Springer.

Mehisto, P., D. Marsh, and M. J. Frigols. 2008. *Uncovering CLIL*. London: Macmillan Education.

Ortega, L. 2014. "Ways Forward for a Bi/Multilingual Turn in SLA." In *The Multilingual Turn: Implications for SLA, TESOL and Bilingual Education*, edited by Stephen May. 147–166. London: Routledge.

Ruiz de Zarobe, Y. & Cenoz, J. 2015. Way forward in the 21st century in content-based instruction: Moving towards integration. *Language, Culture and Curriculum* Vol. 28: 90–96, doi.org/10.1080/07908318.2014.1000927

Ting, Y. L. T. 2010. "CLIL Appeals to how the Brain Likes its Information: Examples from CLIL-(Neuro)Science." *International CLIL Research Journal* 1: 1–18. doi:10.1243/14680874JER511.

Supplementary Material for Chapter 7

How CLIL can provide a pragmatic means to renovate science education – even in a sub-optimally bilingual context

Maria Grandinetti, Margherita Langellotti and Y.L. Teresa Ting

SUPPLEMENTARY MATERIAL FOR CHAPTER 7

First read the instructions of Exercise 1 and Exercise 2 Then do these exercises.

Exercise 1. Circle the correct word to complete the following questions (individual work)

Questions	Answers (see Exercise 2)
1. How *many/much* chambers does the heart have?	
2. How *many/much* blood does the heart pump each minute?	
3. What are the upper chambers *named/called*?	
4. How are the ventricles, the lower chambers, *different from/different by* the upper chambers?	
5. *Is it true/Is true* that the heart shows left-right symmetry?	

Exercise 2. Now <u>write</u> the correct answer next to each of the questions above (there are <u>two extras</u> that you don't need)

   a. Yes it is.
   b. Yes there are.
   c. "Atrium" singular and "atria" plural.
   d. There are four.
   e. They are larger.
   f. Four to six litres a minute at rest and **up to** 30L/min in endurance athletes!
   g. Yes it does.

Exercise 3. Using the information you have obtained in sections I and II, choose the schematic diagram which best represents the heart:

167

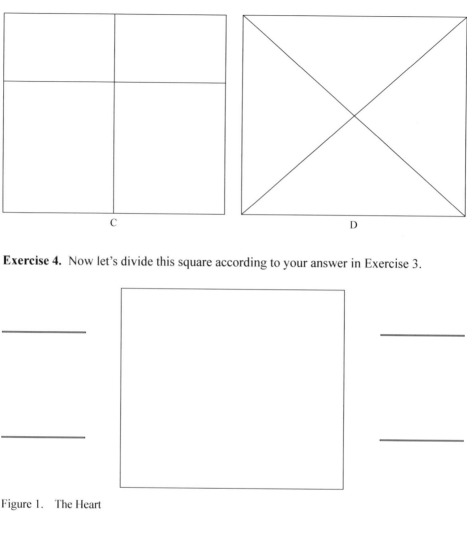

C

D

Exercise 4. Now let's divide this square according to your answer in Exercise 3.

Figure 1. The Heart

Exercise 5. *Before* we label the heart that you have drawn in Figure 1, complete the following text using : (*a*), (*the*) or (nothing).

> Now pretend you are ____ surgeon. ____ heart you are looking at is ____ heart of ____ patient lying on his/her back. So, in figure 1, which is ____ right side and which is ____ left side?
>
> Now label ____ figure 1: write "right" below ____ right side of the patient's heart and "left" below ____ left side.

Exercise 6. Now that you have identified the right and left sides, you can use information from exercises I-V to <u>correctly</u> label the four chambers of the heart by writing the following onto the four lines in Figure 1:

SUPPLEMENTARY MATERIAL FOR CHAPTER 7

- right ventricle
- left atrium
- right atrium
- left ventricle

Now identify and label these two anatomical structures:

- Use a bold blue line to indicate the **inter-atrial septum** which separates the two atria.
- Use a bold green line to indicate the **inter-ventricular septum** which separates the two ventricles.
- Write the name of these structures along the two **septi**.

Exercise 7. Your teacher will now show you how figure 1 should look.

Exercise 8. Let's build on what we know. Put the following sentences in order to form a well-written paragraph:

_____ A. In the lungs, CO_2 is exchanged for O_2.

_____ B. This system ensures that the blood circulating throughout our body contains enough oxygen (O_2), which our cells need for survival.

_____ C. The heart and the lungs form the circulatory system.

_____ D. This relationship between the heart, lungs, body and O_2/CO_2-rich blood is shown in figure 2.

_____ E. To do this, the heart receives blood which contains high concentrations of CO_2-waste from the body and pumps it to the lungs.

_____ F. This O_2-rich blood returns from the lungs to the heart where it is then pumped back to the body.

_____ G. In addition, the circulatory system also removes the carbon dioxide (CO_2) waste produced during cell metabolism.

Exercise 9. What *language* in the sentences helped you decide on the correct order? Work in groups to answer these questions.

1. Give two reasons why sentence C the best way to start the paragraph.
2. Which two words helped you see that B follows C?
3. What words link sentence G after sentence B?
4. Which words helped you see that sentence E follows sentence G?
5. Why is sentence E before sentence A?
6. Which words tell you that sentence F follows sentence A?
7. Why is sentence D a good concluding sentence?
8. Why would sentence D not be a good starting sentence?

Exercise 10. What type of blood is flowing to and from the heart? Complete the following schematic diagram with : CO_2 (x2), O_2 (x2) and LUNGS

Using the information from above, label the six boxes in Figure 2:

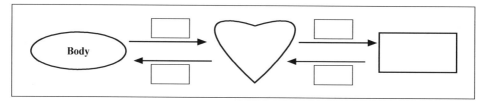

Figure 2. The relationship between the BODY, the HEART and the LUNGS and O_2/CO_2-rich blood.

Exercise 11a. Missing information ... You need to find the missing information. However, pretend you and your friend are in jail, but on different sides of a wall with a very small hole in it. Since your friend has the information you need to complete your text, write the questions you need to ask him/her on a piece of paper and send it through the small hole.

A. Write three questions on a note to ask your classmate for information to complete your text.

The very large vein, called the [_____ _____ **cava**] brings de-oxygenated blood full of carbon-dioxide waste from the **body** to the *heart*, entering at the *right atrium*.

When the *atria* contract, this blood is pumped from the *right atrium* into the [_____ _____], passing through the **tricuspid valve**, which is a one-way valve that prevents blood from flowing back into the *right atrium* when the *ventricles* contract.

When the *ventricles* contract, this de-oxygenated blood leaves the *right ventricle* and is pumped to the [_____], carried through the **pulmonary artery**.

B. Write three questions on a note to ask your classmate for information to complete your text.

The very large vein, called **the superior vena cava** brings de-oxygenated blood, full of carbon-dioxide waste from the **body** to the *heart*, entering at the [_____ _____].

When the *atria* contract, this blood is pumped from the *right atrium* into the *right ventricle*, passing through the [_____ **valve**], which is a one-way valve that prevents blood from flowing back into the *right atrium* when the *ventricles* contract.

When the *ventricles* contract, this de-oxygenated blood leaves the *right ventricle* and is pumped to the **lungs**, carried through the [_____ **artery**].

SUPPLEMENTARY MATERIAL FOR CHAPTER 7

Exercise 11b. Write the answers to the questions on your jail-friend's note.

Exercise 11c. There are <u>five</u> new words in the text, indicated in **bold**: complete the <u>right side</u> of the heart in Figure 1 with these bold words.

Exercise 12a. Listen and choose what you hear:

In the **lungs**, de-oxygenated blood becomes re-oxygenated, *enriched/riched* with oxygen. De-oxygenated blood is dark red but oxygenated blood is *light/bright* red. This re-oxygenated blood leaves *lungs/the lungs* and returns to the heart *through/true* the **pulmonary vein**. *Like/Unlike* all other veins in *body/the body*, the pulmonary vein is the only vein carrying oxygenated blood. The pulmonary vein carries re-oxygenated blood from the lungs to the heart, entering via the left atrium. When the atria *contract/contact*, this re-oxygenated blood is pushed from the left atrium *to/into* the left ventricle, through the **bicuspid valve** which, like the tricuspid valve is a one-way valve that prevents blood from flowing *back/backwards*. When the ventricles contract, this richly oxygenated blood is pumped from the left ventricle *into/to* the **body**, leaving *heart/the heart* via the very *large/wide* artery called the **aorta**.

Exercise 12b. Now insert the <u>four</u> new words from this text to Figure 1.

You have completed Figure 1!!!

Exercise 13. Dino Sauro is a student who doesn't pay attention. His class notes are full of <u>content</u> errors!!! Read Dino's notes and correct them for him. The number of errors per sentence are indicated in (brackets).

Conventionally, the anatomy of the heart is presented with the right side of the heart on the right and the left side of the heart on the left (2). This convention helps dentists learn about the heart and perform surgery correctly (1). De-oxygenated blood from the body enters the heart on the left, at the left atrium, via the inferior vena cava (3). From the right atrium, this oxygenated blood is pumped to the left ventricle, passing through the one-way valve called the bicuspid valve (3). The strong muscles of the right ventricle pump this de-oxygenated blood to the lungs, via the pulmonary vein (1). In the body, this de-oxygenated blood is re-oxygenated (1). Once re-oxygenated, this oxygen-poor blood returns from the lungs to the heart and re-enters the right side of the heart (2). (The pressure that pumps blood from the heart to the lungs and back to the heart is established by the left ventricle (1)!!!) Oxygen-rich blood from the lungs re-enters the heart via the pulmonary vein which enters the heart at the left ventricle (1). The left atrium pumps this oxygen-poor blood to the right ventricle, pushing the blood past the bicuspid valve (2). From the left ventricle, oxygenated blood leaves the heart via the aorta and is pumped to the lungs (1). (Imagine the strength of the muscles of the left ventricle!!! When the left ventricle contracts, it generates enough pressure to pump de-oxygenated blood to all parts of the body and **back** to the heart!!! (1)).

(Knowledge-Transfer HOTS questions)

Use figure 1 which you have completed to answer these questions

1. When does blood from the **right ventricle** mix with that in the **left ventricle**?
2. Is blood in the **right atrium** darker than that in the **right ventricle**?
3. Why is blood in the **superior vena cava** darker than that in the **pulmonary vein**?
4. Which blood is more oxygenated, that passing through the **bicuspid value** or the **tricuspid valve**?
5. What is probably the longest journey through the body that a red blood cell must travel once it leaves the **left ventricle** via the **aorta**?

Answers:

1. Never!;
2. No – they are the same – still deoxygenated;
3. SVC brings in deoxygenated blood to the heart while the PV is carrying oxygenated blood back from the lungs to the heart;
4. Bicuspid which separates the left ventricle and atrium and thus oxygenated blood returning from the lungs;
5. Aorta → longest toe on foot → back to the superior vena cava! This last return route also depends on the incredible pressure with which blood is pumped out of the left atrium of the heart! That is why the muscle walls of the ventricles need to be so thick!

Excerpt 1. Traditional learning material covering the learning objective of the CLIL activities.

The **human heart** is a muscular organ that provides continuous blood circulation through the cardiac cycle and is one of the most vital organs in the human body.[1] The heart is divided into four main chambers: the two upper chambers are called the left and right atria and two lower chambers are called the right and left ventricles. The two superior atria are the receiving chambers and the two inferior ventricles are the discharging chambers. There is a thick wall of muscle separating the right side and the left side of the heart called the septum. The interatrioventricular septum separates the left atrium and ventricle from the right atrium and ventricle, dividing the heart into two functionally separate and anatomically distinct units. The heart acts as a double pump. Normally with each beat the right ventricle pumps the same amount of blood into the lungs that the left ventricle pumps out into the body. Physicians commonly refer to the right atrium and right ventricle together as the **right heart** and to the left atrium and ventricle as the **left heart**.[2] The function of the right side of the heart is to collect de-oxygenated blood, in the right atrium, from the body (via superior and inferior vena cavae) and pump it, via the right ventricle, into the lungs (pulmonary circulation) so that carbon dioxide can be dropped off and oxygen picked up (gas exchange). This happens through the passive process of diffusion. The left side collects oxygenated blood from the lungs into the left atrium.

From the left atrium the blood moves to the left ventricle which pumps it out to the body (via the aorta).

Blood flows through the heart in one direction, from the atria to the ventricles, and out of the great arteries, or the aorta for example. Blood is prevented from flowing backwards by the tricuspid, bicuspid, aortic, and pulmonary valves. On both sides, the lower ventricles are thicker and stronger than the upper atria. The muscle wall surrounding the left ventricle is thicker than the wall surrounding the right ventricle due to the higher force needed to pump the blood through the systemic circulation. Starting in the right atrium, the blood flows through the tricuspid valve to the right ventricle. Here, it is pumped out of the pulmonary semilunar valve and travels through the pulmonary artery to the lungs. From there, blood flows back through the pulmonary vein to the left atrium. It then travels through the mitral valve to the left ventricle, from where it is pumped through the aortic semilunar valve to the aorta and to the rest of the body. The (relatively) deoxygenated blood finally returns to the heart through the inferior vena cava and superior vena cava, and enters the right atrium where the process began.

Index

Entries in **bold** denote tables; entries in *italics* denote figures.

4Cs framework 4, 74–5, 140

academic literacy: and academic success 139–42; cultivating 5, 135–6, 139; multilingual 145, 148, 151, 155–6; teaching 129–30
Action Research 106–7, 116
affective filter 4, 112
Africa, English-medium teaching in 125
agency 20, 153, 155
Andalusia 59, 67, 73, 79, 149, 151
Anglophones: attitudes to other languages 15, 23; and English teachers 46; hosting in classes 65
area texts 148
articles, definite and indefinite 129
at-risk learners 56, 58–61, 120, 135–6, 139
audio recordings 64, 142
Austria: acceptance of CLIL in 37–8, 41, 49; colleges of technology *see* HTLs; educational culture in 42; implementation of CLIL in 43, 50, 58; language management in 9, 37
authentic materials 63

Barcelona: CLIL in 107; teacher education in 104
Basque Autonomous Community 59, 79, 161
Basque language 3, 161
behavioural disorders 56
Belarusian language 93
Belgium, German-speaking community in 3
beliefs, characteristics of 39–40
Bellaterra Model **105**, 106
BICS (Basic Interpersonal Communication Skills) 4–5, 139–40
bilingual, use of term 98
bilingual education: at-risk learners in 58–60; Cummin's theories on 5; in Germany 73, 75, 153; language and content in 145, 161–3; in Poland 91–3, 95; production of texts in 154; teachers adapting to student proficiency 67; *see also* CLIL

Bilingual Education Research Project, Poland 93–6, 102
bilingualism 163; additive 55, 57, 61; *see also* multilingualism

CA (conversation analysis) 104, 106, 120
Calabria 10, 124, 135
CALP (Cognitive Academic Language Proficiency) 4–5, 11, 139–40
Canada, bilingual education in 15, 58, 84, 161–2
Catalan language: in education 104, 109, 118; EU official status of 3
Catalonia 104, 107
CCD (content-cognitive demand) **129**, 130
CEFR (Common European Framework of Reference) 57–8, 77, 107
Centre for Education Development (ORE) 94
Chill and Spill Room 20
Chinese language, seen as useful 2
CIC (classroom interactional competence) 10, 106–7, 115, 119
classroom activities, helpful 63–4
classroom environment 17
classroom events, ownership of 14
classroom interaction, language of 46
classroom observation 62, 91, 95–6, 105–6
classroom practices: evidence base for 15; and LOCIT process 20–1, 31; research on 6–7; and teachers' beliefs 38–9; *see also* pedagogy
CLIL (Content and Language Integrated Learning): and academic success 140, **141**; age of implementation 78, *79*, 84–6; aims of 44, 47–8; in Britain 15; as change agent 14–15; classroom dynamics in 131–5, **132**, 137–8, 142; in classroom practice 6–10, 126–9; conceptualisations used in 118, 120; as educational approach 162–3; in European schools 2–3; genre-based programmes in 147–9, 151, **152**, 154–5; language and content in 5–7, 126, 129–31, 141–2, 145–6; as language teaching approach 161–2;

INDEX

learner-based research on 18–23, *22*, 41–2; learner motivation in *17*, 59; lesson design in 8; mathematical modus operandi of 127, **128**; models of 4–5, 91–2, 96, *97*, 98–100, 160; national profiles for 71–3, 80–4, *81–3*, 86, 159–60; policy and practice in 40–1; regulation and research on 74–5, *76*; scholarship on 159; stakeholder beliefs about 37–9, 45, 49–50; student attitudes to 23–7, *24*, 31; student output in 154–5; subjects taught through 43; success in 28, 48–50; teacher-led interaction in *see* teacher-talk; teacher skills in 58, 60–1, 65, 67, 76–7, 100–1; use of L1 in 112–19; use of term 1, 73–4
CLIL-learning materials 126, 128, **129**
CLIL outputs 18
CMI (Chinese medium of instruction) 59
code choice 104, 119
code-switching 98, 109
CODN (National Centre for Teacher Training) 94–5
cognitive processing 147
collaborative learning 27, 104, 130, 134
communication skills 14, 25–6, 112
comprehensible input 4, 112, 126
comprehension checks 109
content knowledge: arrangement in brain structures 148; integrating with skills development 18
content learning, CLIL results in 7, 41
content teachers: in bilingual settings 148; and language aims 48–9; language competence of 60, 100–1, 125, 141; and learning by doing 45–6
conversations, and learning 4, 106
Counterbalanced Approach 5
Coyle's Triptych 28
creative tasks 63
critical incident analysis 20
cross-cultural communication 9, 68
Cummins' Framework for Developing FL-Proficiency *see* 4Cs framework

Danish language 3
dictionary skills 27
disciplinary discourses 138, 141, 147–8
discourse, and beliefs 40
dual-focused approaches 2, 15, 48, 97
Dutch language 57
dyscalculia and dyslexia 56

education: beliefs of stakeholders in 38, 40, 44; sociocultural view of 106
EFL (English as a foreign language), and CLIL 42, 47–50, 124–5, 130
EIO (European and International Orientation) 57–8, 63, 65–8
El Firmament School 107–8

ELLs (English language learners) 56, 58, 60
embeddedness, multiple 154
EMI (English medium of instruction) 59, 161–2
engineers, use of English 46–7, 49
England: CLIL outputs in 18; foreign language learning in 15, 159–60
English as a lingua franca (ELF) 46, 49, 80, 85
English language: affective factors regarding 48–50; in Austrian schools 43; in Barcelona 107; CLIL student proficiency in 44–6, 57; CLIL teacher competence in 60, 124–5; in European schools 3; extramural exposure to *see* extramural English (EE); in German schools 73; Italian common problems with 129; in mass media 80, 85; in Polish schools 92–3, 95–9, 101; seen as useful 2, 50–1; in Spanish education 104; subject education through *see* EMI; in Swedish education 75; teacher conceptualisations of 44 5
English speakers, native *see* Anglophones
English teachers 7, 45–6, 48–9, 62, 107
ENL (English as native language) 49
ESP (English for specific purposes) 46–7
EU (European Union): implementation of CLIL in 40–1; language diversity in 1–3
European Centre for Modern Languages 4
European Commission: language learning goals of 1, 74; surveys on language learning 2; on teacher education 77
Eurydice Report 94
extramural English (EE) *81*, 160; in Netherlands 64–5; in Sweden 71–2, 79–80, 84–5

familiar language 126, 129–30
Finland: bilingual education in 58; CLIL in 9, 71, 75, 80, *82*, 84; exposure to foreign languages in 78; extramural English in 80; teacher education in 77
first language (L1) *see* mother tongue
fluency, focus on 67
Focus on Form 4–5
foreign languages (FL): attitudes to learning 1–2; content instruction through 4, 91, 127, 129, 136, 162; learner–teacher relationship in 42, 46, 61, 106–7, 128; teachers' competence in *see* teachers, language proficiency of; *see also* target language (TL)
French language: in CLIL classrooms 14; in European schools 3; immersion programs 58–9; in Polish education 96, 99–101; seen as useful 2
fun 25, 27–8, 30, 59, 68

Gaelic language 15, 159
games 25, 64–5, 80, 130
Gdynia 93
genre-based programmes 146–9, **152**, 153

INDEX

genre mapping 8, 145–6, 148–51, **150**, 153, 155
genres: scaffolded use of 8; use of term 146–7
genre selection 146, 151, 153
German language: in Austrian education 41; in CLIL classrooms 14; in European schools 3; in French education 153; in Polish education 96–9, 101; in professional context 50–1; seen as useful 2; in Sweden 86
German-speaking countries, CLIL in 58
Germany: CLIL in 9, 71–3, 75, 80, *83*, 84; exposure to foreign languages in 78–9; extramural English in 80; teacher education in 77
gesture 107, 109–10, 112

history, discourse of 147, 151–5, **152**, 158
HOT (higher-order thinking) 131
HTLs (Höhere technische Lehranstalt) 42–5
humanities subjects 100

immersion: early and late 7; in Finland 72, 75; partial 55; research on 58
immigrant languages 159
instruction language, comprehensible 137, 141
integration, of language and content 145–9, 154, 161
interaction, focus on 4
interactional space 107, 116
Interaction Hypothesis 4
Internet: English language on 64, 80; in language learning 63
internship 104–5, 108, 113
involvement, sense of 27
IRF (initiation-response-feedback) 115, 133, 135
Israel–Palestine conflict 153
Italian language, in Malta 3
ITALIC Report 7, 59–60
Italy, CLIL in 124–5

Kashubian language 93, 159

L1 *see* mother tongue
L2 *see* foreign languages (FL); target language (TL)
language: arrangement in brain structures 148; power of 141
language analysis 127
language anxiety 6, 60
language behaviours, societal mechanisms behind 39
language beliefs 38–40, 49
language chunks 57
language competence: and bilingual education 163; as CLIL output 18, 48, 146; in European countries 160; and genre production 154; as key factor in employment 3
language grading 155

language learning: affective factors in 44, 59–60; age of 85; beliefs about 44–7, 49; including other subjects in 60; literacy/learning model of 26; motivation in 6–7, 15–17, 59; naturalistic 46, 57; reorienting 10; role of L1 in 119; in UK 159–60
language management 9, 37–8, 40, 49–51
language policy (LP): and advanced literacy 146; from below 50–1; and CLIL 1–2, 8, 37, 73, 75, 84; and linguistic dimension of subjects 151; at national and EU levels 38; tripartite model of 38–9, 49
language practices 38–9, 49
language-review tasks 130
language skills: in CLIL students 41; higher order 162; perceived importance of 23
language teaching: genre programmes in 147; good practices in 160; national-level policy on 38; in Poland 93
language use, automatization of 45
Latin language 149, 151
lay theories 39–40, 50
LCD (language-cognitive demand) **129**, 130
learner achievements and gains 17–19, 25–7
learner-centeredness 97–8, 124, 126–7
Learner Conference 20, 22, 25–7
learner-convergent language 107, 115, 119
learner engagement: and LOCIT 21, 28; and motivation 17; and practitioner research 19
learner identities 16–17, 59
learner motivation 7, 15–17, 22–3; process model for interpreting *17*
learner-oriented conversation 109
learner output 28
learners: beliefs of 9; disaffected 124, 135, *136*, 139 (*see also* at-risk learners); as researchers 19–20
learning: language used for 5; *see also* successful learning
learning by doing 47
learning challenges 56
learning moments 20, 23, 28, *29–30*
learning progression: deeper sense of 18; transparent ownership of 26
linguistic devices 130, 135, 155
linguistic diversity 1–2
Listening to Learners 21–2
Lithuanian language 93
LOCIT (Learning-Oriented Critical Incident Technique) 9, 14, 20–1, 23, 28, 31

mask effect 7
meaning: focus on 67; negotiation of 4, 112
metafunctions 5
metalinguistic awareness 163
microlanguage 125
microlearning objectives 126, **127**
minority languages 3, 93, 159, 161

177

INDEX

mistakes, allowing 27, 64
Monitor Model 4
mother tongue: in Dutch vocational education 56, 60; improving use of 26–7; in peer-to-peer interactions 7
mother tongue + 2 objective 1, 40, 73–4, 92–3
motivation, ambivalent 60
multilingual curriculum 149
multilingualism: cognitive advantages of 163; European attitudes to 2, 40
Multimodal Conversation Analysis 104, 108

Netherlands: bilingual education and CLIL in 9, 55–8, 61–3, 66–8; role of English in 160
Norway 3, 84

orality, in Austrian education 42
ownership 14, 20, 26, 31, 129

participant evidence 20
pauses 109
PDS (Professional Development Schools) 113
pedagogy: CLIL approaches to 7–8, 42, 160; innovations in 37–8, 46, 49
peer-to-peer interactions 7, 134–5, 142
personal recounts 153
physics 93, 98, 100, 125
Pilar: experience of CLIL teaching 107–9, 115, 119–20, 120n3; reflective work of 111–12, 116–19; teaching tips from 112–13
PISA (Programme for International Student Assessment) 16, 147, 149
plurilingualism 73, 79, 115, 118; *see also* multilingualism
Poland: CLIL in 9, 91–2, 95–6, 101–2, 160; core curriculum in 93–4; curricular models in 96–100, *97*; quality of CLIL teaching in 100–1
Polish language 92, 97–9
PowerPoint 64
practitioner research 6, 19–21
primary sources 152, 155
professional vision 76
puzzles 64

'real life' 45, 49, 63, 65
rediscursification 145
reflection-on-action 106
respectful discussions 14, 19, 22–3, 25, 28, 31
rhetorical structure 146, 148, 152–5
Russian language 3, 73, 92–3

Sami language 3
scaffolding 115, 118, 130, 142, 145
schools, parental selection of 66–7

science: CLIL in teaching 10, 100; efficacy of learning tasks in *140*; English-medium teaching of 107–8, 125, 131, 142; in genre map 149; Italian school curriculum on **127**; use of language in 134–5, 138, 147
Scotland: CLIL outputs in 18; foreign language learning in 15, 159–60
self, sense of 16–17
self-concept 59, 61
self-esteem 6, 60–1, 68, 107
self-reflective reports 111
semi-structured guideline interviews 43–4
'show and tell' 64
Situated Learning 118
skills development, overemphasising 18
SLA (Second Language Acquisition): interactivist view on 106; teacher training in 104; *see also* language learning
social constructions 38, 40, 45
Spain: bilingual education in 161; CLIL in 9, 71–6, *83*, 84; exposure to foreign languages in 79; extramural English in 80; foreign language learning in 3; multilingual genre mapping in 149; teacher education in 77, 104–5
Spanish language: in Catalonia 104; in CLIL classrooms 14; in European schools 3; in Polish education 93, 96, 100–1; seen as useful 2
speaking skills 26
spontaneity 25–6
successful learning: contributors to *24*, 25; factors in 16–18; investigation into 20–1; meaning strategies for 31; student perceptions of 9, 14–15, 21, *22*
surprises 63
Sweden: CLIL in 9, 71–2, 74–5, 80, *82*, 84–6; exposure to foreign languages in 78; role of English in 160; teacher education in 77
Swedish language, in Finland 72
Swedish National Agency for Education 74–5
Sydney School 147
systemic functional linguistics 5, 147, 153

target language (TL): age of exposure to 78, 85; confidence using 27; contact hours with 94; in Dutch CLIL programmes 57, 63; learner mastery of 127; maximising use of 66–7, 111–12; peer-to-peer discussion in 25; teacher proficiency in *see* teachers, language proficiency of; vocabulary acquisition in 75
task-based learning 124, 131, 139
teacher beliefs 6, 9, 39
Teacher Charter 20
teacher cognition 38, 40
teacher development 31

INDEX

teacher education: academic conversations in 107; beliefs in 39; case study of 107–11, 113–15; classroom-situated 126; dissociative and integrative models of 105–6; formal CLIL training in 41, 100, 104; language proficiency in 77; national differences in 71–3, 76–7, *78*, 80, 84
teacher empowerment 104, 106
teacher input 28
teacher-led enquiry 104, 106
teachers: beliefs of 38, 43–4; collaboration between language and subject 60; language proficiency of 7, 46–8, 60–1, 77, 84, 101, 125–6; qualifications in CLIL 92, 100
teacher self-agency 21
teacher-talk 106–7, 131–4, **132**, 141–2
teaching methods 91–2, 95, 97–8; *see also* classroom practices
teaching strategies 65, **66**, 119, 160, 162
television 63
terminology 28, 46–8, 97–9, 133, 135, 138
textbooks 27, 100, 149, 155

texts: analysis of 27; brain compatibility of 137–8; comprehension and production of 5, 154–5; and genres 147–8, 153
third language 58–60, 75
translation, in CLIL 26
TTO (tweetalig onderwijs) 55, 57
tvmbo (junior secondary vocational education) 57, 61–8, **66**

vehicular languages 72, 145–7
video clips, of learning moments 20, 23
vocabulary, content-specific *see* terminology
vocational education: bilingual 55–6, 58, 61–3, 67–8; English language in 49, 63–4; home languages in 60; teaching strategies in 65, **66**
vocational literacy 7, 61, 68

wait time 116, 118
writing, in CLIL 26; *see also* texts

Zone of Proximal Development 118